IN BUSINESS FOR OURSELVES

Northern Entrepreneurs

McGill-Queen's Native and Northern Series
Bruce G. Trigger, Editor

IN BUSINESS FOR OURSELVES
Northern Entrepreneurs

Fifteen case studies of successful small northern businesses

Wanda A. Wuttunee

The Arctic Institute of North America and
The Faculty of Management of the University of Calgary

McGill-Queen's University Press
Montreal & Kingston • London • Buffalo

Legal deposit second quarter 1992
Bibliothèque nationale du Québec

Printed in Canada on acid-free paper

Publication has been supported by the Faculty
of Management, University of Calgary.

Canadian Cataloguing in Publication Data

Wuttunee, Wanda A. (Wanda Ann), 1956–
In business for ourselves: northern entrepreneurs
(McGill-Queen's native and northern series,
ISSN 1181-7453)
Co-published by: Arctic Institute of North America
and the Faculty of Management of the University
of Calgary.
Includes bibliographical references.
ISBN 0-7735-0924-0 (bound) – ISBN 0-7735-0935-6
(pbk.)
1. Small business – Canada, Northern – Management
– Case studies. I. Arctic Institute of North America.
II. University of Calgary. Faculty of Management.
III. Title. IV. Series
HD62.7.W87 1992   658.02'2'09719   C92-090348-7

This book was typeset by Typo Litho composition inc.
in 10/12 Palatino.

TABLE OF CONTENTS

14 Yukon Game Farm Ltd, Whitehorse, Yukon 257

15 Translation and Interpretation Services, Community
     Unidentified by Request 279

16 Conclusions 287

     Appendix 1: Key Definitions 293

     Appendix 2: Checklists 298

     Bibliography 311

TABLES AND FIGURES

Tables

Figures

FOREWORD

It is a pleasure to contribute the foreword to Wanda Wuttunee's book on northern entrepreneurs. Ms. Wuttunee is an alumna of this faculty, having received her MBA degree in June 1989. She has stated that the entrepreneurship courses that she took during her MBA program have provided a strong information base for her current work. In addition, the Faculty of Management at the University of Calgary, through its New Venture Development Group, has been involved in entrepreneurship education for a number of years. Since 1984, the group's mission has been to promote economic development through entrepreneurial education and research.

In 1986, Allan Gould wrote a book called *The New Entrepreneurs*, the story of seventy-five successful Canadian entrepreneurs from small towns and major cities across the country. They were resourceful, energetic, and creative individuals – just a few of the thousands of individuals across Canada who start their own businesses every year, and succeed. Wanda Wuttunee has now provided us with profiles of fifteen successful Northern small businesses – from the Yukon, Northwest Territories, and northern Alberta – involved in the renewable resource, information, and service industries. The businesses portrayed in this study include sole proprietorships, partnerships, a community development corporation, and a co-operative. The individuals involved are resourceful, energetic, and creative, and they have all succeeded, despite the high costs associated with doing business in the North, the tough competition, the shortage of skilled labour, and small markets.

This book is not limited to a profile of these organizations, however. It is also a handbook. The profiles are case studies to be used as resource materials by potential entrepreneurs contemplating a new business in northern Canada. Many of the profiles include a section of "Advice to New Business," and the final chapter includes a summary of personal skills and business philosophies. A practical checklist is included in an appendix. Starting up a new business is never easy, and doing so in the North makes it even more challenging. The case studies show the necessity for perseverance and flexibility, for diversification to allow for times of economic slowdown, and for sensitivity to the needs of employees, many of whom still hunt and fish part of the year.

In their book, *In Search of Excellence*, Peters and Waterman listed a number of attributes that characterize the finest of large American companies – a bias towards action, closeness to the customer, autonomy and entrepreneurship, productivity through people, hands-on value-driven methods, staying close to the business you know, simplicity, and core values with flexibility. Interestingly, although these fifteen businesses profiled by Wuttunee can hardly be classified as large corporations, every one of them emphasized many of these same attributes – bending over backwards to help customers, putting strong emphasis on quality and service, cultivating a work environment to attract employees and keep them satisfied, diversifying only into other areas that are related to the core business, and having a strong work ethic and sense of autonomy.

Small businesses have an enormous potential for generating wealth and employment throughout Canada and have become an increasingly important part of the country's economy. *In Business for Ourselves: Northern Entrepreneurs* will be of great assistance to those who are thinking about starting their own business in the North but who are not sure where to go for help.

P. Michael Maher, Ph.D.
Dean, Faculty of Management
University of Calgary

ACKNOWLEDGMENTS

Originally conceived by the Arctic Institute of North America's Board and in particular, by Michael Robinson, its executive director, this project is in large part a reflection of AINA's original goal to promote sustainable small business development in the North. I extend my deep appreciation to Mike for the opportunity to write this book and for his enthusiastic support, encouragement, vision and guidance throughout this project.

Financial support for this project came from a variety of sources. Contributions are gratefully acknowledged from the Donner Canadian Foundation, Esso Resources Canada Limited, the Faculty of Management at the University of Calgary, the Department of Indian and Northern Affairs, and the Government of the Yukon.

The Centre for Aboriginal Management (CAMET) at the University of Lethbridge is joint copyright holder of Chapters 1, 6, and 8. They publish a series of original case studies in aboriginal management focusing on individual proprietorships, partnerships, bands, and tribal councils across Canada.

My sincere thanks to Ted Staffen for his organizational skill, assistance, and review of my work in the Yukon. The hospitality that he and his family extended made my work much easier. The key to this whole project, of course, was the participation of the entrepreneurs. It is with gratitude that I recognize their extensive support for this project through personal interviews, telephone conversations, and letters. All brought their unique perspective and candidly shared their experiences so that we may all learn from their insights about doing business in the North.

My thanks to Correna Phillips, Sandra Storm, and Nola Wuttunee for their invaluable assistance in transcribing many hours of taped interviews. Editing and advice were provided regularly by

Trevor Gonsalves and Michael Robinson, who helped keep me on the straight and narrow. Invaluable liaison support was provided by Joe Ohokannoak, regional tourism officer based in Cambridge Bay, NWT.

I wish to thank the individuals who agreed to review the manuscript informally and give me their valuable feedback: Lloyd Binder, Commissioner Ken McKinnon, and Dr Mark Dickerson. Thanks also to Marilyn Croot for her fine drafting of the maps; to Ona Stonkus and Dr Karen McCollough for their superb editing assistance and support.

Finally, and most importantly I must recognize the contribution of my family to this project. To my loving husband Trevor, my son Cody and daughter Drew, the most important people in my life: thank you for your loving support, adaptability and humor in seeing me through this project and for all the hugs and kisses that a mommy could hope for. Thanks to my family for all their love and support, especially Mom and Mom-in-law, Laurie and Nola.

PREFACE

In June 1989, research began on this project in an effort to promote the growth of sustainable, successful Northern small business. The fifteen businesses chosen as case studies operate in northern Alberta, the Yukon, and the Northwest Territories. These firms:

- represent a number of economic activities and geographical locations, with an emphasis on renewable resources, information, and service,
- have operated for a minimum of four years,
- provide local employment,
- operate in culturally and environmentally sensitive ways, and
- are successful.

These cases are presented for the most part in the words of the entrepreneurs themselves and are directed to other Northerners interested in starting a business and to students interested in the concerns of small business in isolated communities.

This work fills a need for case studies of northern businesses. Although good business techniques are straightforward, a northern reader receives a stronger message when reading about the good business practices of neighbours rather than about the usual southern success stories. This handbook presents a qualitative discussion from the business owners' perspective about the challenges and the satisfactions they find in running their businesses. It supplements the more technical information that a prospective entrepreneur might receive from an accountant, bank manager, or local economic development officer. Further, numerous common issues arising in running small businesses and in Native-owned businesses are exemplified for students interested in such topics.

Questions that the reader should be able to answer after reading this case study book include the following: What businesses might succeed in the North or in other isolated communities? What type of technical skills and personality do I need to be a successful business person? What alternatives do I have for financing my new business? How will my family's lifestyle be affected by my new business? What role, if any, can my family play in my business? The main message clearly made throughout this book is that independent, committed people are making a go of their businesses in the North.

Despite high expenses due to isolation and small markets, the businesses that survive and thrive are meeting the needs of their customers. The owners are committed to their clientele and have an excellent reputation in the community. The most common challenge facing these business people is hiring and retaining staff. They must deal with a small local labour force with limited skills. If they do find good staff, then they must compete with the government or big business to keep them.

Profit is only one measure of success for these business owners. Supporting their families in a chosen lifestyle, meeting the needs of the community, and being happy with their choice of occupations are as important, or more so, to these entrepreneurs. Living out their personal principles is also common to these people. They are aware of the importance of clean surroundings to their customers, and they all meet this minimal standard of environmental friendliness. Others go further and sell environmentally friendly products and consciously do their best to operate in ways that are safe for the environment.

I hope that I can convey the enthusiasm, style, and energy of these people. Over the two years I worked on this book, I came to talk about "my businesses." It is my desire that readers go away with the same feeling of connection and inspiration, and that this entrepreneurial spirit will see them through the accomplishment of their dreams.

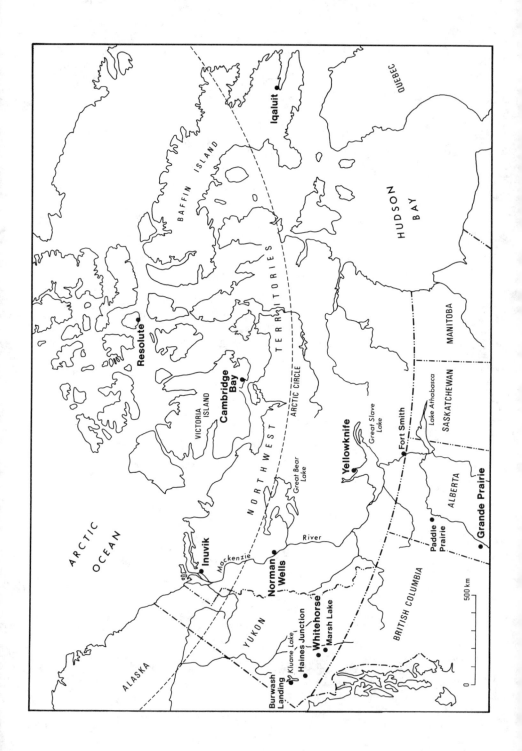

IN BUSINESS FOR OURSELVES

"First, look and see what the place needs
and then go for it. Be prepared to work
hard and try not to reap any financial
rewards right away. Put everything back
into the business and realize it takes time
to make a business work. Don't give up."

Fred Coman
Coman Arctic Ltd.

INTRODUCTION

This book examines a group of successful small businesses based in the North and the people who own and operate them. It is a forum for these entrepreneurs to describe in their own words their personal experiences during the growth of their businesses. To date, no other case study has focused exclusively on northern businesses. This means that northern teaching facilities have had no access to formal northern-based case-study materials. Their courses have relied on southern-based case studies or on informal presentations of local material from instructors.

Potential northern entrepreneurs will find concrete examples of decisions taken in the process of starting a business, of the challenges and benefits of operating one, and of the potential impact a new venture might have on them and their families. This information augments the quantifiable data commonly available from accountants, bankers, and economic development officers. Furthermore, this book provides a means of understanding the entrepreneurial experience for students of entrepreneurship and for those who wish to study the process of operating successful ventures in the North. Arguably, these lessons can also assist rural and small-town businesses in the rest of Canada and developing nations.

The question arises, why study small business? It is important to realize that the continued growth and development of a dynamic small business sector will play a critical role in Canada's future economic structure. According to the 1990 report, *Small Business in Canada,** companies with fewer than fifty employees were responsible

---

* Industry, Science, and Technology Canada. *Small Business in Canada*, 4–5, 11. All information in this paragraph and the next is from this source.

for 76.2% of all new jobs created in Canada between 1978 and 1988. Companies with fewer than twenty employees accounted for more than 60% of these new positions. The shift away from primary resource industries to information and service industries is underlined by the fact that 63% of the new jobs during the 1978–88 period arose in retail trade, community, business, and personal services.

Although trends in the late 1980s indicate that the cycle of rapid growth and job creation in the small-business sector may be countered by renewed activity of large businesses in the 1990s, the federal government is nonetheless committed to fostering the continued growth of the small-business sector across the country. The provincial and territorial governments share this attitude and continue to allocate major portions of their annual budgets to programs studying and serving the needs of small business.

Insight into the factors surrounding the growth of successful small businesses and the common obstacles faced by their owners in the development of their ventures is essential for those who provide support services and those who want to go into business themselves. For many, business ownership is a source of personal empowerment and financial independence. For northern entrepreneurs, this book may be the first opportunity to study the success of their neighbours' enterprises in any great detail.

Although the next questions – who is successful and why – are addressed in the text and summarized in the final chapter, it is crucial to consider the context in which small business must operate in the North. To date, a major factor in northern economic development has been megaprojects directed at development of nonrenewable resources such as oil, gas, and minerals. Many communities have experienced the highs and lows associated with the boom-bust cycles that are inextricably linked to this type of development: for example, increased job and business opportunities and cashflow into communities when projects start, loss of jobs and associated social problems when projects close down.

In the early 1980s, it became readily apparent to the frontier departments (a revealing phrase) of Canadian oil and gas companies working on major projects in the North (or as Berger styled it, the "homeland")* that Native and northern entrepreneurs were having a difficult time both in successfully bidding for work and completing

---

* Berger, *Northern Frontier*.

the contracts they won.* Robinson itemized nine reasons for these problems, some of which are still current today:

1 *Size of contracts*:   Typically, most major construction projects involve a handful of prime contractors and a larger number of subcontractors. Both groups generally have previous business experience and can handle contracts according to standard industry practice. Opportunities for Native and local businesses are traditionally hampered by the size of available contracts.

   As well, the contracts are generally designed for contractors who already have the necessary equipment and manpower on hand. When a prime contractor is unwilling to subcontract parts of the work, then the Native and local entrepreneur often cannot bid.

2 *Access to project information*:   This involves information of many kinds. It starts with information about standard business procedures. In the North, business practices tend to be more relaxed and informal than is usual for urban businesses. Paperwork and record-keeping are often kept to a minimum, and contract requirements may be given a more local than legal interpretation. Information about financing, bidding, legal questions, and labour agreements is often lacking, and answers are hard to get in remote communities. Contractors are often reluctant to treat bids from small local companies seriously, and consequently may not release enough information to enable them to prepare proper bids.

3 *Acquisition of management skills*:   A large proportion of the northern adult population has not been educated beyond grade 8, and very few Native and local entrepreneurs have had formal training in business or administration. This lack of management skills has hindered business development and has contributed to the development of support programs by the Department of Indian and Northern Affairs and many well-intentioned corporate purchasers in the North. Many Native and local businessmen have been taught more about government subsidies, forgivable grants, northern mark-up schemes, and interest-free loans than about sound management practices.

4 *Risk-taking ability*:   Native and local entrepreneurs often lack the analytical skills to forecast the risk associated with new business ventures. Risk-taking ability tends to be learned by successful

---

* Robinson, *Native and Local Economics*.

business people with experience. When artificial factors such as discrimination, bail-out expectations, and community alienation get in the way of legitimate "bottom line" business experience, risk-taking cannot develop as a skill.

5 *Bail-out expectations*: The net result of many business development programs of industry and government has been to create the expectation that firms in trouble will be bailed out. Forgivable loans and grants and no-strings-attached economic development funds have contributed to the creation of this atmosphere in many Native and local businesses. Predictably, businesses founded on this philosophy do not prosper. Another legacy of this approach is the expectance of immediate dividends and capital appreciation – something that few small businesses achieve in the first five years of their operation.

6 *Lack of self-confidence*: A further legacy of bail-out expectations and a lack of management skills is waning self-confidence. To have one's business fail is depressing for any entrepreneur; when a Native business fails, it appears to confirm a "known truth": Native people are business failures. Paradoxically, many traditional values of hunting cultures are those of successful entrepreneurs: self-reliance and initiative, the family unit of production, generalist skills, and friendly competition for high production.*

7 *Discrimination: locality, race, sex*: Discrimination based on locality of business or residence and on race, and sex is probably as old as mankind, but it appears especially prevalent in small populations where positive role models are in short supply. The best way to challenge discrimination is to argue by counterexample, using either your own actions or those of others nearby. Negative stereotypes resist change, and business practices tend to follow "accepted wisdom" in the field.

8 *Alienation of entrepreneur*: In a community with few business people, their merits and contributions may be poorly understood and appreciated. Consequently, even though there are parallels between Native and local "bush values" and entrepreneurial values, these parallels may not be widely understood. In many Native communities, Native entrepreneurs are ostracized in proportion to their success, which may be viewed as alien to the values of the community. For some entrepreneurs, "success" may mean leaving the community for town and the fellowship of other en-

---

* Robinson and Ghostkeeper, "Native and Local Economics," 138–44.

trepreneurs. In town, the discrimination may prevent them from being accepted and having a chance to share interests. The end result for the Native entrepreneur may therefore be disillusionment with *both* communities, and an eventual return home in failure, which only serves to reinforce the Native community stereotype held by non-Native entrepreneurs.

9 *Access to risk capital*: Risk capital generally accrues to the successful risk-takers. Given that the history of small-business risk-taking in Native and local contexts is not glowing, access to money for new ventures is often difficult. Therefore, when a new idea with exceptional merit comes along, venture capitalists may view it with a jaundiced eye. All workable business ideas deserve the same degree of financiers' consideration; in practice the northern experience shows that they do not receive it.

Clearly the experience of Native and local entrepreneurs with the northern oil patch in the late 1970s and early 1980s was mixed. While they gained valuable experience, it was not without a price. And too often the price was a reinforcement of negative opinions about small business as a career and a vocation. Many Northerners were, however, able to learn first-hand about federal environmental regulatory regimes, big business in the industrial economy, and the promotion of megaprojects.

Another major obstacle facing small-business development in the North is the prodigious presence of the Territorial governments and to a lesser extent the federal government. Many bright young northern people are groomed for positions in these bureaucracies through high-paying summer jobs and full-time employment after completion of their studies. This practice leaves very few skilled people in local labour pools available to small business. Some might argue that the economic opportunities available to small business through servicing the government's needs directly or those of its employees serve to counterbalance the employee drain. Other challenges for northern small business are small markets for products and services, isolated communities, limited financial services, and high transportation costs.

Northern communities are mostly small. According to the *Northwest Territories Data Book*, 1990–1, communities range in size from twenty-nine people in Kakiska to 13,000 people in Yellowknife, using estimates made in 1988. Thirty-two communities have less than 500 people, sixteen communities have populations between 500 and 999, seven communities have populations between 1,000 and 2,000 people, and five communities have more than 2,000 people. Statistics for the Yukon estimate a range from 40 people in Keno to 18,385 people in Whitehorse, according to the Yukon Data Book 1986–7. There were three communities with less than 100 people, ten communities with populations between 100 and 500, two communities with 500 to 1,000 people, and three communities with more than 1,000 people.

The positive factors which support small business in the North include: limited competition, the chance to provide essential services to communities, opportunities for those with little or no formal training, and (as mentioned) economic spin-off opportunities from the strong government presence. Other personal factors that might attract entrepreneurs in the North include lifestyle choices for their families and the chance to combine traditional cultural practices and modern business opportunities.

Entrepreneurs

The following section gives a brief introduction to the successful entrepreneurs profiled in this book:

Elmer and Kim Ghostkeeper, Paddle Prairie Mall Corp.
Elmer developed the idea for a grocery store, self-service gas station, and laundromat for introduction into the Métis settlement of Paddle Prairie, Alta. He conducted a market survey, assessed the feasibility of his ideas, and opened up for business in 1986. Kim is involved now as manager in the daily operations of the business. She has successfully juggled family and business responsibilities, as well as managing her employees so as to encourage their loyalty and commitment to their business. The profile examines the experience of this Métis couple from the start-up through four years of operations to the stage where they want to sell their business.

Sandra and Don Jaque, Cascade Publishing Ltd
Sandra and Don publish the *Slave River Journal* in Fort Smith, NWT. In addition, they offer a successful computer graphics service, retail office supplies, and lease office space in the building they own. Regular strategic moves to position their services to best advantage are based on their constant monitoring of trends in the marketplace. They are creative in attracting and keeping their employees, despite the pressures exerted by the territorial government as a high-paying employer.

Fred Coman, Coman Arctic Ltd
Fred came to Iqaluit, NWT, in search of work more than twenty years

ago. Now he is one of a few successful business people making their mark on the community with minimal financial assistance from the government. He provides moving, cartage, and janitorial services to the local and surrounding communities. Fred recently opened an art gallery, an area of personal interest for many years.

William Lyall, Ikaluktutiak Co-operative Ltd

Bill is president of the Co-op located in Cambridge Bay (NWT) and the president of Arctic Co-operatives Limited, the umbrella organization for the forty-one co-ops operating in the Northwest Territories. The Ikaluktutiak Co-op operates an arctic char fishery, grocery store, hotel, taxi, and cable service company, with annual sales in 1990 of $3.5 million. Bill, an Inuk, is a driving force in the organization, and his reflections about the company and its future are presented.

Alex Gauthier and Earl Jacobson, Lou's Small Engines and Sports Ltd

Alex and his brother-in-law Earl operate a repair shop and a retail outlet for sporting goods, all-terrain vehicles, bicycles, and outboard motors in Fort Smith, NWT. They have continued in the tradition established by Alex's brother Lou for excellent service.

George Angohiotok and Bill Tait, Northern Emak Outfitting Inc.

Inuit brothers George and Gary operate a fishing camp north of Cambridge Bay, NWT, with two partners, Bill Tait of Adventure North Expeditions Ltd. and Jerome Knapp, a journalist. Bill books the tourists through his company in Yellowknife and handles the marketing and accounting, while George and Gary manage the fishing camp. Mabel, George's wife, helps with the guests and conducts tours of the town and local area; the majority of her customers are booked through Bill Tait's company. This is a new company and their startup experience is profiled in interviews with George, Mabel, and Bill.

Mo Grant, Raven Enterprises (Inuvik) Ltd

When Mo came to explore Canada for six months in 1972, she never envisioned herself as a successful businesswoman living in Inuvik NWT, almost twenty years later. She purchased Mac's News, a retail outlet for books, magazines, and gifts in 1979. Recently she opened Midnight Express boat tours and Road's End Deli.

Freddie Carmichael, Western Arctic Air Ltd

One of the first Métis pilots accredited in the Northwest Territories, Freddie has been flying for more than thirty years. This chapter

profiles his experience in operating Western Arctic Air in partnership
with the Mackenzie Delta Regional Corporation. He also started a
summer tour company called Antler Tours. Fred recently sold his
share in Western Arctic Air to the Inuvialuit Regional Corporation
and started a new venture called Western Arctic Nature Tours.

Paul Birckel, Champagne–Aishihik Enterprises Ltd
Chief Paul Birckel has been the driving force behind expansion of a
Yukon band-operated construction company. Many band employees
have received training and employment opportunities through this
company. Harold Kane, general manager for the organization, also
shares his views on the company's operations.

Bill and Melody Doehle, Gary and Laurie Putland, Lakeview Resort and Marina
Bill and his sister Laurie are partners with their spouses in a resort
marina located on Marsh Lake, Yukon. Their business serves as an
important focus for the community, as many locals are regular patrons of their restaurant and lounge. They have ten motel rooms,
ten cabins, and an RV park with full hookups, as well as a small
grocery store. They also have a marina with storage and docking
facilities. The chapter profiles their activities since the purchase of
the business in 1986.

John Ostashek, Ostashek Outfitting Ltd
John is recognized internationally for the standards he meets in
offering big game hunts in the Yukon, a reputation he has earned
over the past thirty-two years. He markets his services through
several very successful United States trade shows. In 1981, he
opened another business called Glacier Air Tours, which provides
air trips over local glaciers for tourists. He recently sold the outfitting
company but plans to continue operating the tour company.

Chuck Halliday, Taylor Chevrolet Oldsmobile Dealership
Taylor Chev Olds opened as a division of the Taylor and Drury
trading house empire in 1927. This chapter profiles the Whitehorse
firm's operations since Chuck Halliday joined it in 1966. Charles
Taylor, son of Issac Taylor (one of the original founders) adds some
of his early memories of working in the family firm.

Lorne Metropolit, Yukon Botanical Gardens
Six years ago, Lorne began work on making his dream of a botanical
show garden in Whitehorse a reality. He has developed several

phases of the total project, which involves twenty-two acres of hardy wildflowers, plants, and shrubs, an exotic bird display, and a farm attraction for the family. A garden centre sells seeds, shrubs, hothouse tomatoes, and bedding plants. He recalls the challenges he faced during the startup of his venture and discusses the future of this unique tourist attraction.

Danny Nolan, Yukon Game Farm Ltd

For the past twenty years, supplying top-quality northern animals to zoos and game farms around the world has earned Danny an outstanding international reputation. The game farm was originally conceived as a tourist attraction, but Danny soon realized that there was no market to support his venture, so he changed his focus to breeding. Recently, he reached an agreement with a major tour company, and now busloads of tourists visit his farm from May through September.

Ethel, Translation and Interpretation Services

Ethel, an Inuk businesswoman, started a small business offering translation and interpretation services several years ago. It allows her to use her training while still raising her children at home. Her overload work gives opportunities for other women in the community to earn extra money. (She has asked that her real name and that of her business not be used.)

Although income from small business is never certain, small business is a viable alternative for Northerners who want to break their dependency on externally controlled development projects or who want to work outside large government and corporate bureaucracies. It is essential that new businesses provide products or services that fill a market need that does not depend on megaprojects. This type of sustainable enterprise is further strengthened when environmentally friendly products, services, and operational practices are followed, protecting physical resources for future generations.

A need exists to encourage more small businesses in the North as one way to a more secure economic future. In addition, with land claim settlements looming in the future, economic opportunities and spinoffs for Native and non-Native communities and business people will abound. What can we do to inspire entrepreneurship? One way is to share the experiences of people who are thriving while doing business in the North. The next sections describe the methodology followed in putting this study together and the organization of the book.

Methodology

A list of prerequisites for the type of businesses included in the study was developed, as noted in the preface. Personal interviews were the main source of data, and a questionnaire was developed to use as a guide in the discussions. Ted Staffen, a successful businessman himself and a Yukon resident for twenty years, was hired to assist in the Yukon portion of the work. He identified a number of potential subjects who then were interviewed by the author. The final selection was made after further discussion with Mike Robinson, Executive Director of the Arctic Institute of North America (AINA).

Lists of potential study subjects in the Northwest Territories came from such diverse sources as the Northwest Territories Science Institute, AINA Board members and research associates. Ideally, we wanted businesses at varying times in the business cycle (from startup to maturity) and with a range of organizations (single owner, partnership, community development corporation, and cooperative). Potential participants outside the Yukon were sent letters describing the project, and follow-up telephone interviews ascertained their suitability and level of interest in participating in the project.

The terms of the project allowed entrepreneurs to limit the information they released. One participant preferred to remain anonymous. Two chose to release no financial information, and two provided limited financial data.

Fifteen businesses across the North were finally selected. Each participant signed a consent form setting out the terms of reference for the research project. Draft chapters were reviewed by the author's spouse (who has a small business), by AINA's director, and by the respective participants. Each profile in this book has been checked by the appropriate business owner or team for accuracy.

Organization

Each chapter profiles a business venture and employs a similar style, with a core of common sections beginning with the history of the enterprise. Some chapters include additional subsections, for example, if there is more than one business or if the planning stages of the business were particularly complex. After the business history comes a description of current operations. This section usually concludes with subsections on problems with staffing and competitors.

A brief review of financial practices and some past financial statement information helps to convey the level of financial return generated by these businesses and the size of their operations. Return-on-equity and asset utilization ratios are presented, with total salaries. These ratios are defined in Appendix 1.

Profitability of the businesses varied throughout the sample, depending upon various factors. For example, Champagne-Aishihik Enterprises had a negative return on equity for four of the last five years because of high training costs. Profitability was not a major goal of this operation and they do offer an excellent example of the pressures that a band-operated business commonly experiences. Yukon Botanical Gardens is an example of a start-up operation that survived many challenges but only met its expenses and is now beginning to earn a return. Lakeview Resort and Marina showed no positive return on equity over the four years examined, but major writeoffs were taken to minimize tax consequences.

The next sections identify the reasons for success of the business according to the entrepreneur or entrepreneurial team, and the areas of strength and needed improvement that they identified. Many of the chapters examine company policy regarding both environmental issues and the potential impact a downturn in demand might have on the company's survival. Plans for the future are outlined and some chapters include advice to new businesses. Each study concludes with a summary. The book's final chapter summarizes the study findings and identifies common elements in the data. Appendix 1 presents definitions of key terms. Appendix 2 is a checklist that highlights key issues raised by the case studies.

The following chapters offer an opportunity to develop an understanding of the personal experiences, principles, and ideas from the perspective of these entrepreneurs.

Michael P. Robinson
Wanda A. Wuttunee

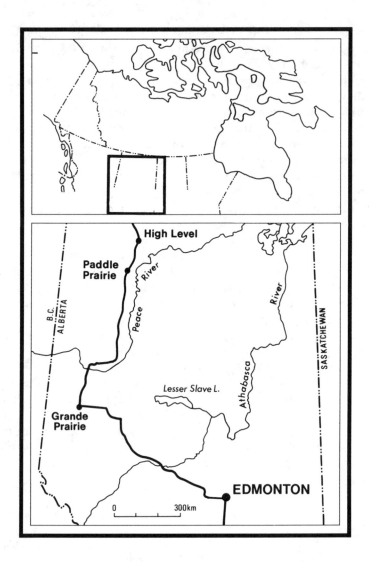

ENTREPRENEURS' ENDORSEMENT

We, the undersigned, acknowledge that we have read our business profile. We approve of the contents of the profile and recognize its accuracy in describing our business.

Dated ⟨signature⟩ , 1990

Elmer Ghostkeeper   Kim Ghostkeeper

1
PADDLE PRAIRIE MALL CORPORATION
Paddle Prairie, Alberta

Elmer and Kim Ghostkeeper own and operate a convenience store, coin laundromat, and self-serve gasoline bar in the small Métis settlement of Paddle Prairie, located in northern Alberta. After two and a half years of planning, Ghostkeeper's Store opened for business in Paddle Prairie on October 28, 1986. This is the only business of its kind operating in a community of 700 individuals.

Elmer was born in Paddle Prairie and returned to the community in August 1986 to begin construction of the store. He operated the store on a daily basis until Kim completed a teaching contract in Edmonton and moved to the community in December 1986. Kim took over daily management, including bookkeeping. Elmer continues to handle overall planning and participates in major decisions. The goal in starting the store in Paddle Prairie was to provide needed services to the settlement through a small business that could be economically viable. The store is a success, with a majority of its business coming from the community. Elmer and Kim point to the convenience and dependability of their service, as well as the friendly atmosphere, as the main factors for their success.

History

Elmer and Kim feel a portion of the success of their business is due to their past training and experience. Elmer is bilingual in Cree and English and earned a diploma in civil engineering technology and a bachelors' degree in cultural anthropology and political science. He has farmed his own land on the settlement, worked as assistant city engineer in Whitehorse, Yukon, and served as president of the Alberta Federation of Métis Settlement Associations.* Elmer also

---

* Robinson and Ghostkeeper, "Implementing the Next Economy," 175.

Elmer and Kim Ghostkeeper

operates an ongoing consulting practice, Ghostkeeper Synergetics, for both industry and Native organizations, as well as a horse breeding and training company called Métis Morgan Farm. "I think an important factor in the success of the business is that I have a good engineering background and a fairly good social science background. My past experience consulting for companies means that I am used to working seven days a week, starting at 7:00 every morning."

Kim also has a diversified background. She holds a Native Communications Certificate and a Bachelor of Arts degree from the University of Alberta. Kim worked in public relations for Native Outreach, has consulted for industry and government, hosted a television program for five years, and acted as Native Affairs officer for the University of Alberta. She also taught in the communications program at Grant MacEwan College in Edmonton. "Most of my work was short-term contracts. That's what prepared me for working in the store. I am used to no guaranteed money, no guaranteed hours, flexibility, diversification of tasks, and deadlines. My communication skills have helped me deal with the public. I think I work very well with all the suppliers and we all get along really well."

The store is highly accessible to highway and local traffic since it is located at the main entrance to the community, at an intersection with the Mackenzie Highway. Land cannot be purchased on a Métis settlement. Elmer holds a certificate of occupancy to the land his store is built on and therefore has the right to any improvements made to the land. Elmer purchased the right years ago. He recalls, "Dad said it would be an excellent idea if I bought the right to occupy the piece of land where the store is now and then thought about a business. He was looking at the future. He said it would be an excellent location and I agreed. So I bought the right to occupy the land, even though I didn't have a business in mind." Negotiations are ongoing and eventually the Paddle Prairie Métis Settlement Association will receive title to the land from the province of Alberta. Once the title to the land is received, then the provincial government and the Federation of Métis Settlements will determine what businesses on the settlement will pay.

Elmer recalls, "When I decided not to seek another term as president with the Métis Federation in 1984, I decided I was going to go back to the settlement, but I really didn't know in what capacity or in what business. At that time the settlement had done a Future Demand Survey, to see what types of services people wanted in the community. Number one was a small store. Number two was a laundromat. They wanted individuals to pursue those ideas. So I did. I did more research and more demand surveys. I found that there was a demand, and people were willing to utilize a store."

Planning Process
The type of questionnaire Elmer used to determine the need for the store and gas bar is reproduced in Table 1.* It asked questions of settlement members that allowed Elmer to attempt a forecast of the success of the business. Since the provincially operated general store closed in 1971, community members have done their shopping in High Level (seventy-two kilometers away) or in Manning (129 kilometers away). The results of his demand survey indicated that 80% of Paddle Prairie households would shop at a community store if prices were competitive with High Level stores.

The next phase of the planning process was to choose a business strategy. Based on the responses to the demand survey, Elmer decided to offer fast, informal, personal service with a good selection of high-quality merchandise. The old government store had left unpleasant memories, and the new store would have to avoid repeating the same mistakes.

---

* All quotations in the next three paragraphs come from *ibid.*, 176.

Table 1
Paddle Prairie Mall Corp. Demand Survey

DATE: January 1984
PLACE: Paddle Prairie Metis Settlement

SURVEY QUESTIONS:
Presently our settlement spends almost all of its income in other communities. This deprives settlement members of business and employment opportunities. This survey is to determine if a general store and gas bar would be successful in getting your support if they were established here by a settlement member.

1. Do you think the settlement should have a general store?
2. Do you think the settlement should have a gas bar selling regular and unleaded gas?
3. Would you support a general store and gas bar by buying groceries and gas there?
4. Presently where do you do most of your shopping?
   High Level _____ Manning _____ Others _____
5. Approximately how much money do you spend in a week in other communities on food? _____
6. Approximately how much money do you spend in a week in other communities on gas? _____
7. If the settlement had a general store and a gas bar, how much do you think you would spend there each week? _____

THANK YOU

Elmer and Kim are proud of their Métis heritage. It was important to them to incorporate the Métis way of doing business into the way their store was operated. According to Robinson and Ghostkeeper, "The Métis way is above all practical, self-reliant, action-oriented, conserving of capital, and very often brilliant in its simplicity." Therefore the new store would rely on its own resources; it would be a profit-making business and the Métis way would be important to the way they conducted their business.

After three and a half years in operation, Elmer notes:

The operation of the store has equaled our expectations, but I overestimated the demand. I estimated that each family would spend $100 a month and they're not spending that. The reason for this, I think, is that there hasn't been a store on the settlement for fourteen or fifteen years and people have built up a pattern of shopping in High Level or in Manning. Over the fourteen years of doing the shopping and making a social trip out of it, as well as a business trip, they just don't want to change.

But now the younger people are shopping more and more at the store, and I find that people that are working shop at the store more than nonworking people, people that are on social assistance or on unemployment or on pensions. These people have the time to go to High Level or Manning or even go as far as Grande Prairie to shop. Even though it's quite a distance, they can manage it on social assistance. But the working people shop at the store because ... they don't have that extra time to run to town whenever they want. So they use the store more often.

*Financing**
The first step that Elmer and Kim took was to limit their personal financial liability by incorporating the Paddle Prairie Mall Corp. (The operating name for the store, as mentioned earlier, is Ghostkeeper's Store.) Elmer and Kim decided that they did not want to borrow the start-up financing they required from a bank. Instead they decided to seek other investors who would purchase shares in their corporation. This money would be used to meet the expenses of building the store and paying for the starting inventory.

The corporation has two types of shares, Class A voting and Class B non-voting. Class A shares were available for purchase by Paddle Prairie residents at $100 per share. Anyone who purchased a Class A share could vote at the annual general meeting and could receive dividend payments at the discretion of the board of directors of the corporation. Class B non-voting shares were offered to corporations at $600 per share. Class B shareholders are not entitled to vote at the annual general meeting and are eligible for dividends at the option of the board. Class A shareholders may choose to buy back the shares of Class B shareholders. This share structure allows the entrepreneurs to raise funds without going to a bank.

A detailed business plan was given to potential investors in Class A shares and a share offering with a prospectus (a legal document which sets out required financial information about the company and its plans) was presented to potential corporate buyers of Class B shares. Elmer and Kim own all of the Class A shares. No one in the community purchased shares because of the risk associated with a new business and the fact that the business would have to earn enough to pay management salaries to both Kim and Elmer.

One hundred Class B shares were purchased by the Native Venture Capital Co. Ltd. and the federal and provincial governments provided two small capital grants for construction. In addition, Elmer made a personal loan to the Paddle Prairie Mall Corp. Part

---

* All information in this section comes from *ibid.*, 177–8.

Ghostkeeper's Store

of the capital expenditures required for the gas bar were picked up by the oil company, which provided the gas pumps and signs, while the operator bought fuel and became partners with the supplier. Each oil company is different, and so Elmer shopped around before deciding to sell gas for Husky Oil.

Once it was clear that the store would be a reality, Elmer began planning its design. He wanted a much more open design than the one typically used by the Hudson's Bay in Northern communities. Working with an architect, they developed a design. "It was decided to use typical northern Alberta farm design elements: a covered front porch, a barn slope roof and wood frame construction. The interior was to be open plan, contain public space for resting and eating and be well lit with both natural and overhead lighting. The chosen colour scheme was to feature Métis reds, yellows, greens and blues in order to reflect the bold traditions of Métis dress (the sash particularly) and bead work."

Elmer acted as the main contractor and hired local people to assist him with the excavation and building of the store. The following year, a small residence was added to the main building. This space will be used for future store expansion. Elmer recalls, "At the end of each day, I did a five- to ten-minute video-log of our progress for the use of other local entrepreneurs. We had good weather and we worked twelve to sixteen hours a day, seven days a week. We started construction on August 3, and by October 26 we had the store open for business, on time and on budget. This experience provided good memories, especially looking at a barley field with nothing there and then driving the first piece of machinery on it and starting to build."

Operations

Kim Ghostkeeper manages the daily operations of the store while Elmer provides general management expertise. He monitors the financial progress of the store, shares the major decision-making with Kim, and plans the overall future course for the business. The store is open seven days a week from 9:00 a.m. to 9:00 p.m.

The store features modern, computerized equipment. The gasoline bar is monitored by a computer and the store's cash register is the latest computerized model. The cash register tape gives Kim and Elmer a daily report of the revenue earned from the sale of groceries, gasoline, cigarettes, and videos. If there are problems with the equipment, the computer blinks to indicate the problem circuits. A new circuit board component can be ordered from Edmonton and Elmer can replace it himself without a service technician.*

Elmer and Kim own shares in their major supplier, the Grocery People, based in Edmonton. Experts from the Grocery People come into the store to advise on how to facilitate customer flow through the store, on what products to carry, and on pricing policies. The store carries canned and fresh goods, automotive supplies, and some hardware items. It also offers fast food and coffee and an area to sit and eat in. The store acts as the bus depot and freight office and has a coin laundromat called Dirt Busters Laundry in an Atco trailer. The laundromat features seven washing machines and eight dryers.

Elmer notes that rural business is simply different: "There is site maintenance that requires extra equipment, such as for snow removal, cutting the grass and garbage disposal. Also we do our banking twice a week in the town of High Level. It's a total of about eight hours, including travel time and doing the actual banking. There's also the added gas expense."

Kim describes her involvement in the store, "It really is varied and in the past three and a half years, my role has changed a lot. In the

---

* *Ibid.*, 179.

beginning, of course, I spent a lot of time in the store. I would work a regular shift myself, clerking behind the counter. That way it gave me an idea of what was happening on a daily basis. Now, I try to be here on Mondays to set the week up and I write all the cheques for what we have ordered from suppliers who are coming during the week. I can get almost anything through the Grocery People. Sometimes, though, it's better to deal with the local suppliers because I'm interested in trying to give as much business to northern Alberta suppliers."

A tight credit policy is in place for individuals and companies. There have been very few cheques returned for insufficient funds. Kim explains:

I have a policy that just about anybody locally can write a personal cheque but with the first NSF cheque I stop that. As a result of this policy, I have about five people on a "Never Cash A Cheque" list because I had a real tough time collecting on the NSF cheque. I'll let them cash a cheque because they don't have any money owing to me, but I just had such a bad experience I won't take their personal cheques. ... I may have lost their business because of it but I don't want to take the chance. It's the same thing with not accepting cheques from out-of-town people; it's a personal decision.

The girls have to have ownership of the cheques that they accept, so each girl signs the back of a cheque when they accept a personal cheque. They are to follow regulations. They are not to accept out-of-town cheques unless they have approval by Elmer or myself. Then the responsibility about the cheque is on our shoulders because we agreed to it. But if it just has her name on it, then the responsibility for the cheque is on her shoulders.

Some small local businesses run accounts with Ghostkeeper's Store. Kim explains, "We bill them twice a month, on the 15th and the 30th. We also have companies like NOVA, and Husky and their subcontractors that run accounts here. The other thing we have are vendor notes which are for government vehicles. They'll pay us with a vendor note which is like a credit note and then we have to invoice the head office. I try to keep the vendor notes up to date. They mean extra bookkeeping but some of my accounts amount to $1,000 per month, so it's very worthwhile."

Kim can recall only one incident where an account was unpaid. "I've had to close one account, which took us for $700. It was rather stupid, but it made me tougher on delinquent accounts. If an account is in arrears my standard letter is that if they don't pay, I have the right to close the account or to fold the account and not let them charge any more."

Kim does the bookkeeping with an accountant out of Edmonton.

I don't know whether it is good or bad to have an accountant so far away. I think if I had it to do all over again, knowing what I know now, I probably would have an accountant who was closer, so I could have had a chance to see them more often. I do everything; then I ship it all down to him. We get on the phone and go over my work. At the year end, either Elmer or I go over the books with the accountant so that we understand the year-end financial statements.

He'll make suggestions and recommendations on how I can improve the system for the following year so it will make it easier for them to do the calculations, and this also gives me more ability to take care of things myself. For instance, in my first year I didn't know how to do cheque reconciliations. They tried and tried to teach me over the phone but it was just a hopeless case. So I never reconciled cheques. I hired somebody to reconcile them and when she did them, I finally understood what was going on. The bookkeeping process gets better and better every year with experience.

It probably would have been helpful to take a basic bookkeeping course prior to trying to do it on the job. I think things would have come to me a lot faster and I wouldn't have been so frustrated in the beginning.

Expectations
After running the store for three and a half years, Kim recalls her initial expectations.

I thought when you had your own business that you were the boss and all the little workers did all the work. I thought I'd have more time to get away to travel, which I don't."

Before we started the business, I was going to have all these policies about what we were going to do in the North – bring all this fresh produce to Paddle Prairie. There's no point in buying produce for the store because people just don't buy it. They'll buy apples and oranges, maybe, but they're seasonal. They're fickle about the bananas we order. Now we order only the staples ... lettuce, tomatoes, cucumbers, celery, potatoes, and onions, and that's about it.

I was going to have some community responsibility and I wasn't going to sell candy to the kids so their teeth would just rot away. Did you notice how much candy I ordered today? Now three-quarters of my store is candy. All your ideas about what you're going to do and what is reality sometimes don't mix.

The perks that we've finally been able to take, I guess, aren't the kind of things that I thought they would be. I thought when we had our own business and it was really successful, I was going to buy things that I really wanted, the luxuries of life. In fact, that's not how it works. In the first couple of years, every cent of profit went right back into the business. Elmer always found things that we needed more than we needed new curtains, more than we needed the dishwasher, which we still don't have. There was always some piece of equipment, gravel, or things for the business that we had to buy.

It's like a new baby. It demands your time, your money, your everything. Finally, this year we've purchased some of the things that a couple would have bought anyway, like new curtains and bikes for the kids. I don't really want for anything any more. Our priorities have changed. When I lived in the city I was too wrapped up in competing with the next person. Now I'm too busy to care what the next person is buying this season. We've become very practical. That's the difference, I think.

Staff

Staff turnover is one of the biggest problems that Kim and Elmer face. Kim recalls, "Over the past three and a half years, I've trained lots of staff. My highest was twenty-four people through the year. Now I have three full-time staff. They are really topnotch staff. Not only do I have good regular staff, I have extra staff who are on call. They've all worked in the store and they know how things run and how I want things done."

In order to encourage staff satisfaction with their jobs, Kim begins by setting out certain expectations for each person as part of a winning team. Then she tries to give them some authority and responsibility and she asks for their input on how to improve the operations of the store. Finally, she offers employee benefits.

Expectations for staff are recorded in the "Store Bible". This is a document that each new staff member reads at the start of the job. It welcomes the new member and outlines the daily operations to Kim and Elmer's specifications. It describes the importance of cleanliness, inside and outside, and of employees' job attitude and appearance. It also covers topics such as the duties of a sales clerk, credit policies, cheque-cashing policies, the importance of the store's public image in terms of advertising, and the role played by the store in the community.

The wage scale and raises are also listed in the "Store Bible." "We were told by the girls that they need to know what they could expect in terms of their wage. They didn't want to go on hoping that I would consider giving them a raise, and deep down I didn't want to have to guess when would be the appropriate time. Now it's written in the store policy."

Kim states, "I try to give the clerks as much authority over things and as much responsibility as I can because I'm not here all the time and because they're capable." As mentioned above, each employee takes responsibility for any cheque that she cashes. Further, Kim encourages them to make a list of inventory they think should be purchased. The girls often develop a strong sense of responsibility and commitment to their work because they have developed a sense of ownership of their role in the store.

But the responsibility can also create problems. In early 1989, the Ghostkeepers tried training an employee for the position of assistant manager. At the end of six months, the woman decided not to stay because she felt that she was given too much responsibility and too much was expected of her. She felt all her energy was going into the business and her family was suffering because of it. Kim comments, "Many women I've met who are in business seem to suffer a major case of guilt. I don't know if it's because we are women or just the nature of business. We all seem to feel guilty that we don't spend enough time with our business or our family and we feel guilty for the amount of time we spend on ourselves."

Kim describes times when she has sought staff input into the store operations.

Problems started when I began feeling like the lowest person on the totem pole. I didn't even feel I had clerk status because I ended up scrubbing toilets and emptying garbage and washing things that people didn't want to wash. I ended up doing all the things that nobody else really wanted to do. I soon realized that there's a lot of things that are not very glorious about this business.

Then I began thinking, "Do I really want to sell potato chips for the rest of my life? I mean, is this what I worked so hard to do? There's no reward there." Then, to make matters worse, I was listening to a businessman talking about starting a business which had eventually developed into a multimillion dollar business. But he said that in the first years he didn't really see any payoff. There's just no payoff and it's a real struggle. I guess in fact we are still in that period where all I see is a lot of work.

It was getting to a point where that's all I saw, just work, and it was just a drudgery for me to come in. But there I was telling staff "I want you to be lively and I want you to feel good about working at the store. You're more than just a clerk and you've got one of the best jobs in the community." But I wasn't feeling that way, so I really had to look at why I was doing this. If I'm making the commitment to stay in this business, then I've got to feel good about it too.

Dirt Busters Laundry

So what I did was, I sat down with my staff and said, "Okay, we've made the commitment to be in this business for another year. So what can we do to give ourselves some goals to shoot for and some way of assessing how we meet our goals? Let's be innovative and if it fails, fine, but we won't know until we try. We say we have the potential to be innovative because nobody else is pulling our strings here, so let's do it." Now we're excited about that. We're thinking of ways to revitalize ourselves.

Let's look at some of the things that we were doing that we're really proud about doing. The *Tamarack Post* was a bimonthly newsletter and was one thing that I was proud about doing and I dropped it. Let's pick it up and do it again because that makes me feel good. Let's do some of the things that the staff thinks makes them feel good. So we're going to try to be creative and innovative and try some things and assess them, evaluate them and see if they are bombs or blossoms. Then we're going to set some goals, some three month, some six month, and some twelve month goals with some payoffs, too. I think that overall the business will be better off for it.

Finally, Kim describes the benefits for an employee. "We have a health care plan through the Grocery People. It covers dental and

medical expenses. It really matters here, because if you get an am-
bulance, it's very expensive. The employee picks up all that expense.
We pick up a small life insurance policy for each of our workers."

Competition

The store's closest competitor is in Keg River, about twenty miles
away from Paddle Prairie. It was completely flooded out two years
ago. Kim notes, "They just rebuilt last year and they have a food
store about the same size as ours. They have a gas station which is
full service as opposed to self service. They have an auto mechanic,
which we do not have. They also have a restaurant and a motel."

Kim does not think that the new store has had a negative impact
on her business. She states, "I think in some ways competition is
good because it forces you to become a better business. They're not
really competitive with us because their prices are higher. In listening
to customers who don't like to shop there, we have better customer
service here, as far as they're concerned. I've actually found we've
increased our sales since they opened. The other thing I think is
that if we had some competition it would help us."

Elmer thinks that competition from another store in Paddle Prairie
would be a good idea. He explains:

I think it would make us a little more keen. Since we have the monopoly
right now there's no reason to be competitive. There is enough business
for two stores. Say, there are 700 people in the settlement and each person
spends $200 a month on food and necessities, you're looking at $140,000 a
month. So then each store realistically makes $50,000 to $60,000 per month.

I think there's room for another store. The thing is, I know there are other
individuals thinking about a business but they can never get past that stage
to actually implementing it. They don't have the expertise to do the demand
survey and the business plan, which you need to get financing.

Advertising

Ghostkeeper's Store has a small advertising budget. Kim explains,
"I use the advertising money every year for such things as T-shirts
with our names on it. We also order a special gift for the store to
give customers at Christmas. One year it was a little calendar with
an owl, that said, 'I wisely shop at Ghostkeeper's.' It also said Paddle
Prairie on it. They're all over the place here. We give them away
and people sent them to their friends and relatives. It's that great."

In the past, Kim has organized a number of promotions, such as
raffles and prizes for customers after they spent a certain amount. She
and her staff will organize more promotions as part of the program

Table 2
Financial Information for Paddle Prairie Mall Corp., Ghostkeeper's Store and Dirt
Busters Laundry

	1987	1988	1989
Return on Equity (%)	25	12	10
Sales/Assets (times)	2.24	2.29	2.40
Total Salaries ($)	35,637	37,101	29,466

of revitalizing interest in the operations of the store, mentioned above.

Financial Information

Total revenues earned since the beginning of operations have averaged more than $500,000 each year over the three-year period from 1987 to 1989. Revenues from the store grew from 58% of total operations in 1987 to 66% in 1989. Gas bar receipts provide the balance of the revenues. Total daily sales earned from the store and the gas bar average between $1,400 and $1,600 per day.

As illustrated in Table 2, the return on equity has declined from a high of 25% in 1987 to 10% in 1989. The store has been profitable since it opened and a variable return-on-equity ratio (ROE) is expected in the first years of operation. In other words, for every dollar invested by the owners, they earned 25¢ in profit during 1987 compared to 10¢ in 1989.

The sales-to-asset ratio indicates the rate of utilization of the company's capacity. This ratio grew steadily over the three-year period. These figures would appear to indicate that the assets are being utilized efficiently to maximize earnings. Total employee salaries have fallen from a high of $37,101 in 1988 to $29,466 in 1989. The lower figure in 1989 reflects the loss of the assistant manager who had worked at the store in 1988. On the advice of their accountant, the owners take withdrawals of cash called drawings whenever they require it. These amounts are not included in the salary statistic.

In 1988, Elmer and Kim decided to decrease the usual markup on grocery items to see if that would increase their sales. They thought that their customers would buy more goods because of the better prices. They decided that the marginal increase in sales did not, however, justify keeping the lower markup, so they went back to their regular markup in 1989.

Dirt Busters Laundry began operations in 1988 as part of Paddle Prairie Mall Corp. It was financed through a loan from the Settlement Investment Corporation. The monthly loan expense is $1,050 which is easily earned from laundromat revenues. Kim and Elmer expect to pay off the loan by October 1990.

Reasons for Success

Elmer and Kim view their business as a success. Elmer states, "The traditional things that point to our success are our financial statements and our profit. That's an indicator whether the business is successful or not in my mind. Another is whether or not you're providing the convenience of your service to the community; whether or not you're fulfilling a need. Finally, I guess the feeling of creating something and being successful is very worthwhile. It's an experience that I couldn't have gotten in a university or anywhere else."

Kim adds, "Well, the fact that we actually have the business up and running is a major success. For two years it was just a dream of Elmer's and so I wasn't anticipating this success from my own standpoint. The fact that I'm here and can actually run it makes me feel that I'm successful at what we're doing. We have recognition by the Grocery People because we've won two runner-up awards for convenience store operations serviced by them. We have recognition from people who have passed by and know Ghostkeeper's Store as a nice place and that tells me, we're a success."

The reasons for their success are varied. Kim and Elmer are proud of their complementary skills as partners, their mutual dedication to this project, and the support of their family. In addition, the cleanliness of their store, the friendly atmosphere, the convenience of the service they offer to the community, and their Métis way of doing business have all contributed to their success in Paddle Prairie.

Kim and Elmer recognize the skills each brings to the business and how they complement one another. It did take some time to recognize and accept each other's capabilities, but in the third year of operation, things run very smoothly. Kim states:

If I had it to do all over again – my famous last words – I think it would have been a lot easier if we'd talked to a professional or another business couple ahead of time. We could have sat down and really been honest about some of the wrinkles we were going to face, such as power struggles, roles, commitment, and responsibilities. Before Elmer and I got married we went to counselling as required by our church. It's too bad the source of our business financing didn't insist on the same thing. Lord knows the commitment being asked of the couple is just as great.

To this day Elmer talks about how I never put a cent into the business financially. To this day, I feel like I gave up a hell of a lot, I took all the risk here. If we split tomorrow, I could well end up walking away empty-handed. But I have a $65,000 guaranteed business loan hanging around my neck, so I've made my commitment. But we see that very differently. I'm sure that an advisor would have said, "All right Elmer, how much do you want Kim to put in here and what's reasonable to expect from her?" As a matter of fact, a year after we started the business the accountant did that.

He sat us down and said "What's the biggest problem?" The biggest problem for me was that I felt as though I had no security and the biggest problem for Elmer was that I was drawing salary and he felt it wasn't right. You are either an employee or you are an owner in his mind and if you're the owner then you don't take salary. The business can't afford it. So I agreed to go off salary, but I wanted signing authority and some sense of security for myself. We negotiated and now we have peace in our house.

Communication and support of the whole family is crucial to the success of their business. Kim and Elmer have four children, two of them adopted from their extended family. They range in age from two to thirteen. Kim comments:

The commitment of the whole family is important, because it affects every-body. My kids suffer; they can't go to rodeos and all kinds of activities, and so they all have to understand and accept the business. There may come a time when they may leave it, but they all have to understand how it's going to affect them. In the case of my family, it's a little bit different because they came into the situation pretty young. But if another couple were going to start a similar business and they had a twelve-year-old or a fifteen-year-old, it's really important to include the kid in the initial stages because it is a lifestyle choice that is going to affect them too. I think that's really important.

The other thing is to include the kids in the business so they have some understanding and appreciation for it. We do that with our staff, but a lot of times we neglect doing that with our kids. Even though we own the store, my kids have to buy everything out of the store just like a regular customer has to do. Once my son filled up his pockets with candy for his classmates before he went to school. He got caught and he certainly got reprimanded for it. I'll bet he will never think to do that again. You just can't have that.

Our niece Tonya, who lives with us, is thirteen. She has run the till, but I've never left her there alone. She's quite capable. She can do just about everything there. She often helps when our grocery order arrives and it needs to be priced and put away. She seems to enjoy the responsibility. My boys have helped in the store as well.

When we used to live in the store residence, we used to give them responsibilities appropriate for their age. Nothing serious. It gave them a chance to be at the store and to work in the store dusting and stocking groceries. If I had to work a shift, they would have to come in the store and be in the store with me. They liked it and they have never balked about having to help out in the store. Their kindergarten teacher once told me, "Your kids are the only ones who would think to make up a bank deposit when playing store."

I think Tonya might sometimes resent the kind of time the store takes because it means that she has to babysit. It means that at 9:00 p.m. she has to be home. I have to close the store and I need somebody to be at home with the other kids. If somebody doesn't show up and I have to go in and do the shift, then she's got to babysit. All through summer holidays that's how it was. She couldn't go to rodeos. We can't be away because rodeo times are a busy time for us. We're hardly a part of any special events because the store is extra busy. So you have to make a lot of sacrifices. Four days is the longest we've been away as a family in three and a half years. A lot of people won't do that.

Kim discusses the other factors that make the store a success. "It really has become a very personal business because we know a lot of our customers by name or face. I can stand behind the till and talk to people with confidence. I have a much broader range of trained staff to rely on; they understand this place and how it runs."

Elmer adds:

I guess our number one strength is convenience. It's convenient not having to go forty-five miles north or eighty miles south or twenty miles to Keg River Cabins to do their shopping for their daily needs. They can get bread, butter, milk, cigarettes, videos, and fast foods. It's a place to socialize and have a cup of coffee. I know some people who used to go to High Level and as a matter of fact stay overnight to do their laundry. Now they use ours. We've certainly provided convenience to our customers, including those stopping off the highway. We get a lot of compliments on the cleanliness and the friendliness of the store. I really feel good about that.

Another strength is that we run a good operation. We have lots of supply so our shelves aren't bare and we look like we're going to be here for awhile. We've brought in some new things. Videos were really new around this area at one time. Now we rent Nintendo games and units.

I like to think that the people can rely on us. They know when we're open and when we're closed. It's not shoddy. It's not, "Well today I feel like opening and tomorrow I don't feel like opening" and so I don't open. That makes a big difference. If you make a commitment to run a business, then run a business. I hope that people think we treat them fairly and that we're just one of them. But on the other hand we're tough too. If you try to pull a fast one on us, I'm not putting up with that kind of garbage. I am taking a hard line on it. That's just treating people with maturity. I don't coddle them because there's no need for it. On the other hand, I will bend over backwards to help my customers, if I can help them. I think that makes a personalized business.

Areas for Improvement

Generally, customers are satisfied with the store, but there is some customer dissatisfaction with the cheque-cashing service and with some products the store does not carry. Kim explains:

I think that in terms of the customer, we're what they expect. It happens in any small business such as ours; the girls are just not doing 100% and the place is not as clean as it should be. Perhaps stock is not rotated and you'll see bad stock out on the shelf when it shouldn't be there.

I think some of my local customers are a little angry that Elmer and I aren't here the entire time that the store is open, so that they can cash cheques at will. When we lived next to the store, they had that service. Since we've moved, it's more difficult to be at the store to cash cheques. But the difference is, you see, we're not a bank. That's an extra service that's provided, but our customers expect it now. Some see it as one less service that we provide.

I don't think that I've lost anybody over it. I understand that we have a good reputation for treating people with dignity and respect. Sometimes they're disappointed that we don't have the product that they want. But then it's because their expectations grow beyond what we are able to provide. We are a small store, we are not a superstore.

Environmental Friendliness

Recognition of the importance of the environment is reflected in their store policies and in the appearance of the store. Kim and Elmer also encourage the children of the community to become involved in keeping the community clean. According to Kim,

We recycle what we can, such as reutilizing cardboard. We've checked into things like the new types of environmentally friendly bags, but at this point they are not economically feasible for us. Economic feasibility has got to be our priority, since we're just a small business.

We're having a big debate in our community about what kind of milk cartons we should be using. Right now the store sells plastic jugs and then cartons. Ultimately it will be the customer that decides what we will sell. They say that the plastic jugs don't break down as quickly as the cartons so environmentally it's probably not the choice we should make.

Elmer adds, "Our grounds are landscaped and they're cut on a regular basis. There's some garbage that's picked up every day and the outside areas are swept. The aesthetics of our store are quite nice. I've gotten a lot of compliments on the design and cleanliness of the building. It's very easy for the customers to go out the door and throw a candy wrapper outside. We do have a garbage barrel on the pump island. So we do try to do our best to keep the environment clean around the store."

Kim describes the community involvement they are trying to generate. "I put a challenge to the high school that if they want any donations from us, then they've got to clean this community from the store to the school. I'll put money towards their projects but I'll refuse to put money towards something for nothing. They have a responsibility too. They put that garbage out there so it's time for them to pick it up. Elmer and I take our responsibility quite seriously to maintain a well-groomed area and it's us out there picking up that garbage, not anybody else."

Profile in the Community

Kim and Elmer made a deliberate decision to return to the settlement where Elmer was born to start a business and raise their family. They embrace the lifestyle and the values that come with living in a small Métis community. Their business provides employment for the community. They have trained staff who have gone on to work in other positions in nearby communities. Salaries and business profits are now recirculated in the community instead of being spent in other communities. Kim and Elmer make an effort to support Northern businesses when they choose their suppliers.

This commitment to their community is also reflected in their volunteer activities. Kim sits on the Northern Alberta Development Council (NADC) and has been involved with the council since she moved to Paddle Prairie. The NADC board is provincially appointed and each member sits for three years. The council travels the northern portion of the province listening to briefs submitted on a variety of topics facing the North and passing issues onto the provincial government. Kim is also an active Chamber of Commerce member and local volunteer.

Elmer is the vice-chairman for the Board for Community Futures. "It is a federal program, funded by Canada Employment and Immigration. The intent is to promote economic development. There's a program called the Business Development Center, which is a place where potential entrepreneurs and existing entrepreneurs can go with an idea or with a problem. The center will help them develop and research the idea. There's a proportionate representation of Native people on the board. I don't know if that proportion will hold true for native people coming to us with business ideas. But certainly that opportunity is there and certainly we can only provide the opportunity."

Elmer sits on the community school board. He notes, "I just gave a speech on the first day of classes welcoming the students, the teachers, and the parents. This year we are offering grade 10 for the first time. There are eleven students that will take a basic core of academic subjects. Our goal is to offer senior matriculation for entrance to university, not just a diploma or a technical diploma."

Elmer sits on the National Action Committee on Race Relations, a subcommittee of the Canadian Confederation of Municipalities. He also organizes wagon and horse trips with his Morgan horses. He notes, "Last year we went to Fort Vermillion. This year we went to Manning. It takes roughly a week. It takes a lot of work to get organized, to exercise your team, and to get all your equipment ready. People from different communities join us. It's word of mouth. Once they come, they seem to stay and finish the trip."

As Kim reviews her stay in the community, she discusses some disappointments.

I thought that the community would want our input, because they had two people who had a variety of experience. I thought they would want our participation and they would actively solicit it. It hasn't been quite that way. In fact, in some ways it's been almost the opposite. In a lot of ways I'm shunned and that surprises and hurts me more because I'm Métis and I have become a full-fledged member of the settlement since I moved here. I've tried hard to be part of the community but I still feel like an outsider.

I think this distance has to do with the type of service business that we operate. I see everybody each day, in all kinds of situations and all kinds of circumstances. They might feel that I have too much access into their lives for them to want me at their dinner table.

I do feel that they respect us and our business. There is a warm atmosphere at the store and people seem to like being there. They say "hi" and they wave. But I'm not thought of as someone to socialize with every evening. Sometimes it makes for a very lonely situation. It is a small community here and I'm a long way away from my family and friends. It's been very hard on me.

Yet things are changing slowly and Kim recalls some special moments. "When the grocery truck comes and I'm unloading groceries, people will come and help me unload groceries. They don't have to do that. It's my business, so it's my job to do that. I don't ask them to help but they do it. I love that feeling that they would want to lend me a hand."

The beginning of a new relationship with the community seems imminent, as Kim notes. "The school phoned and asked me to bake a cake for a goodbye party. Now I'm a busy person, but it really made me proud that they asked me to do it and I really was glad that I could do it too. It's a bit of a breakthrough. It's a bit of acceptance as part of the community."

Kim recalls other special memories.

I love hearing little kids say "Elmer's store." They don't call it Ghostkeeper's store and they don't call it Kim's store, but they call it Elmer's store. I got the biggest charge the very first time that a helicopter landed here from a nearby gas plant, so that the guys could come and have lunch. It's neat to think that there are people who have come here on crosscountry skis, on horseback, in sleigh and horses in the wintertime, skidoos, four-wheel drives, all-terrain vehicles, in helicopters, and regular vehicles. That's pretty special I think.

It's a big thrill for me to hear when I'm someplace else and somebody says, "Oh, you guys own the store in Paddle Prairie. I stop there every time I go up North. It's such a nice store." That makes me feel really proud that maybe we are doing something worthwhile.

I've always said that if I could be a positive role model to someone, then I really was doing something. We are role models, even if it's just for non-Native people because we are perceived to be a successful couple by their standards. They're impressed with this store. Sometimes I lose perspective of that and think well it's just a store. But it's a nice store and we have every right to be proud of it.

Sometimes people will say to me, "You sure gave up a lot when you moved up North." In the beginning, I thought I did too, because of the wonderful career that I'd been working on so hard. But I also appreciate all of the new skills that I've picked up here and all of the skills that I've been able to put to use. Everyday something happens that makes me feel like we were right to do this. Not just for the selfish reason of starting a business and making money but for the unselfish reasons too. It's a good thing.

Kim still finds excitement and challenge in the business.

It's a challenge to see if I can beat my sales from last time and that I can stay on track with sales forecasts. I like to play the game of "Can I guesstimate what people will buy and what they won't buy and the quantities that they will buy or how fast I will turn over the product?" I also like the fact that I've watched children grow up from behind the till. I actually do see them growing as they get closer to the top of the counter.

I think another thing that's fun about the business is watching my clerks grow and mature and hold responsibility. For one of my clerks, this is the very first job that she's ever had. She takes pride in the fact that she balances her cash. That woman never said two words to me in the three years that I've been here and now you can't stop her. I believe that she's really blossomed because of this job and that's a big payoff for me.

Sustainability of the Business

The store is a good example of a sustainable business. Elmer states:

The store had to be a sustainable business which could survive on the business from its customers. If you have to start borrowing money and pumping it into an operation, then maybe that business isn't a good idea. Sustainable development is an important thing to the bush economy.

If you're a good trapper you know which animals to trap at certain times of the year and you know which animals not to trap in a given year because they're at the bottom of their cycle. Most animals are in a seven-year cycle. This year, for example, there's a lot of coyotes and field mice. So coyotes live on field mice. They're right at the peak of their cycle.

In the next couple of years you'll see a downswing in the coyote population and the field mice population and an increase in the rabbit population which will probably increase the lynx. So if you know that as a trapper you can sustain your living. If you don't and you just start killing everything you can't sustain a living. That's what sustainable means to me.

Future Development

Kim and Elmer are looking to their future. Recently they examined the feasibility of selling the store. They decided that it will be another three years before they can consider selling it because of the high debt load they are carrying from Native Venture Capital Corporation. Once they've paid the debt down, another Native business person might be able to qualify for the financing to purchase the store.

Kim and Elmer are committed to remaining in Paddle Prairie for the next few years at least and continuing to improve the success of their store. Elmer notes, "We might expand the hardware section. Sometimes you need a nut or a bolt that's 20¢ and you've got to drive for three hours to pick one up. I think that there's a market for hardware. I don't know if we'll expand yet or not, but I think there's a need for do-it-yourself home hardware. I also think there's a need for a few plumbing and electrical supplies.

If new industry comes into the North, then business will improve. Elmer states, "You have to keep in mind that the North has been in a recession since the oil and gas boom went bust. There hasn't been any industry that's replaced it, but now there's major forestry development. That will increase the traffic on the highway and provide more employment year-round within the settlement, so that will increase sales."

Advice to New Business

If someone was interested in starting a business in a small community, then Elmer thinks that planning is important.

To be successful, a person should like a challenge and be fulfilled in meeting it. Secondly, writing a really good business plan is important. Eighty percent of the time should be spent doing your business plan, doing your demand survey, arranging financing and making certain that it is what you want to do, before you actually implement it. Then if you do that part well enough, you'll find that it takes less time to do the actual construction and to start running the operation.

I guess the most satisfaction for me is doing the business plan, doing all the research, the demand surveys, arranging the financing, putting some management skills in negotiating with the suppliers, negotiating with the government, with the settlement council and really filling a need that wasn't being met.

Summary and Conclusions

Elmer and Kim Ghostkeeper are operating a successful business and raising their family in a small Métis community in Northern Alberta. They are negotiating the obstacles that might be expected with moving to a community where Kim is a newcomer; starting a business partnership, when they had never worked together before; and running a business from scratch, when neither partner had ever run a grocery store.

Elmer was able to identify an opportunity for a business and, after investigating the feasibility of the idea thoroughly, he spent many hours planning all aspects of the operation, from the design of the building through to the financing. Throughout the start-up process and current operations, Elmer and Kim have held true to the Métis values that are important to them.

The building that houses the store reflects the Métis background of the owners. Rather than rely on bank financing or government subsidies, Ghostkeeper's Store is financed through a loan by Native Venture Capital Corporation. Ghostkeeper's Store is not only the major local employer, but it also offers several needed services to the community through the convenience store, gas bar, and laundromat.

Friendly, well-trained staff sell products at Ghostkeeper's Store; prices are reasonable and the store is clean and attractive. The selection of products is influenced partly by their customers but mostly by space limitations. Ghostkeeper's is a convenience store and carries basic foodstuffs, videos, and a limited line of automotive supplies, and offers fast food and a place to have coffee.

In training their employees, Kim and Elmer try to motivate them to take pride in their work and feel that they have a stake in the success of the store. They try to cultivate a team spirit in which employee input and responsibility is essential. Their employees are asked to identify ways to keep their work interesting and satisfying. Kim and Elmer are willing to try new promotional ideas and not to be bound by convention.

Elmer's ability to conceptualize an idea for a business and set it up complements Kim's skill in handling day-to-day operations. The partners share decision-making and short- and long-term planning of the business. Their young family is involved in the operations of the store and co-operate in making the business a success. Other factors in their success are convenience, friendliness, cleanliness, and personalized service.

Kim and Elmer balance economic feasibility with carrying environmentally friendly products. They have strong convictions about keeping their store clean inside and outside. They also try to promote commitment in keeping the community clean. When approached for donations to the school, they encourage children to clean up from the store to the school.

Their personal commitment to improving community life is reflected in their extensive volunteer activities. Given their business success and other interests, Kim and Elmer are excellent role models for young people, Métis people, and to society, generally. They illustrate the success that is possible without compromising basic personal values about lifestyle and the way to do business.

Postscript – 1990

Revenues increased over the year due to a number of factors. The trend away from expensive shopping trips to nearby towns by settlement members continued especially with the recession and the tightening up of the money supply. Prices were increased to reflect the fact that most shoppers use the store as a convenience store. There was no negative response to this move so it is likely seen as fair by the store's customers. The laundromat was paid off on schedule, with a few repairs required due to power surges.

Staffing at the store was somewhat problematic since there was high turnover in two positions. However, one employee has remained in her position for more than a year and a half and has blossomed in her first employment experience. Kim feels that she has accepted responsibility and has an attitude of ownership for the store which takes her beyond the scope of an ordinary clerk.

Kim and Elmer closed the store for a week in August because they recognized the need to take time away from it. They gave the time off to their employees also. Kim reflects on the past year; "1990 was the 'letting go' year for me. Even with the problems, I've come to realize that there's a real sense of pride of having owned the business and it being a family business. However, we chose to shift our focus from the store a bit to our family."

Elmer has developed his Morgan horse farm from a hobby into a potential business enterprise that has reached the point of requiring a business plan, and he is developing special markets. Kim was elected to the local school board, where she acts as vice president.

Another revelation for Kim is that she and Elmer cannot expect the store to meet all their personal needs.

I look at the store as a well of water and unfortunately both Elmer and I have been trying to get all our nourishment from it. There's not enough for both of us from the store. I have learned that we cannot share in such a small, demanding, and time-consuming project like the store that requires a lot of responsibility but gives less satisfaction and personal gratification then one might expect.

In the beginning, the building was a challenge for Elmer. My challenge was becoming comfortable managing the store. I feel good about that and it makes me proud. But we are beginning to get anxious for new challenges. The store is now on a steady course but not meeting our personal desires for new challenges. I was feeling guilty about that but no longer because I think it speaks well of us. Little things won't appease us because we have the capability and desire for bigger and better things. So if nothing else, owning that store was worth it to me as a good learning experience.

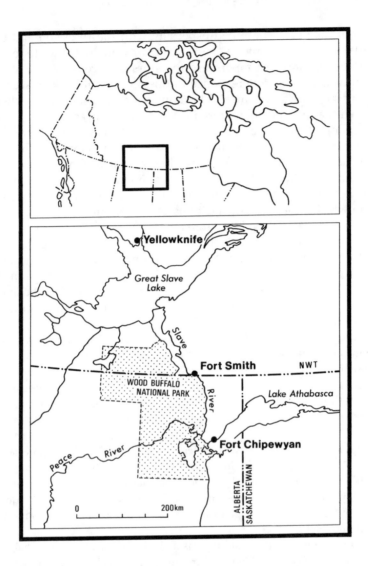

ENTREPRENEURS' ENDORSEMENT

We, the undersigned, acknowledge that we have read our business profile. We approve of the contents of the profile and recognize its accuracy in describing our business.

Dated **Mar 24**, 1991

_____
Don Jaque

_____
Sandra Jaque

2

CASCADE PUBLISHING LTD
Fort Smith, Northwest Territories

Don and Sandra Jaque own and operate the *Slave River Journal*, a regional newspaper serving the area between Lake Athabasca and Great Slave Lake, including the towns of Fort Smith and Fort Chipewyan. The head office is located in the town of Fort Smith, which sits on the west bank of the Slave River at the Alberta and Northwest Territories border. They also offer a computer graphics service and retail computing and office supplies under the operating name of Cascade Graphics.

The husband and wife are equal partners and serve as publishers for the weekly newspaper, which they started in 1978. Each partner handles the areas that reflect their expertise and interest while acting as a team on general issues of management and strategic planning. Don's main duties are overseeing the operation of the newspaper, handling staffing requirements, writing articles and editorials, and managing their office building. Sandra heads the production team on the newspaper and is project manager for Cascade Graphics.

Strategic positioning and diversification in the marketplace are the key factors in the success of the Jaques' ventures. Their attention to the needs of their staff put them ahead in the competition for skilled employees. Finally, their slow, steady growth and aversion to debt helped them earn a reasonable profit and establish an excellent credit rating. These policies provide the means to accomplish many of their goals. Their first venture was the newspaper, and the record of that initial experience is described in the following section.

History

The idea for running a newspaper happened to come at a time when Don and Sandra were considering their next project. They had operated a group home for teenage girls in Fort Smith for four years but had decided that it was time to try something different. Sandra had taken some time off and Don had studied welding at the local college.

There had always been a community newspaper of some sort in Fort Smith. In 1978, there were two newspapers operating. One, the *Slave River Journal*, had been operating for a year, and the other, owned by a local man named Joe Mercredi, had been in operation for about five months. *News North*, a territorial weekly newspaper based in Yellowknife, wanted to expand and its owners approached Don and Sandra. Don recalls, "We had been looking at buying the *Slave River Journal* but were reticent about the deal. Somebody else in town bought it and their kids ran it for a while. *News North* figured that chances were that these kids wouldn't last very long, so they decided to start a newspaper. They approached us to do it. At that time, we were quite interested in doing a newspaper but we didn't have the expertise ourselves. Our attitude was that if there was no risk involved and they were going to teach us, then let's give it a try. If nothing else we'll have an interesting experience and learn some new things."

Sandra has an arts degree with a major in sociology. Don explains, "My background was political science and I could write fairly well. I found that out in university when I used to make a little bit of money on the side writing people's term papers for $20."

They started a newspaper called the *Fort Smith News* and were affiliated briefly with *News North*. Sandra recalls, "We collected the information, wrote the stories, took pictures, and gathered the ads together. We sent all the material with a mock-up dummy of the newspaper to Yellowknife every Tuesday and they put it together. We distributed our newspaper on Thursdays."

Don recalls their rapid expansion in the first year. "Mercredi's newspaper folded about seven months after we were in operation. About that time we bought the *Slave River Journal* and used that name, since it was the oldest publication. It had been a tough period until then because a newspaper is not eligible for government advertising for the first nine months of operations. Advertising is the major source of income, which is the base of any newspaper. In the first nine months, we were losing money every week and working very hard for nothing."

They survived the first year operating out of their house. Their circulation was about 1,200 and has grown to 1,950 in twelve years. Sandra recalls how they split duties in the early days.

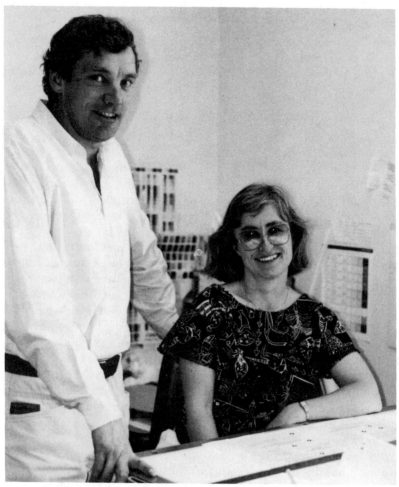

Don and Sandra Jaque

Don sold the advertising, did all the writing, and developed the photos in the darkroom. I organized his work into a format and looked after the books and the circulation. We would work all week then we would be up all Tuesday night, so we could get the paper to the airport at 7:00 the next morning.

We made money because we didn't have any expenses and we only had several part-time staff. The territorial government, Fort Smith businesses, and the government of Canada were our main advertisers. By 1980, we had bought another house and we moved the business there and out of the basement of our house.

We had help in the early years from the Federal Business Development Bank's program. They had retired people from all professions who were available for consulting. Three different fellows came to give us ideas about running a newspaper, organizing the books, and how to handle advertising.

After several years, the next area they expanded into was graphic arts. Sandra states, "Some of our equipment wasn't used on Thursday and Friday, so we could handle other projects. We've slowly evolved into that area." Until this expansion, they had operated as a partnership. On the advice of an accountant, they incorporated Cascade Publishing Ltd in 1982. They had reached a sufficient revenue level, planned to continue operating, and could reduce the level of taxation through this legal move.

Sandra notes: "We did our own books and taxes in the first years because we were always careful about spending large sums of money on people. We were always very frugal and so we paid $50 or $75 and incorporated the company ourselves." The next step was to buy land for their own building. About three years later, they built the building and moved in.

Sandra recalls, "We thought that it would be a good idea to add a little extra space and rent it out." Don drew up the initial designs of the building and then acted as general contractor. The 4,000-square-foot two-storey building is located on Fort Smith's main street. The newspaper office is on the upper floor and takes up one-quarter of the building.

Don assesses the changes in the newspaper since 1978. "The quality of our publication has grown significantly, in large part because we have hired university grads from the south. For the first year or two we tried hiring local people with a general arts degree or a teachers' degree. We found that there's turnover after one to two years. So we were training people and then they would move on. I decided to hire trained journalists who are committed to the profession."

Don does have some favorite memories. "When we first started out, the equipment was very antiquated. For example the typesetter that we used had one type style and one type size. When you typed you couldn't see the copy. You didn't know what you were typing until it came out on a ticker tape. Then you took that tape and fed it into another machine that put it on typesetting paper. If you made a mistake then you had to go back and do it again. Now our machines have hundreds of type styles and hundreds of sizes at the press of a button."

Operations

The *Slave River Journal* prints 1,950 copies each week for 51 weeks of the year. Sandra says, "Close to 500 go to different vendors in almost every community in the Western Arctic." The major source of revenues is advertising. Less significant income comes from newsstand sales and classified advertising.

Advertising is handled by a full-time employee. Sandra notes, "Advertising comes in the mail every day; it comes on the phone and it walks in the door. Our advertising person conducts various campaigns, such as our high school graduation campaign for congratulatory ads from businesses and family of the grads."

The office is open Monday through Friday. The staff put the newspaper together "camera ready" late Tuesday night. Then it is printed in Yellowknife on Wednesday. Sandra notes, "It goes out on the 8:00 a.m. flight to Yellowknife and it comes back at 7:00 in the evening. They do a good job and this is the best turnaround we've ever had."

Promotion of the newspaper involves a variety of methods. Free papers are given to the local airline and are distributed in several smaller communities in order to increase circulation. The newspaper gets additional publicity by sponsoring community-based events that attract people to Fort Smith from across the country.

Don states, "We do support a lot of tourism and sports activities to bring people into the community. We sponsor sporting events, including a triathlon. I personally am very active in promoting tourism on the Slave River. I'm in the process of negotiating with Canadian Airlines to bring in some very high-profile whitewater paddlers and set up the western Canadian championships in 1991. I believe that within five to ten years we're going to see a large influx of American and European whitewater paddlers. There are a tremendous number of very wealthy whitewater paddlers who would come to a place with an uncontrolled, unspoiled river with magnificent rapids, in a wilderness setting."

Interest is not charged on overdue accounts, mainly because of difficulty administering a penalty. Statements are mailed, but if a bill is outstanding after sixty days then a telephone call will be made to the customer. They have tried to recover several debts in small claims court but have never been successful because the customer left town. Don notes, "If it is a new business, we might ask for cash up front for advertising. We are getting stricter and asking people to pay before the ad runs because it's easier on our bookkeeping."

The newspaper's major advertising customer is the territorial government. The government will make interim payments on big projects, but otherwise they only make the final payments within thirty days after receiving the invoice. Don states, "There are a couple of departments that are slow and we have to phone them. But it's common for invoices to go astray in the government because they are so busy."

Recent cutbacks in government advertising budgets have affected the newspaper. Don describes their strategy in dealing with this threat. "We have to respond by exploring new market areas. If you don't stay flexible and you lock yourself into one market then you run the risk of that market drying up and running into financial trouble." One area that has grown steadily is Cascade Graphics.

As mentioned before, the newspaper's computer use is negligible on Wednesday and Thursday. The slack is taken up by Cascade Graphics. Don and Sandra decided to diversify rather than cut staff to part-time during the weekly slow period. Cascade Graphics offers a wide variety of services including newsletters, business cards, letterhead, logo design, and flyers.

Sandra and a production person work on the newspaper and on Cascade Graphics. A part-time office staff member works with printers and customers. Sandra states, "We have made arrangements with six different printers in Yellowknife, Hay River, Edmonton, and Winnipeg." The choice of a printer depends on the project and the quality required. With the recent purchase of a desktop publishing system, Sandra says, "We'll have more options to work with and it will definitely enhance our Cascade Graphics area. We will be able to offer some of those services much faster." Don spent the better part of a year researching the best system to purchase and shopping for the best deal.

Don describes some of their other services. "We've expanded our darkroom operation and now do passport photos and photo orders. For example, I just did a shoot for a lawyer who had a court case and he wanted two sets of twenty prints. We've also done a few slide shows, which is an interesting area." No deposits are required for orders except on large jobs and full payment is made when the jobs are picked up. Regular customers are allowed thirty days to pay their accounts.

Don recalls that one of their more interesting display projects was a series of panels for display at the Northwest Territories pavilion during Expo. "We did panels with graphs, charts, and big photographs for the Renewable Resources department. It described the different things that Renewable Resources does for wildlife management and fire fighting."

Staff

In addition to Don and Sandra, the business employs two full-time reporters and one full- and one part-time general office staff. The full-time office person handles advertising, circulation, and reception, as well as providing photocopying and fax service. The part-time person does the bookkeeping and manages some of the job printing. They also have a full-time summer student. There is one full-time production person and the Jaques' teenage son handles darkroom duty and janitorial services after school.

Sandra works very little overtime. She says, "I like to spend some time with the three kids now and be involved in their school. I try to take it a little bit easier now. I don't work past eleven on Tuesday nights. I can't stay up all night anymore because it's too tiring." They currently have well-trained and reliable staff so they were able to take an unprecedented month of holidays in 1990. Sandra says, "Don and I went away for two weeks for ourselves and then we took the kids for two weeks."

Staffing is the major ongoing problem for Don and Sandra. There is a limited skilled labour pool to draw from locally, but the turnover among the people who are brought in from the south is high. There is strong competition from the government for skilled people, and there is a scarcity of trained Native reporters. The Jaques cannot match the salary or the benefits offered by the territorial government. As a result, it is difficult to attract and keep skilled employees.

The local labour shortage is one of the main reasons that the Jaques are putting off further expansion. They have thought of opening a retail outlet or doing consulting work but are hesitating because of the anticipated staffing problems. The journalists and graphics people they require for the newspaper and computer graphics service are usually brought in from the south. Local people are hired for the other areas of their business.

Sandra points out, "We really prefer to have local people because they have houses and are raising their families in the community. When we bring somebody in from outside, we have to find them a place to live and it is a hassle. People from outside aren't committed to our community for the long term. We've had some really good people come through who have used us as a stepping stone to further their career. At the same time we've drawn on their expertise, and the quality of our publication grows with each person we hire."

The Jaques are interested in hiring more Native employees to reflect the views of the local Dene and Métis population. To date, they have had Native employees in advertising and administration but as journalists only on a sporadic basis. They have a standing offer to help train and employ any interested Native person. Unfortunately no person has accepted their offer for help in training and employment in this area. In fact, the journalism course at the local college is being discontinued due to low student enrollment.

The Jaques employ several strategies for dealing with their staffing problems. Don states, "Turnover is a major problem. It's a tremendous loss to have someone leave who has excellent skills that you know is reliable. Minimizing the problem is critical to the survival of our business." To meet this challenge, they have cultivated a unique working environment to attract and keep their employees satisfied.

A conscious effort to differentiate the business and capitalize on its strengths as compared to the government's is a major part of Don's management philosophy. He says, "We sell our office to prospective employees on the basis that our office is a comfortable, relaxed, and friendly place to work. I tell people as a matter of course, when they come to work here that they do not have a job description and are expected to work in all areas. I try to maximize their capabilities because it is to our mutual benefit. I find that is attractive to people who need to grow in their jobs."

In trying to tap the local labour market, the Jaques discovered that a number of educated women were raising families but were interested in getting back into the work force. Over the years, several women have worked part-time at the newspaper. In this way, the Jaques were able to draw on a segment of the labour market that had been underemployed. Don recalls,

We've had situations where our employees who had small children bring them to work. There were children playing underneath the light table with toys or sleeping here. We offered job sharing before anybody even talked about it.

I'll never forget one time when we had three pregnant women working for us at the same time. Everybody in town teased me that it was my fault. The women were all in their later stages of pregnancy, with great huge fronts. It was just like being in bumper cars trying to get around because they kept running into each other. My wife was one of them. Anyway, we found great success with this over the years because these people were a tremendous resource. One of them worked with us for ten years. Another one we trained worked with us for about six years and then moved to the coast and continued on in her new career.

Competition

There are no other local newspapers operating in Fort Smith. Their main competitor is *News North*, but the *Slave River Journal* has the advantage of its local focus. Their reporters are able to cover a wider range of topics of interest to the local readership. In 1990, the Jaques mounted an aggressive marketing campaign to increase circulation. Sandra explains, "We sent papers to schools and all the government offices for a few months. We generated some subscriptions and increased our exposure."

The major competitor for local advertising dollars is the local television station. The owner offers a channel of continuous business advertising for a very low price. His major source of revenue comes from subscribers and television rentals, and so he can offer excellent advertising rates. Don and Sandra admit it is a problem but hope to try several ideas to overcome it.

The services offered by Cascade Graphics are not duplicated in Fort Smith. Other graphic arts firms operate in Hay River and Yellowknife, so that Cascade Graphics has to keep its prices competitive. They do have the advantage of access to the local market. Sandra notes, "We occasionally get our competitors to do something for us, if we have a job that they can do better. Many of our printers do graphic arts as well, so we may send things to them. But the nice thing about Cascade Graphics is once we've done a good job for somebody, they come back for reorders and that's a nice way to make money because there's not too much work involved."

Financial Information

Very little funding has been received from the government except for one building grant and a grant to cover 20% of the cost of upgrading their computer equipment. Canada Manpower has also provided assistance for training staff on the new computers and it used to help fund transportation and relocation costs of employees brought up from the south.

The Jaques have taken a few bank loans and have a mortgage on the office building. Don explains.

I have a different sort of approach to banks. I don't like dealing with banks and being in debt. I've always tried to stay away from deficit financing. For

Table 3
Financial Information for Cascade Publishing Ltd

	1985	1986	1987	1988	1989
Return on Equity (%)	24	0	23	14	18
Sales/Assets (times)	2.34	1.94	1.09	1.04	1.08
Total Salaries ($000)	130	134	145	159	147

example, when we financed our building we took every cent we had, including our kids' university education money and their family allowance savings. We put the money into the building, thinking we were investing in our own future.

We have one mortgage on the office and we're paying it off as fast as we possibly can with all of our excess revenue. I just don't like to be at the mercy of the banks. Our credit rating is excellent since we always pay our bills quickly. When we went for a mortgage, the bank manager was excited about getting us as a client.

Table 3 includes financial information from the newspaper and the graphic arts service for the five-year period from 1985 through 1989. The return-on-equity ratio (ROE) fluctuates between 0% and 24% over the period. Major repairs to the old house which served as the office were undertaken in 1986 and contributed to the small loss that occurred in 1986. It should be noted that throughout this period, management salaries were taken in each year, including in 1986; these are not reflected in the ROE. If the bonuses were added back into net profit figures, then the ROE ratios would range from 35% to 72%.

The sales-to-assets ratio trends indicate that every $1.00 invested in company assets generated sales rates varying from 1.04 times to 2.34. High sales rates of 2.34 in 1985 and 1.94 in 1986 provided the necessary capital to finance the new building, which is included in the 1987 financial statements. This addition almost doubled the value of company assets, but the utilization ratio still did not drop below one. Total salaries include management bonuses and have climbed by 13% over the five-year period. This slow increase is an indication of salary increases rather than additional staff.

The following sections describe the reasons for the success of Cascade Publishing Ltd, future plans for the business, and advice to new businesses.

Reasons for Success

Don and Sandra have worked together since they married. This partnership has worked because of their mutual respect for each other's skills and opinions. In addition, their marriage and family have been enhanced by the business partnership as well as their shared business philosophy. Finally, their emphasis on high-quality service for the best price helps them maintain their competitive edge.

Sandra and Don feel that their business is a success. According to Sandra, "I think that we're doing something with the newspaper that is important to the community. We keep track of events and we have an amazing file of photographs of the town's history. We've managed to survive even though it's hard work. We're also financially able to do things that we want." Don agrees and adds, "We have come a long way with the material things. We're very proud of our building. Newspaper offices are usually messy, crowded, disorganized places that are fire traps. We made our space clean, organized, and friendly, with a positive character. We're always expanding in different areas of business that are fun and exciting. We're doing a good job at it and making money, which is our recipe for success."

Don and Sandra share a common philosophy. Don states, "We concentrate on quality products, good service, reliability and long-term commitment. With the newspaper for example, we've always said that although advertising is the basis of our operation, that editorial content will always come first. It's a point of integrity. We've lost advertisers because some people try to manipulate editorial content by threatening not to advertise. That has hurt us at times but we've stuck by the policy."

Sandra adds, "With the newspaper, we try not to make too many people mad at the same time or else we are dead in the water. Don has to be especially careful because he's the one who's usually on the front lines with his editorials."

Don and Sandra's partnership works in their business and benefits some aspects of their family life. Don says, "The key to our success is our partnership. Sandy and I have lived and worked together since we were married. It's part of the nature of our relationship. Our skills are complementary, since I'm more management and she's more administrative. We look out for each other. We lost our highly skilled graphic artist. She was a good artist and she was knowledgeable in typography and design. She helped raise our skill level in terms of our services. When she left, there was a vacuum that

Sandy stepped in to fill. She has blossomed in that area and she shows a talent that none of us realized that she had, even herself, in design and graphics."

By operating their own business, the Jaques had some freedom to meet the needs of their children, which they might not have had if they worked for somebody else. If the children were sick when they were small, Sandra could look after them, or she could drop everything and take an afternoon off. Sandra says, "I've always thought that we would involve them in the business. They will get training and experience in learning the life skills associated with being a part of a business. Our older son started out being a paper boy and now he does darkroom and the janitorial work. He's quite good in the darkroom; he has taught a course at the college. Now the nine-year-old has started delivering papers. My daughter likes to come and sit at my desk and work on her little projects. She's also learning some things on the computer."

In spending the day working together, Don appreciates how hard Sandra works and this affects his role as a husband and father. "I have had some strong second thoughts about what I do and what my place is at home. I don't cook, but I'm not a traditional father because I do a lot of housework too. I'm making an effort to play a stronger role in being around when the kids need a parent. I want to free up my wife so that she can have a chance to do her hobbies. I'm quite conscious of how hard she works and then she has the other job of mother and a homemaker. I try to do as much as I can to lighten that load."

Personal or family conflicts at home might spill over into the workplace, but Don and Sandra try to keep both areas of their lives separate. They try to act professionally at work with each other and with their children. They identify this as an important area to cultivate in a family business.

Another reason for their success has been their ability to identify the type of atmosphere they want in their business and to cultivate it by hiring people who can work well together. Don states, "We try to have a casual atmosphere that is still productive. We try to have a good time with what we're doing. I think the kind of people that fit in our office are people who like to work hard and accomplish things. They like to have freedom to be creative. They get along with other people and aren't clock watchers. They don't mind if they have to put in a little extra effort. In turn, we like to accommodate time-off requests."

Don tries to be fair in dealing with staff. Sandra notes, "Sometimes Don will sit down and have a little chat with somebody about their performance. If he's got something negative to say, then he also tries to discuss positive things too. They usually work out all right, but if they don't after a chat or two then that person will leave quietly because they didn't fit in."

Finally, Don and Sandra strive to stay competitive by constantly offering the best prices and services they can. They research the marketplace regularly and select suppliers who allow them to offer their customers the best value for the dollar. They recently expanded and updated their own computer system with the same diligent research. They are open to new services that they see a need for, or that their customers suggest, in order to maintain their competitive edge.

Areas for Improvement

Several areas in the business could be improved. Don admits that their collections practices could be more aggressive in order to protect their cash flow. The marketing of Cascade Graphics could be increased. However, the balance between increased sales and the high quality of their service must be maintained or customer satisfaction will suffer.

Don states, "We need to improve our organization's efficiency especially because we're expanding into new areas. We don't want to alienate customers by giving them poor service. I want to sell our capabilities in the graphics area more, but I am holding off on promoting Cascade Graphics. We're currently working at our maximum capacity in terms of what our staff can handle. We're going to get to a point where we're overloaded and then I will hire someone else to pick up the slack. We're just in that transition period right now, and I don't want to be flooded with something that I can't handle."

Environmental Friendliness

Don and Sandra designed their building to conserve energy and to be aesthetically pleasing. They try to minimize contamination caused by disposal of chemical by-products and they are a major supplier of recycled paper. They commonly address environmental issues in newspaper editorials and give environmentally friendly hints to their readers. Finally, they write articles which feature any community efforts to clean up Fort Smith.

Don was the general contractor on the building:

I was very conscious of energy conservation in the construction of the building. We used good materials in the ceiling insulation, triple glass, and more windows on the south side. We also angled the building so it's directly facing south so we benefit from the solar input. Our heating bills for this building are very, very low because it's very energy efficient. In fact, we spend less in January heating this building than we did to heat the old house we used to operate in. It is sealed carefully, which included caulking the vapor barriers.

We made a few innovations that weren't standard. There were potential problems due to lack of fresh-air and from poor humidity, so we have a fresh air intake into the furnace vents that increases the fresh-air flow in the building. We put a vestibule in the front, which is good to have in cold climates, because then there is a trap for the cold air. It's glassed in and is heated from the sun in winter.

We have lots of windows and most of them open. Even though we have air conditioning, we wanted to have that option. People who work in sealed buildings aren't happy. We also spent extra money getting full spectrum fluorescent lights. You can get cool white or warm white or full spectrum lights. The cool white lights are the blue end of the spectrum, which are the most common and give people headaches. The warm white lights are at the red end of the spectrum. They have a warmer pinkish light. In our graphic arts work we wanted to have a true rendition of colour so we chose full-spectrum lighting, which is generally healthier.

The colour scheme [of the building] is pink, grey, and blue and is carried from the interior to the exterior in a unified concept. Plans are set to use crushed gravel from the local granite rock that is pink, blue, and gray on the driveway and exterior surfaces below the windows.

The Jaques try to minimize air and water pollution in their business. For example, they have instituted a non-smoking policy in their office. Don notes, "One of the reasons we went to a laser printer is because we don't like the chemicals that are required in the photo-typesetting process."

The Jaques sell recycled paper and are one of the main suppliers in the Northwest Territories. They offer Cascade Graphics customers a variety of recycled paper for any printing jobs. It is not only an environmental issue but, as Don explains, they are also positioning themselves for future orders with the terriorial government: "With all of the market tied up by existing paper suppliers, we knew that the government would set a policy of purchasing recycled paper. We worked to get in on the ground floor and become suppliers. We're marketing ourselves to the government on a small scale in order to get our foot in the door. When it comes to larger purchases, then we hope that they're going to come to us."

The Jaques also initiate, encourage, and support environmental awareness in their community through editorials and articles in the *Slave River Journal*. Don says, "We've done numerous free campaigns to eliminate garbage and to clean up the environment. We put little reminder messages throughout the newspaper. Fort Smith is generally environmentally conscious without that kind of stimulus."

One problem that the community does have is with a large amount of garbage in the schoolyard. Don explains, "One person who writes for us is a grandmother. She is organizing a group of grandmothers to pick up that garbage. They want to try to shame the kids into being more careful. We will include that story because we are always on the lookout for that kind of thing."

Their interest is often reported in editorials. Don continues, "We're the ones who broke the story on the Alberta pulp mills two and a half years ago. We were writing stories about it a year before anybody ever heard of it. As a result, I think that the environmental groups got turned onto it too."

Sustainability of the Business

How vulnerable are the Jaques' businesses to changes in market demand? Would they survive if there was an economic downturn? The Jaques feel that they would make it through. They are building a solid economic base through diversification of products and services. It would also be easy for them to cut back on expenses if revenues declined dramatically, since they have a flexible lifestyle and keep their business and personal debts to a minimum.

Don explains his philosophy about doing business in the North. "For a business to succeed, you usually have to push through a large volume of business. We don't have a large population base in the North, so a northern business has to offer a number of different products or services that generate volume and profits." The newspaper could survive, but Sandra feels that the graphics services might suffer during an economic slump. While customers would likely reduce their expenditure on graphics, they might increase advertising in the newspaper in order to attract customers and survive the slump.

The second point reflects Don and Sandra's personal philosophy. Don explains, "Since Sandy and I are the major actors in the business, we can cut back personally on our expenses. We would eat the losses and revert to a meagre lifestyle. We keep our own lifestyle flexible so that if we have sufficient money to take a two-week vacation in February, we spend it. If we don't have the funds then we don't take a holiday. Those are the breaks."

Profile in the Community

Don and Sandra are active members in the community. Their commitment to the community gives them personal satisfaction and undoubtedly enhances customer loyalty. Don sits on the Board of Governors for Arctic College and travels throughout the North in performing his duties on the Finance Committee. He has sat on the Board of Directors for the local Chamber of Commerce for the past eight years and served for several years as president.

"I would like to help our Chamber of Commerce become much more active in promoting Fort Smith aggressively. I keep pushing for this development and poking people in the ribs to try to foster good things for the community. I'm also working at the formation of a regional Chamber of Commerce. We would unite with Hay River and Fort Resolution and use the group to lobby for improved community services."

Despite his other activities, Don feels that his greatest involvement in the community is in the area of sports. He says, "I was a cross-country ski coach for the last six years. In the last two years I've switched into coaching biathlon, which includes shooting as well as skiing." He is working on a shooting range and a fifteen-kilometer trail system.

Don has been president of the local whitewater club for the past eight years and is proud of its achievements. He states, "We've got twelve fifteen- to seventeen-year-olds who are really keen on kayaking. For the last two years, we've hosted the terriorial championships." The club also sponsors clinics and trains judges and rescue people, as well as organizing a training camp held during the championships which brings in young people from across the territories.

Sandra teaches piano. She involves their own children in piano, skating, ballet, and hockey and belongs to several clubs. She has taken a variety of evening courses including public speaking, computers, crafts, carpentry, Native sewing and cooking, and Chinese cooking.

Future Development

Don and Sandra have a number of options for diversifying their services. They plan to maximize the use of their resources through the newspaper and the graphic arts service. They are expanding their retail sales operation. They also hope to rent out the rest of their office building in the near future. Finally, if they found that it was time for a change then they would sell their business and start up another in Fort Smith or elsewhere in the North.

Given the photographic and writing skills at the disposal of the newspaper, several potential projects include expanding their current wedding and special-event photography service and providing additional audiovisual services. Don is currently researching the purchase of video equipment and is also examining the market for professional slide show presentations. The Jaques have an extensive historical photographic record of the community, which could be material for a book or at least a new column in the *Journal*.

The new desktop publishing system will expand the type and quality of services that they will be able to offer the customers. Don is considering offering consulting services to other community newspapers for the purchase of their own systems. He is assessing the feasibility of expanding their retail operation of business supplies. They would set up a separate operating name and market stationery, office supplies, office equipment, computers, and software.

Don notes, "We're fully set up with wholesalers and suppliers. We have Sharp Canada's fax machines and office equipment, and we have about five major computer hardware and software suppliers. We also have a number of suppliers for stationery, office supplies, and office furniture."

Two obstacles to this expansion that Don has identified are staff turnover and the complications arising from the new goods and services tax. He would have to be able to step in if the sales clerk quit. He also admits, "I am afraid of getting into retail business when I'm faced with a challenge like the GST. If it is simply a matter of buying a cash register that adds it on, it might not be too bad, but it could mean that customers won't buy."

The fourth area of interest is rental of their extra office space. Don says, "We have about 3,000 square feet of space right now that we have to fill. If there is no interest from either government on a large scale or from small businesses, then we will have to fill it ourselves. It would make sense to expand the retail office supply business. Another alternative we have is to set up a conference centre or a secretarial service for out-of-town businesses that need telephone and mail service."

Advice to New Business

Starting a newspaper in a northern community would require, in Don's estimation, a minimal market of approximately 1,000 people in one community or several communities in close proximity. There would be an initial cost of $40,000 to $50,000 for basic desktop publishing equipment and three computer terminals. Additional investment would be necessary to upgrade equipment in approximately two years.

Initial staff would consist of an administrative person to answer telephones and handle the bookkeeping, a reporter, and a production person. All staff should have good typing and spelling skills. There are few northern communities with a large enough private business sector to generate a reasonable amount of advertising revenue. Therefore local advertising would have to be supplemented by government ads.

Don and Sandra suggest that the owner expect little in the way of profits, be frugal, and be prepared to do most of the work in the beginning. He or she should have an interest in the newspaper business, if not actual journalism or business training. Don and Sandra did not have specific training, but in Sandra's words, "The idea of a newspaper really caught our imaginations."

The lack of training was a mixed blessing for Don and Sandra. On the one hand, they were not bound by traditional newspaper policy. They developed their own style that met their personal standards. Don says, "When the retired newspaper fellow from the Federal Business Development Bank came to assess our operation, I found that I was teaching him new things. I think I really opened his eyes in terms of how we make money. I also felt that our quality of editorial content was higher because his old paper placed advertising above editorial content. It was a whole different approach to journalistic integrity."

On the other hand, Sandra remembers, "It was pretty terrifying in the beginning, with a young family and not making any money. We were working so hard and spending our savings. There were probably some things we could have done differently that might have made the experience easier."

Once the newspaper was operational, the reasons for staying in the business have changed for Don and Sandra. Sandra gets personal satisfaction from the people she works with and the new challenges she faces. "It's fun to work with people who are having fun doing their job. Once a week we produce this creation that's quite amazing. With the graphic arts, we are producing a variety of projects that make it challenging."

Don still finds it very interesting. "I would have a real difficult time considering leaving it even though there might come a time when I should move on to something else. I might at some point study for my masters' in journalism. However, I find the business so interesting because we're involved in so many areas that are exciting, creative, and dynamic."

Another secret to their longevity in the business is giving themselves an occasional break. Don says, "You absolutely have to make sure that you don't overload yourself. We've gone through cycles where we've found that we were getting burned out. We had to pull away, take a vacation, and rejuvenate. If you don't, you cease to be creative and stimulated."

Summary and Conclusions

Don and Sandra Jaque offer a set of complementary products and services that utilize the resources of their newspaper, the *Slave River Journal*. They are constantly researching new ideas to increase volume and even out the revenue "hiccups" that are inherent to doing business in the North. They support each other in developing policies that encourage their staff and themselves to develop fully their personal potential. This is done in a milieu that is in keeping with their personal philosophies.

Although neither had directly relevant journalism or business training, they undertook the business of a community newspaper with dedication, hard work, common sense, and frugality. They relied on the expertise they acquired from their early association with *News North* and the Federal Business Development Bank. They have, however, brought a fresh perspective to the business of running a newspaper, and they chose to put editorial content before advertising revenues, contrary to the practice of their business advisor.

Don and Sandra are constantly examining new ways to build up their business. With the newspaper, they expanded their market from their home base of Fort Smith. They also offer photographers to record local events, including parties and weddings. Recognizing the extra computer capacity they had several days a week, Don and Sandra added a computer graphics service.

The quality of service that Cascade Graphics offers was recently upgraded with the addition of state-of-the-art computer equipment. They also retail business supplies through Cascade Graphics. They offer supplies on a small scale and will not commit to an expansion unless there is sufficient demand and suitable staff and until they are sure that this would be an efficient use of their resources.

The Jaques strive for a professional product in their newspaper and in their computer graphics venture. Don will not compromise his journalistic integrity, despite pressures from advertisers. Sandra strives to satisfy the computer graphics customers through high-quality products at competitive prices.

Don and Sandra have achieved success without compromising their own personal values. They are able to teach their children about the responsibility that comes from being part of a family business. They cultivate an atmosphere in the office that is stimulating, creative, and exciting and that promotes personal development. They use the newspaper as a forum to promote issues of importance, including environmentalism.

Financial success allowed them to design and construct a building that incorporates energy conservation and is aesthetically pleasing without incurring major debt. The bank financing that was required for the building construction is being paid off quickly in order to minimize their debt load and maintain their excellent credit rating.

Thoughtful diversification of services, low debt, high-quality products and environmental sensitivity are the necessary ingredients in the strategy that will ensure the continued survival of their businesses. Creative but reasoned risk-taking in expanding their services will help them to maintain their competitive edge, as well as their personal interest in their businesses. Their continued efforts of community service will enhance the quality of life for their family and business, with benefits flowing to the rest of Fort Smith.

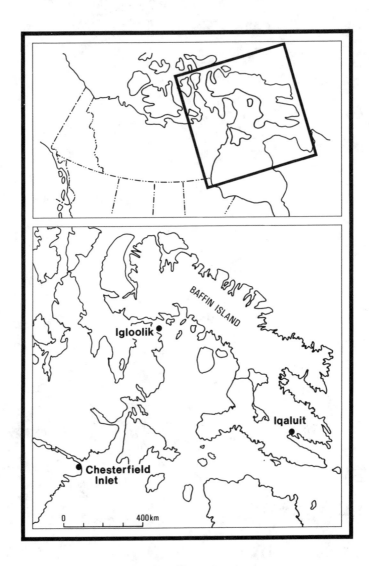

ENTREPRENEUR'S ENDORSEMENT

I, the undersigned, acknowledge that I have read my business profile. I approve of the contents of the profile and recognize its accuracy in describing my business.

Dated _Sept 15_, 1991

Fred Coman

3
COMAN ARCTIC LTD
Iqaluit, Northwest Territories

For more than twenty years, Fred Coman has been providing office and warehouse leasing, cartage, moving, and janitorial services in Iqaluit and the Baffin Island region. He recently opened an art gallery called Coman Arctic Galleries Ltd, which serves tourists and the local community.

Fred is sole owner of his companies, but his brother Mickey handles the accounting, some of the art purchases, and hiring the janitorial staff. Fred built his business up slowly without government assistance. He attributes his success to making business decisions carefully and thoughtfully while taking advantage of opportunities, once he feels comfortable with them. Fred has established a solid reputation in the community for friendly, reliable service at a reasonable price. He is active in local politics and a strong supporter of local community activities. The details of his early years are set out in the following section.

History

Fred lives with his wife and two children in Iqaluit. He received a grade 8 education in Kirkland Lake, a small town in northern Ontario, before moving to Iqaluit in 1961. After getting out of the airforce, he was offered a job with a company that handled refueling of European flights. In 1963, he was hired by the Department of Indian Affairs and Northern Development as a foreman for road maintenance and water, garbage, and sewage service. He recalls, "I convinced them that I could do it, so they agreed to try me for one year. They started me at $1.81 an hour and I worked my way up to $2.10 an hour. At the end of the year they put me on full salary at $4.25 an hour."

Fred Coman

Fred continued in that position for eight years, including five years after the work was taken over by a private contractor. In 1968, Fred bought an old movie theatre and ran it in the evenings after work. He went on his own in February 1970. He recalls, "I ran the theatre and started a janitorial service; then I brought three trucks up from the south. Next I bought out the existing moving company for about $2,500. We handle the whole Baffin region and some of the central Arctic."

With the advent of television, the movie theatre had to be shut down. It closed in the mid-1970s when revenues could not cover expenses. Coman Arctic Ltd is federally incorporated. The main focus of the business for the following years remained the janitorial and local cartage services and the moving business.

In 1985, Fred applied for membership with United Van Lines. He recalls the stringent selection process, "We had to be financially sound, as shown in three years of financial statements. We had to meet facility requirements and we had to have $5 million in insurance because they don't want just anybody representing them." In 1989, in terms of volume his company ranked 40th among 290 movers across Canada.

The community of Iqaluit, which now has a population of 3,000, has changed considerably over the past thirty years. Fred recalls,

"There were few private businesses here except the little local hotel, a taxi company, a barber shop, the local co-op's carving shop, and a Bay store. Today it has grown, with the territorial government as the biggest industry and all the economic spin-offs associated with servicing the government. We need more stores to supply goods to the families of the personnel that are in government and those who are hired to look after the government employees. It's a big chain of spin-off opportunities."

One thing that Fred is struck by is the fact that all the clerks he worked with in Finance and Public Works during the mid-1960s, are either deputy ministers in Yellowknife now or directors of their branches. He wonders, "If I had stayed with the government, would I have gone that far? I don't know, but I chose my road."

Living in the North can be eventful in the winter. Fred remembers an eight-day storm that left him snowed in at home with his wife and children. "I told my wife that if it got to 35° below, I would smash the washroom window out and take the kids across the road where there was an old coal stove. We were scared that we wouldn't have electricity. Two times during that week, it went down to 40° then 45° below. We dressed everybody, but ended up waiting to see what would happen. Then the third time the temperature dropped, we got everybody dressed because the power was off. I took a chair and as I raised it to smash the window; the lights came back on and we stayed."

Operations

Coman Arctic and Coman Arctic Galleries carry on business in a new 10,000-square-foot building, directly across from the airport. Valued at $1.1 million, the building required the first bank financing that Fred has ever taken in all his years of business. The loan amounted to 30% of the total project cost. The art gallery occupies approximately 900 square feet, with the balance taken by Fred's office, short-term storage space, and storage of packing materials.

Payroll, accounting, and all the paperwork associated with the various businesses are handled by a secretary, by the office manager, and by Fred's brother Mickey. They work out of another office building that Fred owns. The land is leased, since some land in the Northwest Territories is no longer available for purchase until land claims are settled.

Fred notes, "The office staff handle the majority of paperwork there. Anything that has to be signed or looked after, they send to me at this office every morning. I do it and send it back. We meet everyday and it is like a family business because Mickey has worked with me for so many years." Revenues are split evenly between janitorial, moving, and cartage services.

Regulation of the majority of Fred's businesses is limited. Generally, all he needs is a business licence. However, there is more extensive regulation regarding the moving of dangerous goods. Fred explains, "We have to abide by all federal regulations. Three employees and I have taken courses on special packing requirements. We pack and ship dangerous goods for all the local companies."

Regular cartage customers include the Northern Store, Arctic Ventures, and some hotels, since they regularly have goods for pickup from the airport. Fred notes, "We make deliveries every afternoon. The rest of the time is filled with packing and moving. One complements the other. We do office moving from one building to another, moving new people in or moving people who are leaving the area."

Fred has nine trucks, five which are used for the moving and cartage business. "We use three trucks every day with two spare trucks to handle any overload. I have step-in vans with fourteen-foot platforms that are covered in and with roll-down doors at the back. I also have a couple of older ones that I keep and several window vans to pick up staff or for transportation."

Packing material must be ordered annually and is brought in by boat. "We order material based on the previous two years. We have to rely on our experience because there is no one to ask about how many teachers are going to leave or how many government staff are going to quit or be transferred in the year."

United Van Lines sets the schedule of territorial rates across the west, central, and eastern regions. The prices are set so that Fred earns a reasonable rate of return. He explains his personal pricing philosophy: "My attitude is, what difference is $10,000 going to mean to me? Will I live any better? I have a roof over my head, a vehicle to drive, my kids go to school, and I take a holiday when I want. I could increase my prices another 30% and my customers would squawk for a month, but then they would pay it. I won't do that because as long as I'm personally satisfied with what I am earning, I can live, pay my bills, and show a profit, then I am happy. If you get greedy it can work against you, so it is not worth it."

The steadiest source of revenue is the janitorial services. "I have had a verbal contract with Frobisher Developments since 1970. I have the contract as long as I do the work. Our projects include apartments, the shopping mall, Bell Canada, and the RCMP."

Fred never had a master plan of the types of businesses that he wanted to operate. In his words, "I just saw opportunities and took

Coman Arctic Moving Van and Employees

advantage of them." Another venture Fred is involved in is leasing buildings that he has built. He currently owns ten buildings in Iqaluit and he leases them to individuals or government agencies, usually as office space.

Finally, Fred recently opened an art gallery in his new office building. It represents a personal interest he has pursued for many years.

I always liked art and I've always dabbled in it. I bought and sold pieces through friends and people who came into the office. The art gallery is just starting and I think it is going to be successful. The art is the most expensive business I am in, particularly because the prices are high. If I make a mistake and I buy a piece that I can't sell then, I've just inherited a piece for life.

My brother and I buy the inventory based on many years of experience. I supply soapstone to a number of local artists – which I have no problem getting, contrary to what the media might say. I have a couple of local artists that I look after by paying their rent, phone, and power bills and buying a new machine when they need it. They come and collect money every day and I keep a bank book of their account. When they carve a piece, that pays down their account. I've been doing that for fifteen years. I think I've just about broken even with all the pieces I've sold recently. I lost quite a bit of money in a camp that we tried to get going where a couple of artists wanted to camp out on the land. It just didn't pan out. They spent money but didn't pay back enough in carving, so now they stay in town and work.

Fred has watched the influence modern tools have had on traditional carving techniques.

Some people label traditional carving techniques as when the artist uses only a hatchet and file. Today artists use electric tools and a saw but I think that they're still creating a traditional piece. The new tools save time. An experienced carver can shape a block of soapstone so the four legs of a polar bear are square and save 80% of the time it took to chip with just a hatchet and a file. It still comes out in the same form and saves him a week's work. All the final work is done with his little hammer and his file.

I don't think that the final product is influenced by the use of these tools. In fact, with the finer tools available today it should be better quality. However, I don't really see that change yet. The older guys used to make hands with fingers and fingernails but now the figure has gloves.

In 1989, Fred was asked to supply 180 sculptures as prizes for the Ladies Pro-Golfers Association's DuMaurier Golf Classic in the United States. It took three months to fill the order, and the customers were pleased with them because no two sculptures were the same. Now they buy 36 sculptures a year from Fred for various tournaments. Other customers have included Peter Pocklington, owner of the Edmonton Oilers, Glen Sather, their coach, and the coach of the Winnipeg Jets, Bob Murdock.

Staff

There are a total of twenty-three people working for Coman Arctic Ltd. As mentioned earlier, there are three office staff; in addition, seven employees handle cartage and seven others work for the moving business. Three couples are employed for the janitorial service.

Fred's brother Mickey has been with him for a number of years, handling accounting and assisting in operations. Fred notes, "His wife has arthritis so they decided to move south several years ago. Now he works seven months a year for me and he has five months a year off. He comes up at the end of each month to handle the books. We try not to do anything without letting the other one know about it. He looks after the business when I take holidays." Fred's office manager has been with him for three years. She has signing authority for all cheques.

Fred does not dwell on problems in business. "Problems here are the same as for any business down south. I don't think there's any great big problem, other than what you want to create. I guess staff is about our biggest problem up here but I've been lucky over the years. I haven't had that many staff problems and I have guys that are still with me after nine years."

Fred attributes low staff turnover to the type of employee that he hires and the operation that he runs. He looks for employees who are reliable and honest and who can get along with other employees.

Staff stay, maybe because I treat them how I would like to be treated. Maybe that's the secret. I try to make work enjoyable and fun. We joke a lot. I am not strict about coffee break and my guys have coffee all the time as long as the work's done at the end of the day. I pay competitive hourly wages and we give bonuses at Christmas.

Most of the staff are Native except in the janitorial services. I always allow the guys to hunt caribou or seal or go fishing unless we're really busy and then I'll explain that fully to them. Some want to go together but that's hard. I will ask them to rotate and take turns, when one comes back then another can go.

Minor discipline matters are handled by constant reminder, or Fred may have a discussion with an employee to determine the cause of the problem. Discipline may also be handled with staff participation. "I don't like disciplining my staff; instead I like to have a chat with the person. Maybe there's a problem at home with their marriage or finances. I try and iron it out because we're like a family, since we're together every day. I remember one young guy who had a bad temper. I called him and the other guys in and said, 'Okay, it's up to you, do you want me to fire him?' They said, 'No, not really because we like him and he is a good worker but he has to learn to hold his temper.' It's been a year and that session worked."

Fred encourages his staff to stop by and discuss any concerns they have with their job anytime. He describes his management style, "Just being myself and using common sense. I don't consider myself the boss or manager."

Fred tried hiring local people for janitorial services but had a lot of problems. He explains:

The staff work from midnight until 8:00 in the morning. It is not a popular time because most people want to be with their families and friends. I had no luck finding reliable staff. I had a special clause put into the contract that I would only hire local people for extra help. I was tired working all day and then working all night when staff didn't show up.

Now I hire couples strictly from the south. We advertise in various cities in the south and then go and interview the married couples. They each earn $1,400 per month. They stay in a fully furnished apartment, so all they need is their clothes. I pay their holiday out once a year, and if they want to go out on excursion trip, I give them time off.

Competition

There has been competition but it did not last. There is not enough business in town to support two moving companies. "There is enough work to keep busy, but if there was competition I wouldn't be able to keep the guys on for a full year. I keep all my employees on, and if it is slack, they're guaranteed seven hours a day in wages."

Fred advertises his services in community papers and in a southern airlines magazine. Word gets around about the art gallery. Fred notes, "I get letters asking for a catalogue very regularly. But I try to explain that I can't because the inventory changes all the time. Some pieces come in and go out within five minutes or an hour, or some stay a year."

Financial Information

Fred has financed the vast majority of his business himself. Any business expansion has been accomplished by reinvesting earnings. Several minor government grants were used to cover a small portion of expenses associated with his interest in art.

Fred discusses his philosophy. "I worked my butt off but I never drew a salary for ten years. I just took money when I needed to buy something or take a vacation. It has only been in the last five years that I have taken a salary. I never took grants because I know what I have is mine, and I earned it with sweat, tears, and blood. It wasn't given to me and I can hold my head up and say that's mine."

Fred does shows in the United States to promote the art. He explains the extent of government grants he has received, "One year it cost me $29,000 to finance a tour and I got $2,200 from the government. Another year I received $1,500 when we took an artist down south for a whole week's show. We paid for his airfare, accommodation, and meals for ten days and we sold a few carvings."

Fred's brother and the office manager are in the process of putting the accounting onto computer. Fred generally knows the financial picture and does not look at monthly statements. He says, "I trust my brother to keep me above the water. He keeps a very close eye on all our expenses."

Coman Arctic Gallery

Reasons for Success

The factors that have contributed to the success enjoyed by Coman Arctic Ltd include using common sense to develop a reputation for good service, a reasonable pricing strategy, relying on personal experience, and taking pride in delivering high-quality service. Fred has made the policies of his company a reflection of his personal attitude about the way he would like to be treated. He also has a long history of supporting the community through charity events and by holding a political office.

Fred has capitalized on his past work experience in developing his current business practices. He feels strongly that he received a lot of opportunities because he decided to work in the North. "I don't think that a southern company would have given me a chance without the education that they always ask for. I think education is very necessary in today's world and both my kids will go to university, but there are exceptions, too. I think that a lot of bright people in this world do not have a formal education. Their education is on the road."

One important philosophy he follows is reflected in his pricing strategy. For example, he prices his art to sell quickly. He feels that he can turn over twice as much product as his competition. He is also willing to bargain. Since he pays cash for his inventory, he is able to generate good returns on his investment through the higher volume of business that he does.

With regards to the moving business, he uses the rates set by United Van Lines as the guide. He does offer advice to those people who have to pay for the move themselves and are not having the move paid for by the government, which is the usual case. "We've helped a lot of people that have had to pay their own way out. We cut prices and give them information about air freight and how to cut corners. I may even suggest that they don't use the moving company in the south because it is cheaper to rent a truck. I'm talking against myself because I'm losing that money."

Fred delivers good service and ensures that his staff follow this policy with the customers.

You have to give your customers good service. I tell the fellows to pack the customer's goods like they're packing their own things. You would want to receive it well-packed and in one piece.

We train our employees. We have our own way which is much better than the United Van Line's way, which I have mentioned to the head office. I have refused to deal with some United Van Line agents because they don't pack properly. Packing for shipment by air is different than if the move is from house to house. In the North, we pack for shipment by jet to a Twin Otter, and into a small settlement where furniture and the boxes are likely thrown around. We also separate our shipments into freight and personal effects. We use heavy cardboard, blankets, bubble paper, and shredded paper to wrap furniture and other goods.

The reasonable prices and high standard of service have made it difficult for other competitors to gain a share of the moving business. Fred states, "We're hard to compete with once we show our customers our storage facilities and explain our packing methods. Our building is heated and has smoke detection. If the air gets too warm or if it gets too cold the alarm goes off. I have a motion detector that sets off an alarm if someone tries to pry open a window or enter the building. It's connected to the fire hall; a call goes to the RCMP immediately and then to me. We also have insurance on the facilities."

The art business is competitive because of his pricing strategy and the types of products that he purchases. Fred relies on personal experience built up over the last sixteen years to select the pieces that he thinks will sell. He notes, "There are people who like abstract carvings but the big money is in realism and nice pieces."

Fred has also established himself as an active community member. He has sat on town council for four terms. He says, "I create a lot of shit sometimes and some people are scared of me but it's usually when someone is trying to pull the wool over the eyes of the community. I want to see development here but it has to be fair." He is a member of the Chamber of Commerce, has assisted the RCMP, and helps with local projects. Fred received awards recognizing his help in improving police-community relations, his work with a sports camp, and his financial assistance in making possible a parish hall renovation.

"I've had undercover agents work for me busting people with drugs. I sometimes give them apartments or vehicles to use to help keep drugs out of the community. The sports camp is for local kids. In 1990, ten university students were brought in to put on sports programs in baseball, soccer, and other sports. I helped organize that with the RCMP."

When asked why customers use his services, Fred replies modestly, "Because they like me. I smile. I don't know."

Areas for Improvement

Fred would like to train more of his staff in the proper techniques of packing and he would like to spend more time developing the art gallery. He notes, "Right now I rely on only two men who are fully trained in packing. If they got sick, then I would be slowed right down, but it takes time to teach. I'd also like to go into art more since I really enjoy that. I would need a couple of million dollars to do it properly but I think I could make it pay."

Environmental Friendliness

Fred is active in minimizing the impact his businesses have on the environment. "We try to recycle everything we can and we'll burn what we can't. We try not to burn anything that's going to be toxic and usually it's just cardboard paper. We pick up the cardboard deposited by the sealift operations and try to recycle it. Finally, we supply garbage bags and pick up shredded paper from any office who calls us, and we reuse it."

His interest in Inuit art supports the community and their way of life through his art gallery. Further, he sees opportunities for growth in this market through increased tourism in the North. The increase in tourism will only work, though, if proper environmental protection measures are taken right from the very beginning. A big attraction of the North is its natural unspoiled beauty.

Sustainability of the Businesses

An economic slowdown, Fred feels, would affect his businesses. "We would feel it, but we don't have everything in one basket and most are essential services. Some would slow down but others wouldn't. The janitorial business is steady because it has to be done every day and generates the same revenue winter or spring. The moving business might drop if program budgets were cut. The art gallery is definitely susceptible, but lawyers and doctors do continue to buy. If things were bad, all our guys would do anything to keep going, including digging ditches or washing windows."

Advice to new Business

It takes a great commitment to get a business off the ground in the North. People who want to start a new business should look at what role, if any, government subsidies will play in their businesses. Fair pricing over the long term is important to the business and its reputation in the community. Successful business people enjoy what they are doing. Finally, Fred sees a role for government in business, which should include controls on the number of competing businesses starting up in a small market.

Fred believes that there are many obstacles to overcome for new businesses in the North. "It takes a lot of guts to make it in the North. You have to work much harder than business people in the south. The costs are higher, competition is tough, few skilled people are available to work, and markets are small. If you're in a community of 600 or 900 people, then that is pretty much your market. If you start a small store on the outskirts of a town down south, then you've got 20,000 people. You have to try and get local people coming in and coming back."

Once the business is established in the community, then it is important to maintain a fair pricing strategy in order to have a good business reputation. "We always get the new businesses that give a good price. They say, 'We're going to give everybody a break and we're going to charge $30 or $35 dollars an hour.' Then two years later their prices are up to $50 dollars an hour, which is what the other guy they kicked out was charging. So it's a vicious circle when greed sets in."

Fred's personal convictions would not allow him to use government subsidies to any great extent in his businesses. He comments on the problems that subsidies can cause for inexperienced business people.

The big question today is whether or not you can start a business without subsidies from the government. A fellow gets $20,000 from the government to start a little business. Next he orders $20,000 worth of goods and sells them and has $25,000. He's doing well so he decides to buy himself a nice new skidoo for $7,000 and a few other things. He has $14,000 left but that's not bad. Then he starts ordering more goods and before you know it he notices that he doesn't have much on his shelves and no money in the bank.

A new business can't make it like that because you have to keep your shelves stocked and only spend a little of the profit for yourself. A lot of people spend their working capital and their profit and are bankrupt in six months or a year. You have to work hard, limit personal spending, and put most of the money back into the business. It seems that if the money comes too easily then a person does not appreciate it and looks for more from the government when the money drys up.

Fred is very committed to his businesses. He has fun just coming to work. He says, "I'm here from 8:30 in the morning until evening. When I was single, I used to work until 1:00 in the morning packing in the warehouse. I cleaned floors on Christmas Day. As long as I can pay the bills now and take a trip once in a while, I'm happy. I enjoy my art. I don't have any art at home because then I would want to keep all the pieces and it would be difficult to sell them at the gallery."

Fred's main advice to new businesses is to meet a need in the community that no one else is meeting. "See what the place needs and then go for it. Be prepared to work hard and try not to reap any financial rewards right away. Put everything back into the business and realize it takes time to make a business work. Don't give up."

Fred feels strongly that new businesses should provide products or services that are not already available in a community. "There's room for every little business, but I would like to see it controlled. We don't need ten plumbing, carpentry, hauling, or contracting businesses in this community or any other small community. I think competition should be controlled in the North." The market plays a role in controlling the businesses that survive but the present cycle – new businesses being competitive for a few years and then charging the same high prices that the original businesses were charging

– is frustrating because there seems to be no long-term benefit to the community.

Future Development

In the short term, Fred would like to market the janitorial service positions using a video. It would introduce prospective employees to the type of working conditions they could expect if they decided to work in Iqaluit. In the long term, Fred plans to retire and pass the business on to his daughter once he has taught her the business and she has received university training. He would concentrate on his art business and expand the facility to include workshops. He would like to bring artists in to learn from master carvers. His job would be to think of ways to make money to finance the project. He plans to stay in the North.

The future of the North is expansion, through economic development, population growth, and tourism in Fred's opinion. Tourism is the wave of the future, he believes. "I think it's up to the people in the North in every hamlet, town and municipality to develop projects to bring tourists here. We have visitors from all over the world who come and visit our parks. They buy our arts and crafts. It is our responsibility to explain how these tourists are expected to behave in order to protect our environment, but we can all benefit."

Summary and Conclusions

Fred Coman is a self-made man who has made his businesses a success because he has followed his personal beliefs. His guiding philosophy is treat others the way he would like to be treated. Fred seized business opportunities that made sense to him. He lived frugally and reinvested the majority of revenues earned in his businesses. Until recently, he did not take a regular salary. This philosophy allowed him to avoid bank financing and government grants to any great extent. He recently took a loan to pay for only 30% of the cost of a new building and he has received several small grants in support of marketing his artists' work in the south.

His reputation in the community is excellent. Fred is seen as a friendly person who provides good service for reasonable prices. He is willing to negotiate prices for artwork or moving services. He is one of about four business people in the community who quietly stoke the fires of economic development with little government involvement.

Fred loves his work and is very committed to it. His wife helps him to balance the time spent at his businesses and with his family.

He admits his habits have changed since he married. Fred plans to continue with his art project and develop it more fully, especially when he retires.

His staff numbers approximately twenty-three and there is very little turnover. Fred pays a competitive wage and is sensitive to the needs of those employees who still hunt and fish on the land. He encourages open communication and makes himself readily available to discuss problems. He passes his high standards of service on to his employees and encourages them to handle their customers' goods like their own. He inspires their loyalty and commitment through his own example and feels they could weather any economic downturn together.

Fred has a close relationship with his brother Mickey, who has worked with him for many years. Mickey handles all the accounting matters and keeps a close eye on expenses. Projects are brought in on budget with Mickey's constant monitoring of finances. Mickey assists Fred with some of the operations and in hiring janitorial staff.

Concern for the environment is reflected in Fred's policy of recycling paper and cardboard as much as possible. He asks businesses in the community to pass on their shredded paper for use in his moving business. Another aspect of his concern for the community is his support of local artists, which enables them to keep a part of their culture alive. He is a patron of several artists and finances their living expenses so that they can practice their craft. He takes an interest in local politics and sits on town council. Fred also supports local charity events, including a summer sports camp for the local children. In these ways, Fred is making his own mark on the community of Iqaluit.

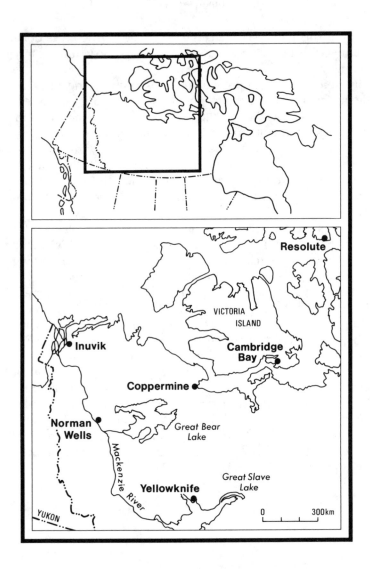

ENTREPRENEURS' ENDORSEMENT

We, the undersigned, acknowledge that we have read our business profile. We approve of the contents of the profile and recognize its accuracy in describing our business.

Dated _April_ , 1991

William Lyall
William Lyall

4
IKALUKTUTIAK CO-OPERATIVE LIMITED
Cambridge Bay, Northwest Territories

A commercial arctic char fishery was started in the late 1950s and marked the beginning of the co-operative movement in Cambridge Bay, a community on the southeast coast of Victoria Island. More than thirty years later, the Co-op is thriving and operates a number of businesses in the town: a retail outlet that sells groceries, dry goods, and hardware; a twenty-four room hotel; a large commercial fishery; an arts and crafts outlet; a taxi and freight service; a commercial bakery; and a cable television service. During the peak summer season, the Co-op employs forty-five to fifty full-time staff and is a major employer of Native people in Cambridge Bay.

William (Bill) Lyall has been involved in the operations of the Co-op store in Cambridge Bay since 1974. He was elected to the board in 1981 and now serves as president. Bill attributes the success of the Co-op to the support of the community, which has grown over the history of their operations. He feels that the personal service he and his staff are able to offer to family, friends, and neighbours in the community of 1,000 people makes all the difference. The Co-op has been able to return a healthy proportion of its savings, when annual profits were available for distribution, directly to their customers as dividends, in recognition of their dedicated support.

The Cambridge Bay Co-op is a member of Arctic Co-operatives Limited (ACL), an umbrella organization which serves forty-one member co-operatives operating in the Northwest Territories. A history of the co-operative movement in the territory and the Co-op in Cambridge Bay is presented in the following section.

History

Co-operatives began over 150 years ago in Britain and have grown and even flourished in some parts of the world. They are a means for economic activity to be controlled by the workers or co-op members and they operate on significantly different principles than those followed by private enterprise. Co-operatives adhere to six main principles described in a brochure entitled, "The Co-operative Movement in the Northwest Territories: An Overview 1959–1989":*

1 Membership in a co-operative is open to anyone who uses its services and willingly accepts membership responsibilities.
2 A co-operative is administered by people who are elected or appointed by the members and are accountable to them.
3 Members are issued shares but receive little or no interest on those shares.
4 When a co-operative has a surplus of earnings from its operations then this surplus may be reinvested in the business of the co-op, invested in common services, or distributed among members in proportion to the value of their transactions with the co-op.
5 Education of its members, employees, executive and the general public in understanding co-operative principles is a priority.
6 Co-operation among co-operative organizations is encouraged on a local, national, and international basis.

A co-op exhibits a number of unique features which differ from a privately-owned business. A co-op is owned by its members, who are often its employees. Profits are distributed according to the directions of its members, and a percentage is usually returned to its members in the form of patronage refunds. Each member has one vote, and co-operatives thus provide a means to introduce democracy into the decision-making process. As other parts of rural Canada successfully established co-ops, the federal government introduced co-ops to the Northwest Territories in the late 1950s. It was an attempt to establish an economic base for the indigenous population.

In 1972, twenty-six of the existing NWT co-ops became founding members of the umbrella organization which later became Arctic Co-operatives Limited. ACL is a central organization which provides services to member co-ops, including accounting and auditing functions, purchasing and marketing assistance, management support and advisory services, and training and education for managers and directors. Its mission statement is: "To be the vehicle for service to, and co-operation amongst, the Northwest Territories co-operatives; hence, providing leadership and expertise to develop and safeguard the ownership participation of the northern people in the business

---

* Arctic Co-operatives Ltd., "The Co-operative Movement," 4.

William Lyall

and commerce of their country, to assure control over their own destiny."*

As depicted in the graphs set out in Figure 1, assets and equity in ACL reached an impressive $14 million and $5.9 million respectively over the ten-year period from 1980 to 1989. Revenues have grown steadily to more than $35 million in 1989 and net earnings have reached more than $1.6 million.

---

* *Ibid.*, 15.

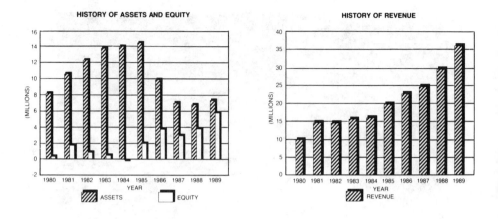

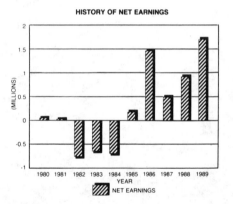

Figure 1. Arctic Co-operatives Limited: The Decade in Review, 1980–1989

Source: Arctic Co-operatives Ltd., "The Co-operative Movement in the Northwest Territories: An Overview, 1959–1989. Winnipeg: Arctic Co-operatives Ltd., 1989, appendix 5.

It is clear, however, that the major recession experienced in the Canadian economy had a great impact on the financial health of ACL in the three-year period from 1982 through 1984. In order to meet this challenge, ACL consolidated operations, moved its headquarters from Yellowknife to the less expensive city of Winnipeg, and sold several buildings. These decisions helped reduce operating costs by more than one-third. In October 1986 the Government of the Northwest Territories wrote off more than $1.4 million in debt owed by ACL. Many member co-ops organized aggressive membership drives to ensure the survival of co-operatives in the territory. ACL has regained financial stability and is set to continue growing in the future.

Its minimal financial resources created difficulties for ACL and its members in raising funds to meet the capital needs of member co-ops. To deal with this situation, the federal and territorial governments provided $10.2 million in capital contributions to the Northwest Territories Co-operative Business Development Fund in 1986. The fund is itself a co-operative, owned and controlled by Northwest Territories co-ops. Loans are made available to member co-ops for expansion, refinancing existing debt, and short-term financing for annual resupply inventory. Interest from the loans goes into the fund and patronage dividends are issued to its members. For example, for every dollar of income received by the fund in 1989, 64¢ was issued as patronage dividends. There have been no loan defaults in the history of the fund, which grew to $11.4 million in 1989.

The consolidated financial history of Northwest Territories co-operatives is illustrated in Figure 2. They are clearly an important source of revenue and employment for Northerners, with revenues of $44.6 million in 1989. In 1989, ownership by individuals in their local co-operatives was at 27.4%, which indicates a reasonable level of equity invested in the co-operative movement in the Northwest Territories.

On an individual basis, the Ikaluktutiak Co-op has built up a healthy group of successful businesses. As previously mentioned, the fishery was the first co-operative endeavor. It led the way for the construction of the hotel by local labour in the mid-1970s and then the retail outlet in 1981.

Bill Lyall was hired by the Board of Directors in 1974 to manage the Co-op, improve services, and reduce pilferage. At that time, Bill had closed his taxi company because he had been recently elected as a member of the territorial legislative assembly. He recalls, "We only had four meetings a year in those days so I had lots of time on my hands to get involved with the Co-op."

Bill has taken an active role in the community at the local, regional, territorial, and national level. He is president of the local Co-op. He represents six communities at the ACL Board meetings and sits as President of the Board. He is also president of the territorial Co-operative Business Development Fund. Bill sits on the board of Tuttavik, a joint-venture between ACL and La Fédération des Co-operatives du Nouveau-Québec wholesaling northern arts and crafts to southern Ontario. He is also a member of the board of Northland Utilities and Canadian Airlines North. He is a past member of the Water Board and the Native Economic Development Program Fund board and past president of the Arctic Coast Tourist Association.

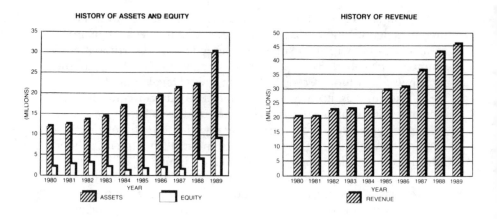

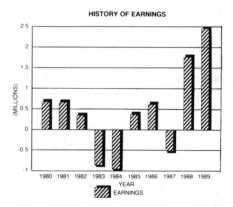

Figure 2. Northwest Territories Co-operatives: The Decade in Review, 1980–1989

Source: Arctic Co-operatives Ltd., "The Co-operative Movement in the Northwest Territories: An Overview, 1959–1989. Winnipeg: Arctic Co-operatives Ltd., 1989, appendix 4.

Bill was elected president to the board of ACL in 1981 when 80–85% of the co-ops were on the brink of bankruptcy. One strategy to deal with the crisis, and one which worked for the Cambridge Bay Co-op, was a membership drive. The Co-op now has approximately 460 active members, close to 50% of the community and 90% of the adults.

Bill recalls, "We tried to get more interest in the store but it wasn't working. In the beginning, people used us when they couldn't charge any more at the Bay. We finally got through to quite a few people that this is their own business and profits stay right here. We proved that with the dividend payments." The majority of co-ops survived the three-year slump in the early 1980s and have gone onto accomplish many of their goals. This has brought Bill a great deal of personal satisfaction.

Bill enjoys his various positions especially his involvement in ACL. "There's always some new thing that comes up so it's an interesting job. I am also very proud that the whole organization of co-ops is the second largest employer of native people in the Northwest Territories, after the territorial government. I think one of the biggest thrills Eskimo people have with our business is that it's our own business. Generally native people in the communities own the co-op, but we hire white people to run the biggest part of it for us. People see at last, we're not working for the white man, but the white man is working for us."

Operations

A lifetime membership in the local Co-op is available for $15 to anyone over eighteen years of age with no residence requirement. As previously mentioned, there are approximately 460 active Co-op members in Cambridge Bay. Once a member builds up his equity through store purchases to $1,500 then he is eligible for dividends based on a proportion of total purchases. Equity is allowed to build up to $7,500 and then the member receives cash for any excess equity that is earned above the ceiling. Each member receives one vote and may attend the annual board meeting.

There are nine board members from the community who are elected for one, two, or three years at the annual meeting. The board executive includes the president, first vice-president, and the secretary-treasurer. There are no honoraria because membership is a volunteer service for the benefit of the community. The board guides the Co-op's operations and recently drafted a five-year plan incorporating suggestions from the membership. Bill notes, "This is one of the new things that we try to encourage all the co-ops to adopt so that they can continue their success."

The board meets once a month and handles complaints, policies, planning, and other issues of interest, with management handling the follow-up of these matters. Bill states, "I might talk to drivers going too fast or to a kid who is stealing stuff out of the store. The board of directors give a lot of direction to management."

The major source of revenue is generated from the retail grocery outlet. In 1989, retail sales were 69% of total sales, with the hotel revenues at 15%, the fish plant generating 9% and general contracts, including the cable service and delivering mail between offices and the airport for the government, accounting for 7% of total revenues.

Ikaluktutiak Retail Store

Retail Outlet

John Senow, a merchandising specialist with ACL, is the temporary general manager in the retail outlet. He has thirty-six years of experience in wholesale and retail sales and store engineering. He freelances for ACL when a store needs his help, for example with staffing, cash flow, or low sales. He expects to be in Cambridge Bay until September, 1990, when they hope to have hired a general manager and a produce manager for the Co-op.

John is streamlining operations. "I will do a stock relocation which means relocating all similar products together and generally improving the functional end of the business." The retail outlet is 10,000 square feet and carries groceries and dry goods. It has a loading dock, storage space, an office, an arts and crafts outlet, and a sewing centre. It is the second largest retail co-op in the territory.

Any Co-op member may have an account with the store. The usual amount charged is $150 every two weeks. Very few people have accounts over $500 and Bill monitors account levels very closely. He says, "We do not send bills that accounts are overdue the way that Northern Stores does. It is a personal touch, because if you keep sending somebody bills marked overdue they won't pay. If someone is slow in paying then I go personally and see what payment plan can be worked out. Generally they respond positively."

The craft shop is handled by the administration office. Two staff people order crafts from Canadian Arctic Producers for the tourist market. (Canadian Arctic Producers is the arts and crafts wholesale marketing arm of ACL and Northern Images handles the retailing of these goods.) There are four local carvers but they do not create a large number of items. Bill notes, "The government tried to start carving here with the attitude that all Eskimos are carvers. That's not true. They soon found out that we weren't all carvers. We hire women to do some sewing in the wintertime. We don't mass-produce products like we used to because it tied up a lot of cash. What we do now is produce smaller items, for instance, lots of duffel bags that can be sold quickly."

John adds, "Right now we have quite an inventory of fabrics and skins. We've already got some ladies started on using sealskin for men's vests and we'll see how they turn out. [The vests] don't require much time and there is a demand for them. Now, with the weather turning colder, we can go into more products such as seal-skin slippers, mitts and gloves. We also buy finished products from the community if we think that there is a market for them."

Fishery

Bill manages the fishery, which operates seven days a week from the first week in July until the first week in September. He is the only person with the expertise to maintain the equipment, so he is on call throughout the whole season. Seven to ten fishermen are hired to net the arctic char. The fish are gutted and gilled before being flown to the fish plant and trucked in to be weighed, washed, hung, and freeze-blasted. After freeze-blasting, they are graded according to size: two to four pounds, five to seven pounds, eight to ten pounds, and over ten pounds.

The fish are boxed in packages of seventy-five pounds each and stored until there is enough inventory to be shipped to the Fresh-water Marketing Corporation in Winnipeg or to fill orders from other communities. The Freshwater Marketing Corporation is a Crown

Co-op Fishery

corporation that was formed to market all fish caught in the North-west Territories for export to markets in Canada and the world. Orders are filled as promptly as possible due to high power costs associated with plant operations. The fishery provides seasonal employment for about seventy people in the community, including the fishermen. All age groups are hired to work at the plant, including students, as long as they can see over the sink to wash fish.

Hotel

The hotel has twenty-four rooms and operates a dining room geared to the needs of its hotel patrons. There are no choices on the menu and meals may be purchased by townspeople. The cook is encouraged to offer home-cooked meals. Country foods may be ordered by the guests in advance and include caribou, musk ox, and arctic char. The hours of operation are 7:30 a.m. to 7:30 p.m. There is an in-house bakery which provides baked goods to the hotel and sells the rest to the public. Ten people handle the cleaning, cooking, and baking in the hotel. Most receive on-the-job training, since few have any previous experience. No liquor is served in the restaurant in compliance with a motion supported by local Co-op members banning alcoholic beverages. A liquor license can be obtained for special occasions, for example for a wedding reception, in the meeting rooms.

The bakery was started in the hotel seven years ago as a government project. People who showed an interest in that area were given training. Turnover is high because it is a hot, demanding job. After the Co-op took the bakery over, they tried supplying other communities with baked goods. There was a strong demand for their products but the transportation costs were prohibitive. Bill explains, "I shipped the same type of seventy-five-pound package to Resolute Bay, Calgary, and to Norman Wells. It cost $208 to ship to Resolute Bay, $123 to Norman, and $87 to ship it to Calgary. The freight rate from Cambridge Bay to Winnipeg is $1.00 a kilo and to Spence Bay is $3.25 a kilo. The freight rates killed us. They had to start selling a loaf of bread for $6.00 which is too expensive."

Taxi, Courier Contract, and Cable Services

Bill organizes the taxi service which is offered seven days a week from 9:00 a.m. to 8:00 p.m. The Co-op has three vehicles. Two are used for fares from the hotel, from the airport, and around town. The third vehicle is used to deliver mail from the airport to the government buildings. In the summertime, there are two full-time drivers, with Bill filling in as required. They have four full-time cabbies in the wintertime.

Prior to the purchase of the cable company, the hotel received one television station. It now receives thirteen channels.

Licensing requirements are specific to each Co-op business. The Co-op has licences for import and export, radio, tobacco, fur dealing, food, as well as a local business licence. It also carries a firearms certificate.

Bill is heavily involved in all operations at the local and the territorial level. He enjoys travel to other communities but does find the demands on his time with the fishery to be trying at times. He says, "I try to take the weekends off but it's very hard unless I go and hide. My wife is a teacher and usually takes extra courses in the summer so she and I are busy at the same time. She sits on the local Co-op's board of directors and is involved at that level."

Staff
Locating and keeping reliable, skilled employees is the major problem facing the retail outlet, the fishery, the taxi service, and (to a lesser extent) the hotel. There are twenty-seven full-time employees, with seasonal employment at the fishery adding forty or fifty more. Turnover is constant, and people rotate through companies in the community. They will work at the Co-op, the Northern Store, then for the government or a private corporation.

There are few trained local people for the more skilled positions. Many of the people who have been trained work for the government. The Co-op's policy is to hire locally if possible; to bring someone into the community is second best. John describes the difficulties in attracting someone to the community. "I think one of the hardest things is to get mature people for management positions in the North. We want more mature people, but a person in their late forties is usually set in their life. They don't like to move to the North, so it is very difficult for us to find suitable candidates."

These problems of high turnover and a finite skilled labour pool have implications for the five-year plan. The Co-op cannot expand or try business opportunities that require a large number of employees. It seems to have reached a plateau where it can operate successfully with the staff situation. Several strategies are being employed to address these staffing problems.

Education and training are promoted among the young people and adults in the community. A greater number of skilled people to draw on locally will mean more options for further development of Co-op businesses. Bill comments:

Arctic College provides different courses. There are problems however, because first of all, people have to want to go to take upgrading and other courses; and second, once they decide to try, often the courses are too hard because they don't have the required background. For example, to take a good bookkeeping course you need grade 10 or more. I took two courses but I just couldn't go through the whole thing because it was tough.

Older people seem to have a greater desire to upgrade their education than a number of young people, who drop out of school and don't have the skills to get good paying jobs. The kids that have graduated from

Co-op Hotel

grade 12 and want to go on to college or university are now working for the government at wages between $11 and $17 an hour. We just can't afford to pay them that kind of money when they come back to the community.

Other strategies include increasing salaries and benefits to compete with the government, better staff recognition, and increased staff responsibility. Bill states, "With better profits, we plan to start paying better salaries. For reliable and loyal staff, we will try to accommodate their requests for holidays and sometimes may help pay their airfare."

Bill describes a new policy. "We are trying to let people know that they are doing a good job by presenting awards at our annual meeting. ACL is encouraging all co-ops to recognize their staff in some manner."

Bill will hire anyone who can handle the job. This includes handicapped people and members of the same family. All employees are treated equally and are given a chance to work through any problems. Bill notes, " We try to work out difficulties but we keep that code in mind about three times late or three times not to work without a reason are grounds for divorce between you and your job."

Bill describes his philosophy. "I try to give staff responsibility because it gives them input into the operation and they will be encouraged to perform. It takes time, but it will happen. I have a deaf and dumb girl on the checkout there. I've given her a little responsibility and she's really picking it up. We also have handicapped people in the hotel and at the fish plant. They are tremendous people to work with and if you give them a little bit of responsibility you see them meet the challenge. It's almost like a football player that you work with closely and in the end, you get results."

Competition
The Northern Store is the only competitor operating in Cambridge Bay. The Co-op store prices its goods to remain competitive, with a 15% to 25% mark-up to cover expenses and to contribute to a fund for future expansion. Bill would never engage in a price war with the Northern Store because the Co-op would not gain any advantage. The Co-op relies on local ownership and patronage refunds to build customer loyalty. They also advertise their monthly specials in flyers that are delivered to Co-op members.

There is one other hotel in town. It has five rooms with kitchenettes but no restaurant. Another hotel is being built that will have approximately sixteen rooms, but it will probably not operate year-round. Bill does not know how this will affect business but he hopes that the hotel restaurant will help attract customers. Advertising for the hotel is carried in regional magazines that are distributed on aircraft, and travel agents receive quarterly updates through ads in large newspapers. There is no other fishery or bakery in town. There are two other taxi companies, but they are not very active.

Financial Information

The Co-op relies on a variety of funding sources for meeting its needs. Revenues generated by the various business interests are reinvested in the businesses according to the direction of the board. Government funding plays a role in expanding existing services and investing in new business. Finally, the Co-op seeks funding from the territorial Co-operative Business Development Fund or a bank when it is necessary.

Daily reports are compiled and faxed to the ACL office in Winnipeg, where payroll and monthly financial statements are generated on a computer. The Cambridge Bay Co-op receives its information reports in about thirty days; these give detailed breakdowns of revenue flows by product and business. Reports are generated for

Table 4
Financial Information for Ikaluktutiak Co-operative Limited

	1986	1987	1988	1989	1990
Return on Equity (%)	83	40	44	42	30
Sales/Assets (times)	1.97	1.85	1.94	2.14	1.41
Wages ($000)	232	265	392	438	456
Patronage Refunds ($000)	164	163	107	236	325

every Northwest Territories co-op so that problems can be identified quickly and remedied immediately.

Table 4 presents some consolidated financial information for the co-op's businesses over the five-year period from 1986 through 1990. The return-on-equity (ROE) ratio gives an indication of the return from business profits on the shareholder investment by comparing profits with shareholder equity. As indicated in the table, the ROE for 1986 is very high at 83%. Revenues from the various businesses were very good, and the gross margin was reasonable, and these were reflected in the net profit. In fact, the net profit in 1986 is similar to the net profit earned in 1990, but the shareholders' equity was almost three times greater in 1990. This explains the declining but still healthy ROE. The rate of growth in shareholders' equity outstripped the steady but slower rate of growth in net pre-tax profit over the period. For every dollar invested by a co-op member, revenue earned ranged from 30¢ to 83¢. Even though ROE has declined, a 30% ROE is an indication of a healthy business.

The sales-to-asset ratio indicates how many times each dollar invested in company assets generates revenue. If the ratio is low, then the company may need to invest in more assets to build the capacity to generate more revenue. The co-op businesses in aggregate generated close to twice the revenue for every dollar invested in assets for the first four years recorded in the table. This ratio dropped to 1.41 times in 1990, which reflects the increased investment in assets during the year. Increased revenues from this investment would not yet be recorded in the financial statements.

Salaries have grown steadily and peaked in 1990 to more than $456,000 in 1990. This is a 180% increase over 1986 salaries and reflects the increased business activity. Patronage dividends were declared in each year of the five-year period and ranged from $107,000 in 1988 to $325,000 in 1990. Patronage refunds range from 36% to 92% of net profits after taxes. This is a healthy return on the investment made by co-op members. The next sections will identify a number of reasons for the success of the co-op and areas for improvement.

Reasons for Success

The Cambridge Bay Co-op has one of the most viable operations of its type because of the volume of business it generates through the strong support of the community. It is a major presence in the community as an employer and promotes circulation of money in the community through its patronage refunds. Bill Lyall has had a continuing positive influence on the operations of the Co-op. He promotes a friendly, family-type atmosphere with his employees and customers.

Bill comments on the success of the Co-op. "The Native lifestyle works very much around co-operation so that the community will survive. For example, we share meat amongst our extended family. The Co-op banks on the support of the community for its continued success."

Bill also notes, "Every part of this organization complements the other." The restaurant and bakery complement the hotel business. Customers staying at the hotel are encouraged to shop at the retail outlet. The retail store provides a needed service to the community, which is complemented by the arts and crafts centre. The fishery provides a means of livelihood for individuals following a traditional lifestyle or who want seasonal employment, while also meeting a demand in the marketplace for arctic char. The cable system provides a service that meets a desire of local Co-op members.

It seems to be in the community's economic interests that the Co-op businesses succeed. Bill notes, "In the first five days of opening the fish plant, we made out cheques for over $11,000. With the other businesses, the Co-op contributes a lot to the local economy with a payroll of about $10,000 every two weeks. Patronage refund cheques are another example of money staying in the community and benefiting local members."

Bill tries to follow a philosophy of personal service.

I know the people that shop with us personally and I always try to greet them or help someone out who might be short of cash one month. It's just temporary, so I think that kind of help goes a long way in a small community. I try to keep our staff happy and I encourage our staff to treat our customers well. We listen to everyone's suggestions on how to improve our service, but everybody has to work together to have a successful business. If I have a good manager, I try to keep at arm's length from their activities and only become involved if they ask for help. This policy does tend to keep good people here. By giving somebody full authority, they know you trust them and they try harder to make it work.

If someone is sick or wants extra time off, we try to have that flexibility in every part of the Co-op, as long as we have a little notice. My job is to make sure everything works right. I work a seven-day week because I always try to have a firsthand look at everything that is happening. I still enjoy my job and the best part is being around people. Nothing else really counts but people. Another big satisfaction is when everything is working like clockwork and everybody is pulling together.

The community benefits in other ways from the presence of the Co-op. It is very common for the Co-op to donate food or raffle items to local classes or community events. Bill notes, "We have never refused anybody yet." Another project sees the history and philosophy governing co-ops taught in the local schools from a curriculum developed by ACL.

Areas for Improvement

The areas for improvement are mainly human resources and administrative procedure. Bill sees a need for help at the senior management level and for a more educated labour pool. John also sees a need for strong management to fill several open positions and for streamlining operations and redefining responsibilities to increase productivity. These efforts would be enhanced by office computerization.

Bill is very busy running the local operation and meeting his ACL duties. He sees a need for one or two additional general managers to help oversee operations. As discussed in the previous section on staffing, a better educated workforce would benefit the Co-op's business ventures. Grade 6 is the highest education level held by current staff in the Co-op, except among management.

John identifies a need for strong management to move into two unfilled positions in the retail outlet. He explains, "Strong management is needed in order to maintain the retail operation's viability. There are confusion and wasted efforts among staff, which can be remedied by good management. We want to make operations easier so more responsibilities are shared and better productivity is achieved."

He continues, "All administrative work is done by hand. If somebody comes in for the value of their shares, it is very time-consuming to give them an answer. Computerized checkouts would remedy that situation and also help with inventory control. Pricing merchandise would be improved and we wouldn't have to go through countless files to do an invoice."

Environmental Friendliness

Bill feels that Native people have been raised to be aware of the environment and minimize any negative impact. He sees that more people are becoming aware of the need for better methods of garbage disposal and better filtration for sewage disposal in the community.

Bill states, "I think that we have been leaders in Cambridge Bay for bringing in biodegradable materials. We're always looking at new products, especially to replace plastic bags. I must say that disposable diapers are one of the worst pollutants in the Arctic. I see a lot of diapers out on the tundra when I go hunting." Another item of note is that by keeping the fishery going for the shortest period of time possible, the Co-op is minimizing any waste products, which might create pollution for the community.

Sustainability of the Businesses

After weathering the slump in the 1980s, Bill is cautiously optimistic about their chances of surviving another economic downturn. He states, "I've got to go through a slump to know if we could survive because people don't spend money. They always have to buy groceries though. We may not suffer as much, but we would suffer."

Future Development

Any plans for future expansion would be contingent on the impact of competition and the availability of skilled labour. Additional services in the short term, might include a pizza or fast-food outlet in the store or the hotel. In the long term, a new retail outlet and hotel expansion are possible. Bill explains, "The building which houses our retail operations, is ten years old now, but buildings don't last with the kind of weather that we have here. The board of directors are looking for a new piece of land to build a store and perhaps a daycare centre. We may expand the hotel, but we have to see the impact that the new hotels will have on our business first."

Bill has no firm plans for the future but he knows he will always support the Co-op, at least as a member. He plans to retire someday.

I've been with the Co-op almost ten years. I took on a challenge that I think has come to an end because the business is successful. I would say get out while everything is working right and then if they get in trouble, they can call me in to help with it. I'm getting to that age when I have to look for something else rather than doing this all the time. I might start a tour operation and live off the land. I like fishing, hunting, and walking. I want to do something that interests me because there are a lot of parties and you could end up an alcoholic quickly. I really don't want that for myself.

I think we have people in place who have the ability to continue operations. However even when you cultivate people as successors, you never know what you are going to get until they take over. I've seen many problems, not only in the co-op system but in other Native organizations, where new people take advantage of their positions.

Summary and Conclusions

The Northwest Territories' experiment into co-operatives has proven to be successful over more than thirty years of operations. There were obstacles to overcome, and these eliminated some of the weaker co-ops, but in 1991 the co-operative movement is thriving in the territory. A major employer and recycler of capital in local communities, the forty-one co-operatives in the territory seem to be meeting their objective as a means of independence and self-determination for Native people.

Native people are the main source of labour for local co-operatives and the movement has been inspirational and a matter of pride for Northern people. Although co-ops must compete with the government in attracting skilled employees, they offer fellow community members the chance for employment in traditional and modern pursuits.

The Ikaluktutiak Co-op in Cambridge Bay is one of the movement's success stories. Under the leadership of Bill Lyall, it has become one of the largest co-operatives. With a payroll over $456,000, this co-op provides employment for twenty-seven full-time staff and an additional forty or fifty people during the summer.

By offering personal service and products at reasonable prices, the Co-op has built up community support over the years. Close to 50% of the local community are members of the Co-op and benefit from patronage refunds amounting to $325,000 in 1990, a significant proportion of net profits. Nine local community members volunteer to assist in the management of the Co-op's businesses as board directors.

Through the Board of Directors and the annual meeting, the quality of services is constantly under review and steps are taken to remedy any problems which may arise. Input is also sought from members about new products or services they would like to see added to the Co-op. Bill has been instrumental in promoting friendly, personal service to customers and supportive policies for employees. Good employees are well-treated and given responsibility and flexibility for time off. Employees who require discipline are dealt with fairly but will be asked to leave if the problems are not resolved within a reasonable period of time. Another policy worth noting is the Co-op's concern for environmentally friendly products and its leadership role taken in this regard.

In a recession, the types of services offered at the retail outlet would remain necessities while the hotel might face a decline in business. In any case, the lessons learned from the recession in the early 1980s will likely see the Co-op through any economic downturn.

The future looks bright for the Cambridge Bay Co-op. Expansion plans for products and services are being contemplated, including a fast-food outlet, a new retail store building, and an extension to the hotel. Bill's role may change in the future, although he will always support the Co-op as a member. He has been active at the local and territorial levels for a number of years and he may decide to move onto other projects. In any case, he feels confident that there are skilled people who would be able to take up the duties of president without any difficulty.

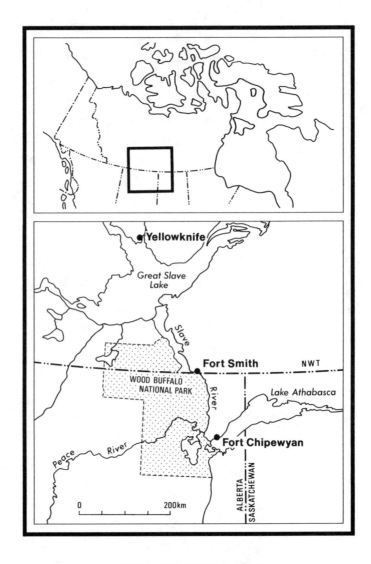

ENTREPRENEURS' ENDORSEMENT

We, the undersigned, acknowledge that we have read our business profile. We approve of the contents of the profile and recognize its accuracy in describing our business.

Dated ___MAY 13.___ , 1991

Earl Jacobson

Alex Gauthier

5

LOU'S SMALL ENGINES AND SPORTS LIMITED
Fort Smith, Northwest Territories

For the past nineteen years, Alex Gauthier has worked as head mechanic for Lou's Small Engines. He started working for his brother Lou, and then nine years ago Alex and his brother-in-law Earl Jacobson bought the business. It is a family business that sells and services dirt bikes and snowmobiles, as well as selling hunting and sporting goods to the 2,500 people in the Fort Smith area. The firm also offers courier and car rental services. Recently, Lou's Small Engine became an outlet for Sears catalogue sales.

Over the years, the business has built up a reputation for excellent sales and service. This reputation and the company's ability to streamline its staff without affecting service have enabled it to survive tough economic times. The business allows its owners to work at something they both enjoy while paying the bills. The history of the operation is reviewed in the next section.

History

Twenty years ago, Lou Gauthier opened up a small shop called Lou's Small Engines in the town of Fort Smith, a town of 300. He had his journeyman papers as a motor mechanic, diesel mechanic, and welder. His wife handled the company accounts. One year later, he hired his brother Alex, who was in the middle of completing training as a motor mechanic.

Alex recalls those early years, "When I first started with Lou, he had the skidoo dealership, the Honda dealership, and the Homelite dealership for chainsaws. We also handled repairs. We still hold the dealership for skidoos. Eventually, Earl came to work in the sporting goods section of the store. It has stayed a family business."

Earl worked at the store for about four years and then Lou decided to sell his business. He offered it to Alex and Earl. Earl recalls, "For me, I wanted to keep my job. We weren't sure who was going to buy the business and if we would be kept on. Then Lou suggested talking to Economic Development with the territorial government about grants that might be available. With the help of Economic Development, we put a package together for the purchase of the store and it was approved."

In making the decision to purchase the business, Alex and Earl went through the financial information of the business. Alex recalls, "I didn't really know the expenses but I knew it was a profitable business." Part of the funding application included a five-year projection of business financial statements. With the grant funds, Alex and Earl purchased equal shares in the business. Earl states, "Lou and his wife stayed for a year as part of the deal and helped us run the business and make the transition smoothly." Earl now handles the accounting, ordering, and sales, while Alex looks after the repair work.

Earl had no bookkeeping experience. Lou's wife taught him basic bookkeeping skills after they bought the store. After managing the store for some time, they ran into trouble. Earl recalls: "We did have a lot of problems because I wasn't getting enough financial information and the government let staff go in town. It snuck up on us before we knew what was happening, and we had a cash flow problem. We had to borrow money to consolidate all our debts and we laid off four full-time staff. However, we kept our inventory at the same level." The government layoffs and the decreased demand for fur, which led to lower demands for hunting equipment and snowmobile servicing, meant that their actual revenue was less than that forecast in the grant proposal.

Since buying the store, Alex and Earl have added the courier service and the Sears catalogue department. The store also has the dealership for Tilden Rent-A-Car. Since they hold a Honda dealership, they are invited to attend annual trade shows. They rarely attend these events, since new products do not generally affect the type of inventory that they carry in the store. However, the first show Earl and Alex attended in Calgary provided some interesting memories.

Earl recalls, "They paid our way to Calgary and we expected that it would be first-class. It was still shocking and we were flabbergasted. When we landed in Calgary, there was a guy with a Honda sign and we went to see him. They put our bags in a limousine and drove us downtown. We were casually dressed in jeans but every-

Earl Jacobson and Alex Gauthier

body else was in a suit and tie, so we changed right away. It was only two days but we still talk about that show periodically."

Self-employment is a Gauthier family tradition: Alex's father had his own business and served as a role model for his sons. Alex also owns a hauling company called A & R Hauling. He purchased the truck from another brother and has the contract with the Northern Store to haul their garbage to the dump. His son picks up the garbage and Alex handles the accounting. Alex notes, "My son is seventeen and he earns his own spending money. This job keeps him out of trouble and gives him some work experience."

Operations

Located on the main street of Fort Smith, Lou's Small Engines and Sports operates out of a two-storey office and sporting goods shop which has a repair shop attached to it. There is also a cold storage warehouse on the property. The shop is open from 8:30 a.m. to 6:00 p.m. Monday through Friday and from 10:00 a.m. to 5:00 p.m. on Saturday, year-round.

The sporting goods shop carries lawn mowers, skidoos, chainsaws, bicycles, motorcycles, and dirt bikes. Earl comments, "We carry a little bit of everything including fishing, hunting, and camping gear and team sports equipment for baseball and hockey. We don't carry a large inventory of sporting goods but it does not take us very long to fill orders."

The other main service is the repair shop. Alex notes, "I service anything that has to do with small motors." Earl adds, "The repair shop is the bread and butter of the whole business. It pays our wages, mortgage, and electricity." They carry a good parts inventory and receive calls from Cambridge Bay and other areas of central Northwest Territories for parts. They had to cut back on this service because customers often failed to pick up their COD orders when they arrived and the shop had to pay the round-trip delivery costs.

Earl's mother looks after the Sears catalogue orders, which are filled from the head office in Regina. Lou's Small Engines earns a percentage on the total amount of sales. They are agents for Tilden Rent-A-Car and Buffalo Courier. Two other agencies in town compete for a share of a very small car rental market. Earl and Alex are contemplating discontinuing this service if demand remains low. Buffalo Courier ships packages from Edmonton across the North, on Canadian Airlines. Earl and Alex deliver the packages shipped to the Fort Smith area.

Trappers have provided a significant demand for skidoo purchases and servicing in the past, from October through February. This demand has decreased in the past several years with the drastic drop in fur prices and its negative impact on the fur-trapping industry. Business picks up in May, when motorcycle sales pick up and government fire fighters require regular equipment maintenance. The territorial government is a major client. Wood Buffalo National Park and the territorial government have their own fire fighters. The shop also services equipment for the RCMP. As is common for many small northern communities, Earl notes, "Take the government away from here and you have nothing since at least 80% of the people are employed by the government."

Most of the inventory is paid for immediately by the store. One supplier of skidoos, Bombardier, has a finance company and allows its wholesale customers to pay over a period of time. Recently this supplier instituted a new type of payment system called curtailment fees; under it, Lou's Small Engines orders twenty-five units in the fall but instead of paying the total inventory cost in the usual thirty days, the retailer makes monthly payments that go towards the cost of the machine, not towards interest charges. Bombardier hopes that sales outlets will be encouraged to order more units while sharing in the ownership of the units with the suppliers.

The partners must make guarantees that leave them personally liable for all debts to the suppliers. As Earl notes, "Any lawyer would advise against signing personal guarantees but that's how these bigger companies protect themselves. As a customer, I am stuck if they've got a product that sells and I want to sell it." Dealership agreements must be renewed each year. If sales quotas were not met, then Earl and Alex negotiate with that supplier and explain the problems they face with the demand in the local market. They communicate regularly with their suppliers by telephone and with sales representatives, who make infrequent trips to Fort Smith. Many suppliers offer sales incentives such as reduced inventory rates or free trips when target sales levels are reached.

The level of accounts receivable is strictly monitored so that their operating cash flow is not jeopardized. The general rule is cash-and-carry, but Alex and Earl give established customers some latitude in paying within thirty days. If payment is not made on time, then the customer's account is cancelled immediately and interest is charged on the outstanding balance. Earl will write and visit the customers with outstanding balances and has taken some delinquent accounts to court for settlement. The territorial government is a special case: they know that the account will be paid, but sometimes it takes up to forty-five days to receive the payment because of the bureaucracy involved in processing invoices. Bank financing is available to customers on big-ticket items but is arranged by the suppliers of those items.

The demand for their products has shifted over time. As mentioned, trappers are no longer major customers. Demand for dirt bikes has also dropped, from forty-five or fifty units when Alex's brother first acquired the Honda dealership to one or two a season. Earl comments, "These are recreation vehicles that if you can afford it, you buy it. Kids used to be our big customers but now they want cars not dirt bikes." By diversifying into other product lines, Earl and Alex hope that the demand for new products will replace the dwindling demand for some of the established products.

With the shift in demand, Earl has to monitor inventory more closely. His ordering patterns have changed. If something does not move in a reasonable time period, then he puts it on sale and does not reorder it. Inventory is not on the firm's computer and he does a visual check once a month to make up the stock order.

Although sales have slowed, Earl recalls their delight in winning the top dealership award from Bombardier for sales and service in 1988. Earl recalls, "They monitor your purchases of parts and units in order to select a winner. They also talk to different customers.

Lou's Small Engines

They paid our way down to their annual skidoo show in Edmonton and gave us a plaque. It was a surprise."

Several licences are required in order to operate Lou's Small Engines. Earl and Alex have a business licence and must comply with the requirements of the Worker's Compensation Board. Alex has his journeyman's licence as a mechanic, which is a necessity when bidding for government contracts. They also carry fire and theft insurance but have never had to make a claim.

Staff

In the nine years Earl and Alex have been in business, they have had four full-time employees. When they had to downsize several years ago because of a downturn in demand, they had to lay off these employees, who were never rehired. They hired Alex's sister to do sales, but she has moved away. Currently Earl and Alex are helped by Earl's mother, who handles the Sears catalogue orders, and by Alex's son, who is training to become a mechanic.

Working with family has been a success. Earl and Alex share the conviction that treating each other and their employees in a businesslike manner has contributed to their success in this area. If they were in the position to hire new employees, they would look for qualified staff who required little supervision, were committed to their work, had high work standards, and were capable of handling customers in a friendly manner. According to Earl, "They would have to be conscientious about their work. No short cuts on repair work, because we've established our reputation based on service and we don't want to lose it. They could not leave tools lying around because it's a reflection of sloppy work and gives the customer a bad impression."

The difficulty in running a small operation arises when there is a serious illness or the owners want to take holidays. Earl and Alex have not had to deal with illness: Alex has taken only three sick days in the past eighteen years. But physical problems may increase now that he is getting older. Holidays in the past have meant taking only long weekends, staggering their time off and covering for the other partner, or occasionally hiring previous employees or relatives to cover for them. They try to take a proper holiday every second year. Alex explains, "Since I'm the only mechanic here, it is tough to take regular holidays. Our customers are used to quick repair service and I can't let my customers down." The benefit of owning the business is that the partners have the flexibility to take a few days off if business is slow. Alex is able to leave his son to handle the repairs on some Saturdays.

Competition

There are some competitors offering similar services in Fort Smith and the surrounding area. These businesses could take away business, but Lou's Small Engines has built up a fine reputation over the years, and this has served to protect their share of the market.

There is one small engine shop which sells Polaris snowmobiles in Fort Smith. Another sporting goods store operates in town, and two other sporting goods stores are in the planning stages. Alex notes, "Competition is getting stiff. One new store will be run by an ex-schoolteacher who plans to carry team sports equipment. The other store will concentrate on hunting equipment, but won't have our reputation."

Earl adds, "We've built our reputation over a number of years and that includes Alex's good reputation in the repair shop. If customers have any problems we'll stand up to our mistakes and make sure that the customer is happy. We're established in the sporting goods area. We know who are customers are and what to sell, so I don't lose sleep over these new competitors. I just make sure that we've got the proper stock and that we're competitively priced. We don't offer real low prices and hope to move a large volume of business because there aren't enough people in this town."

The repair shop has little direct competition. Alex comments, "I do not service cars or trucks. Local garages do that work, and they don't service small engines. It's an understanding we have with the other businesses here. The town is too small to support all of us in the same business."

When the territorial government seeks tenders on certain jobs, Lou's Small Engines also faces competition from Bombardier dealers operating in nearby towns such as Hay River and Fort Chipewyan. On the whole Lou's Small Engines has done well in bidding on government contracts. Earl explains, "Alex and I have established a minimum gross margin that we must earn on a contract. If we don't get that margin then I don't want the contract. If we're not going to make a dollar then it's not worth doing. We're in business to survive and make money."

Advertising of the firm appears in the Business Yellow Pages and the local newspaper. In Earl's opinion, Lou's Small Engines does not need to advertise unless new inventory has just arrived or a sales event is planned. Most people in town know about the business already.

Financial Information

The purchase of Lou's Small Engines and Sports was accomplished through personal investment, a territorial government grant, and a bank loan. The territorial government has been very helpful over the years. Other government assistance includes a loan when Earl and Alex consolidated their debts and a grant to purchase a computer and training for Earl.

Earl is far from positive about their relationship with their local bank. He recalls, "The bank is very difficult to work with when trying to negotiate a loan. Ask any business; the bank won't lend money to anybody in town. You have to go in there and fight for it. They have to get permission from Calgary, but Calgary doesn't know our situation here at all. They just flat-out refuse so that's very, very hard. Even when the government approved our initial purchase of the business, the bank loan would not be processed until we received the government funds, which took a year."

The accounting system was recently computerized. Earl enters

Table 5
Financial Information for Lou's Small Engine and Sports Limited

	1985	1986	1987	1988	1989
Return on Equity (%)	5	4	18	0	14
Sales/Assets (times)	1.67	1.34	1.34	1.80	1.60
Total Salaries ($000)	84	96	80	70	60

sales information on a regular basis and their Hay River accountant handles the year-end financial statements. Earl notes, "I had never dealt with computers before, so initially it scared me. Once I got into it, though, I got a handle on it. I will generate monthly reports that show sales by product, labour, and unit costs, accounts receivable, and accounts payable. We will know what is selling and what isn't, so we'll know where we have to improve."

Five years of financial information is set out in Table 5. The return-on-equity ratios, which compare profit before interest and taxes to total owners' equity, fluctuated throughout the period from 0% in 1988 to 18% in 1987. This variability reflects the turbulent local economy, which has included a recession. In 1989, for each $1.00 invested in the business, Earl and Alex earned 14¢.

The sales-to-asset ratio fluctuated throughout the period in a narrow range between 1.34 times and 1.8 times. This ratio indicates the capacity to generate revenue based on the company's investment in assets. For every $1.00 invested in assets, Lou's Small Engines generated more than an equal rate in sales, with a high in 1988 of 1.8. Total salaries declined steadily throughout the five-year period, reflecting the company's general strategy of retrenching in order to survive the tough economic times.

Reasons for Success

Earl and Alex define their business as a success because it is profitable, they enjoy it, and it provides a needed service to the community. Many factors have contributed to their success and to the longevity of their business, including excellent service on all their products, active care for customer satisfaction, a strong partnership, and their longtime residence in Fort Smith.

Alex comments, "It's fun because I get to play with the toys around here. I really like that I can come here any time of the day or night and work. It's relaxing by myself and nobody bothers me. I'm glad our wives are working, though, because if they weren't working for the government, we couldn't support our family in the slow times."

Customer service and satisfaction is still their number one goal; Alex notes, "Customer service has always been first since Lou started the business. Our service is known across the North and people really appreciate it. We try to satisfy the customer in a timely manner. It is the service and the smile you give them that brings in new customers and brings back the old customers."

Earl adds, "Customer service has to be your goal or forget owning a successful business. For example, there are six outlets in town that sell peddle bicycles. Every year we sell up to eighty bikes, which is more than our main competitor, the Hudson Bay. I use our after-sales service as the sales pitch to attract customers."

Another important factor in the success of their business is their strong partnership. Although they are related through marriage, each treats the other as he would any other business partner. Alex explains, "Business is business and pleasure is pleasure. We do mix the two, but we try to be open and honest. We've had our ups and downs but we have worked through them. We go hunting together and discuss business issues."

Earl adds, "I guess we just understand each other and get along. It helps that we had a natural division of duties from the beginning. Alex has always handled the repair shop and I had nothing to do with it. I run the front counter and handle sales. We did find out the hard way that we have to communicate all the time. Sometimes I get into a routine and forget about discussing a problem or I'll put it off for a while. The problem continues and then all of a sudden, everything comes to a big crunch, then we have to sit down and deal with it. Partnerships can split over things like that, so communication is number one."

Finally, Earl and Alex go back a long way in Fort Smith. Alex points out, "People know me very well. I was practically raised with all our customers. They know my work is good and we stand behind it."

Areas for Improvement

The major challenge facing Lou's Small Engines is remaining competitive. It is crucial to watch the competition, and Lou's Small Engines' pricing strategy is fine-tuned as required, so that they remain competitively priced. As new competitors enter the market, this will become even more important.

Earl thinks that more training in the computerized bookkeeping package would be beneficial. "If more information is available to us, we can be on top of problems quickly. I think we are on the right track with the new computer." Alex would like to hire another mechanic because the work is very steady for one person. The pressure would ease his working hours, but the question is whether or not they can afford another person at this time.

Sustainability of the Business

The business has successfully weathered some tough times. Some of the factors that have contributed to this sustainability include the firm's solid reputation, the stability of the territorial government departmental customers, and the flexibility available to a small business.

Their reputation has seen them through the tough times according to Earl. "We have a good name that has been around for nineteen years. When times are tough, people will have their broken items repaired rather than throw them away. We've always given them good service."

When the marketplace is slow, the government's level of demand is fairly constant. This acts as a safety buffer. Earl notes, "A lot of our business is dependent on the government. They basically run the same budget every year with a slight increase. This does give us some stability when the market fluctuates."

Finally, flexibility in making changes in order to survive has seen them through slow times. When they had to consolidate their debts, they let staff go and they were able to rely on the stability of their wives' salaries to meet family budgets while they took cuts in their salaries. They have diversified into services that the community needs in order to bring in customers. Earl states, "I think we are well established and many people depend on us. We provide an essential service to the community. People keep on coming no matter what, and the loyal customers are the main reason we are still here."

Environmental Friendliness

The environmental movement and the recession are encouraging people to reuse or repair goods rather than continue to consume new products. The repair shop provides the service to local people who are interested in maintaining their old equipment.

Earl and Alex try to keep the area around the store as clean as possible in order to attract customers. They take their garbage to the dump and are going to try recycling some of the waste products from the repair shop. It is very expensive to recycle used oil and there is only a small demand for it in Fort Smith. Previously, Alex disposed of this oil in a dugout on their property but it seeps into the soil. He has decided to store the oil in drums and give it to anyone who wants it for their driveways or highways. Alex is quite concerned about the proposed pulp mills in northern Alberta. "It wouldn't help us at all. It just sends their pollution this way. I'm not for it."

Future Development

Alex and Earl would like to build the business up and then sell out in the next couple of years. If they cannot sell in the near future, then they would build up revenues and hire a manager so that they could get away more often. Both partners feel that the business must have several more years of stable earnings before they can hope to sell it. Alex comments, "I'm due for a change and I want to take my wife out of the North. I'm starting to find the winters are too damn long. If we did sell, I would go work for somebody else. It would be tough but there would be fewer headaches."

Earl would stay in the North if they sold the business. "I have been up here all my life and I enjoy it. Once we sell I'd take a break and just work for wages. I would do something that's not too hard and just enjoy life for a while. If we couldn't sell, then I could see us hiring a manager and a mechanic in the back. We would get away more and let them run it. However, we need a stable industry to come in so that the population will grow and then our business will grow otherwise I don't see us getting any bigger."

Advice to New Business

Alex and Earl have learned a number of lessons from their own experience. Before purchasing an existing business, the entrepreneur should consider working for the owner in order to learn the business and avoid surprises. Government programs should be checked for applicability. It may make sense to have the past owners stay on to help with the transition after the purchase of the business. Bookkeeping skills are crucial in the success of the new business. In starting a new business, the entrepreneur should closely examine the market in the community. Once the business is opened, then inventory control should remain a priority.

Earl and Alex purchased a business in which they had a total of fourteen years' experience between them. As a result, there were few surprises, except when they did not keep close watch on their inventory. Their experience with the government has been very positive and they would recommend that a new business apply to relevant funding programs.

The major expense in their type of operation is the investment in inventory and buildings. Earl estimates that their buildings and inventory are valued at $500,000. Alex adds, "You may get stuck with units that you took in on trade and you have to pay your suppliers every thirty days for the new units."

If the business person is contemplating a similar but untried business then Earl would suggest their type of operation would do well where the community numbers 2,500 to 3,000 people. Alex adds, "It depends a lot on the people and how they pay their bills. Many northern communities have a problem with that. I've known a few places where a person tries to start a small engine shop. It's almost a necessity because many people depend on snowmobiles, bikes, or outboard motors for their boats, which need servicing, but the customers don't know how to pay."

Earl notes, "If I started a new business somewhere else I would check with other businesses and see what the people are like. I would want to know who pays their bills and who doesn't pay, and then I would have quite a strict cash-and-carry policy." Alex adds, "You have to make sure the market is there and is stable enough to support your business. You have to be prepared for hard work and to just keep plugging away. You have to be willing to work long hours without holidays and you might succeed."

The question of whether or not the new business should be a partnership is answered by Alex in the negative. He explains, "If I was to start again, I don't think I would have a partner. Although Earl and I have a great partnership, if I could do it on my own I would have a very small business. It would be just big enough to survive and when I wanted to leave, I would close the doors and go. It's tough with a partner because you've got to split profits and the losses fifty-fifty. It is hard when times are slow to pay two salaries."

The partners get a lot of personal satisfaction from their business. Earl notes, "I like to see the business coming along through rough times and that we have been able to survive. Business has

turned around and we are starting to make money again. It is satisfying."

Summary and Conclusions

Earl Jacobson and Alex Gauthier have continued a tradition of excellent after-sales service of their products, a policy established by
Lou Gauthier when he started Lou's Small Engines nineteen years
ago. Earl and Alex have survived tough economic times and shifts
in demand through their excellent reputation, improved inventory
controls, and streamlined operations.

It is a strong partnership that has seen them through the past nine
years. They both had experience in different aspects of the business,
and these added up to a near-complete package of skills. They were
able to purchase the business with assistance from the Territorial
Government and the bank. Their relationship with the government
is good; government agencies are solid customers and have helped
them to consolidate their debts. Their relationship with the local
bank has not been as positive. They respect each other and treat
each other in a businesslike manner. Earl and Alex try to communicate regularly about problems before the problems get out of hand.
They know where the other person stands and share similar work
ethics and standards.

Neither partner takes their customers for granted. Customer service and satisfaction is their main goal, a policy that any new staff
would have to follow. They are in tune with the needs of their
customers, and this understanding is reflected in their purchase of
inventory. They have diversified from skidoos and dirt bikes to
camping, hunting, and team sports equipment, as well as gardening
accessories. They offer Sears catalogue sales and courier and car
rental services to the community. This strategy of diversification
brings new customers into the store, increases their profile, and acts
as a buffer if sales in their more established product lines decrease.

Their ability to cut back on staff and personal salaries when economic times have been poor has helped them survive. The steady
income that their wives earn in their government jobs has eased the
financial burden at home. The relatively stable demand from their
government customers has lessened the impact of changes in the
demand of their other customers. Earl and Alex take pride in maintaining a neat workplace for the aesthetic value to their customers
and the benefit to their environment. Recycling of waste products
from the repair shop is going to play a greater role in the future.

After nineteen years in the business, Alex and Earl are looking forward to a change. After several more years of good earnings, they plan to sell the business and move on to other projects. If the store is not sold then they would like to hire staff which allow them to take more time off and enjoy life.

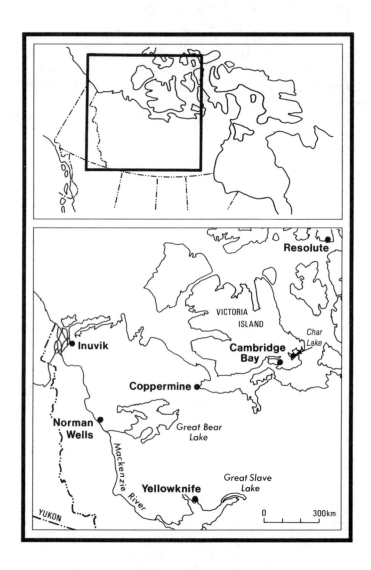

ENTREPRENEURS' ENDORSEMENT

I, the undersigned, acknowledge that I have read my business profile. I approve of the contents of the profile and recognize its accuracy in describing my business.

Dated _May_, 1991

George Angohlotok
George Angohlotok

6

NORTHERN EMAK OUTFITTING INC.
Cambridge Bay, Northwest Territories

On a remote coastal lake on the east side of Victoria Island, which lies 200 miles north of the Arctic Circle, brothers George and Gary Angohiotok operate a fishing camp. They are majority partners in a company called Northern Emak Outfitting Ltd. "Emak" is the Inuit word for "waters." They offer fishermen from around the world an opportunity to catch arctic char in Char Lake.

Bill Tait, who operates Adventure North Expeditions Ltd (previously called Canada North) in Yellowknife, and Jerome Knapp, a well-known journalist, are the other partners in Northern Emak. This is the first venture in which Bill and Jerome have formalized a partnership agreement. In addition to booking the fishing trips, Bill's company handles the bookings for tours of Cambridge Bay, a village of 1,000 people on Victoria Island, as well as tours to look for muskox. Mabel, George's wife, conducts these local tours.

The business is a success because each partner brings a complementary set of skills to the operation. Bill's tour company handles the bookings and does the accounting; George and Gary hire the guides and ensure that clients are well looked after. After only four years of operation, they find that customers come back and refer others. A review of the planning process and the start-up of the company is presented in the next section.

History

The idea for the Northern Emak partnership evolved out of Jerome's experience with George as his hunting guide over the course of several years. George's expertise as a guide reflects his upbringing. George was born sixty miles west of Coppermine, at a little place called Bernard Harbour. He recalls, "A small group of Natives lived there and we followed the migrating herds of caribou. In the spring, we hunted seals. When I was six, I went away to school in Inuvik with the other kids in my family. Then I went to Yellowknife and I completed grade 8 and little bit of grade 9. But I felt a strong urge to come back and be on the land, so I did." George continues to hunt during the year and provides his family with their meat supply.

Northern Emak is not George's first business venture. "About ten years ago, I started a little company that sold snow machine products and bikes. I stayed with it for about three years. I had two partners and we sold equipment and did repair work. It was okay, but the place that we were working out of was a little too small. We couldn't really afford the overhead and it was difficult to expand in this small community. So we sold that business and it's still in operation today."

Next George started to guide for the Hunters and Trappers Association. Many customers booked through Adventure North Expeditions, and this was the beginning of the relationship which resulted in the formation of Northern Emak. Bill Tait recalls, "It all started because George was an extraordinary top-notch guide. About five years ago, we wanted an arctic char fishing operation and we thought George would be a good prospect for a partner. Adventure North is a company that does anything it can in tourism that we think will be profitable. We delve into all kinds of package tours. I handle the western Northwest Territories and we have an affiliated company in Iqaluit that does the east. We also have another operation in Ottawa that books the eastern Arctic tours and other tours in Africa and Europe."

George recalls when Jerome approached him with the idea. "Gary and I always knew that fishing was good at Jayko and Char lakes. Every year a group of us would get together and charter a plane out and do some fishing there, two or three times a summer. We knew the fishing would be good, so we decided we'd give it a go."

A partnership agreement was drawn up, with George and Gary holding a majority position, and the company was incorporated. Bill notes, "We work with Native people on many of our tours, but the arrangements are not formalized as partnerships in any other case. We decided to follow that route because we have a lot of faith in George. He's probably the best hunting guide we've ever run into across the Arctic."

The local Hunters and Trappers Association and the town council approved the new business. George recalls, "It was quite easy to approach them. We had long discussions, but I guess by showing interest in getting something like this business started, they were

George and Mabel Angohiotok

quite willing to support it. We started negotiations in November and everything was in place by the time we started in August." Northern Emak has a ninety-nine-year lease of 200 feet of shoreline that does not include the water itself.

No business plan was necessary because the first year of operation was financed by Bill and Jerome. Bill recalls, "Although it was a bit of the seat-of-the-pants type project, we know enough about the business to know what will work and what won't. I've been in it for over twenty years, and Jerome is well experienced too. He's one of the top outdoor writers in Canada. Indeed, Canada North is probably number one in booking tours around the Arctic. In any case, a lot of business plans and feasibility studies are just justification for disaster."

George recalls, "From the first moment I spoke to Jerome, Gary and I discussed it pretty well all year and planned how we'd go about doing it. We took it step by step and bought some boats and equipment. Then in 1987, we brought ten customers up to Jayko Lake, which is about twenty miles north of Char Lake. The pilot project went pretty well that week, so we decided to give it a shot. The fishing wasn't that good at Jayko Lake so we moved to Char Lake the following year."

Operations

Northern Emak clients may book their tours through Adventure North Expeditions in Yellowknife or at one of the trade shows Adventure North frequents in the United States. Clients fly from Edmonton to Cambridge Bay, where Mabel meets them at the airport. She takes them into town to get their fishing licences and then to the charter aircraft from Adlair Aviation, which flies them to Char Lake for a one-week stay. Tours begin in July and run through until the end of August.

George and Gary look after hiring the cook and the guides for the two-month period. The ratio is one guide for two clients. Groups average seven people, but the largest group (in 1990) was fourteen people. The majority of clients come from the United States, but, as Mabel notes, "We've also met people from Australia, Germany, Switzerland, and Canada." The tours attract both beginners and experienced anglers.

George states, "The number of clients has quadrupled since our first summer. This year we built five new prefab boats. The largest is a sixteen-footer. My brother and I are easygoing. We understand each other quite well. We usually start the season off together, and then I'll spend time at the camp and he'll come back to Cambridge Bay. He's spent the last bit of this season without me."

Clients stay in a simple tent camp on Char Lake. It can be moved from year to year so that it is close to the best fishing. Wooden bunks with foam pads and heaters are supplied and the clients bring their own sleeping bags. The fees have gone from $1,900 to $2,400 over a three-year period for a one-week stay. Clients make a $500 deposit on the trips and the balance must be paid sixty days before the tour date.

According to their advertising literature, the price of the package includes the client's accommodation in camp, all meals, the services of Inuit guides, round-trip airfare from Edmonton or Yellowknife to Cambridge Bay, and the air charter from Cambridge Bay to camp. Hospitality is free.

Their brochure is comprehensive in listing the type of clothing and equipment that are recommended for a stay, but George recalls, "Some people still had to borrow extra clothing because it's quite cool."The average temperature in July and August ranges from 6° to 8° C.

Clients are informed that their fees are not refundable if the weather is bad or if they don't catch any fish. George states, "It's nice to get them out the first couple of days especially if it's good weather. Since they spend eight to twelve hours fishing a day, they don't mind sitting in camp for an extra day if the weather is poor. This summer (1990), we only had two days of bad weather and we couldn't do anything. No one has ever left without catching a fish in the years we've been operating." In fact, clients find that the arctic char and lake trout fishing is excellent. According to their brochure, char weighing up to twenty-four pounds have been caught on lure and line. The largest char caught in the summer of 1990 weighed about fifteen pounds.

The weather can be unpredictable, and George recalls how once, in the first year, they almost blew away. "We just had tents attached to a plywood platform with ropes. One big tent was a kitchen and dining room. It was about the fourth day and the winds picked up and were howling. The cook came to get me about 4:00 in the morning because our kitchen was falling over. Three of us went rushing out and managed to save the tent in winds that were blowing about fifty miles an hour."

Fish is frozen for shipping out with the client. If the client wants the catch mounted, George recommends a taxidermist in Winnipeg and will ship it out to the client once the work is completed. He notes, "We recently found out about another taxidermist in Yellowknife and we're looking into that for the future."

Plant and animal life are abundant by Char Lake and include lichens, arctic poppy, and moss campion. Besides muskox, there are arctic foxes, wolves, hares, lemmings, and Peary and barren-ground caribou. Common birds include the red-throated loon, Sabine's gull, golden plover, snowy owl, rough-legged hawk, arctic tern, and ptarmigan.

A number of lodges across the Arctic Coast offer fishing, hiking, photography, and big-game hunting. High Arctic Lodge is an established venture and the only other lodge operating on Victoria Island. They have five guest cabins and a modern lodge.

Bill and George are pleased with the way their business has developed. George is pleasantly surprised at how quickly it has grown. "We didn't think it would grow this quickly. We were going to take it really slow. Our overhead was somewhat higher in 1990 than we'd planned because we bought boats and more tents and equipment to try to make it a little more comfortable. I think that with the improvements we are going to get even more people next year."

Bill organizes the marketing of the fishing packages through advertising and attending trade shows. He has a one-page flyer that describes the package and the Char Lake camp. In addition, they have listings in some of the government tourist publications. A colour brochure is planned for the 1991 season. Bill regularly attends trade shows in Denver, Colorado, and other shows in the western United States, since 90% of their business is from the States.

Bill also markets the community tour that Mabel handles as another activity of Northern Emak. "We send clients with Mabel to view muskox at Mount Pelly and tour Cambridge Bay on our Victoria Island weekend package. We send them up there from Friday to Monday. They get out on the land and have good photo opportunities of the muskox. The potential for that kind of tour is very good. I'd like to make Cambridge Bay the muskox capital of the world."

Wildlife sightings cannot be guaranteed, but in the 1990 season no one was disappointed. The tour to Mount Pelly is about four hours and includes a lunch stop. The tour of the town includes a stop at the original town of Cambridge Bay where several historical sites are located. It lasts about an hour. Mabel has handled the tours for two years. She finds that it is both a challenge and a satisfaction to make a success of something she has never done before. She enjoys meeting the people from all over the world. In the off-season, Mabel has a full-time job teaching handicapped children.

Training

In the 1990 season, Northern Emak employed seven guides and a cook. George notes, "I look for people with experience. The last few years we've had experienced guides, but they're getting jobs with better pay at other places, so they aren't available when I need them. So this year we decided to go with a young group. Most are in their teens and they've done quite well. I was happy with them."

George gives an orientation to the guides at the beginning of the season. He outlines their responsibilities and his expectations for their behaviour with the clients. He states, "Before we went out, I explained that I know they're kind of shy but I want them not to be so shy. They should try to communicate with the clients out there and show them a feeling of warmth and welcome. It worked pretty well this summer." This sort of experience will benefit these young men in many ways because they will feel at ease in new situations and with new people.

George states, "We work from eight to sixteen hours a day following the fish for our clients. We pay a flat rate to our guides, but towards the end of August I knew I couldn't keep them going those long hours so I cut it right off. I told them to guide only during the day. They could guide in the evenings if they felt like going out. It made it a lot easier on them. In addition, they each get a week back in town."

George and Gary do hire family members and it has worked out well for them. Problems are avoided by talking openly with their employees about their expectations. Both brothers are certified guides and do not require that their guides be certified. However, they do encourage them to think about getting their certification, since that will improve their employability as guides.

The certification course is available from Arctic College. It offers a guide training program in two levels. The first level is a three-week training course that includes four or five days gaining practical experience on the land. Topics covered include the tourism industry, the guide's role as a professional and employer, safety and first aid, tour preparation and regulations, menu development and cooking skills, and finally, proper sanitation and hygiene. The second level is a four-week course on guiding for big game hunters. There are approximately thirty-five to forty licensed guides in the region.

Every northern tourism operation must meet the regulations of the Travel and Tourism Act, which is administered by the local Tourism officer. Northern Emak also carries liability insurance and bonds its employees and must qualify for a Tourist Establishment licence. Records of each client and the bookings for the year are required. Equipment must be maintained in good condition and the damage to the environment must be minimized. The Renewable Resources officer and the Tourism officer make regular visits to the camp and check that licences and all regulations are met.

George enjoys the business. He states

In the beginning, it's a hard task for the new fellows to look after the guests properly when they're out on the lake. Usually they catch on quickly and as the season gets on they have other things to worry about. For instance, we have to work a little harder to find the fish since fish move around.

I'm not a very aggressive guy and most of the guys that have worked with me know when I'm not pleased with something. It doesn't really happen very often and I don't show it too much emotionally. On a couple of occasions I've just come out and said, 'You know, it should be done another way, or it shouldn't be done at all.' Things seem to work out and I think this year's group all want to come back again next year.

Financial Information

Bill Tait's company does the accounting for the business. Separate financial statements are prepared for Northern Emak's operations. Bill is in touch with George regularly, but only on an informal basis. The fourth partner, Jerome, was the one who originally conceived the idea but does not take an active role in the daily operations of the business. Bill states his philosophy, "I've worked with Eskimos for over 20 years in developing tours. I'm a firm believer in, 'If it works, let them do their thing.'"

No external financing was necessary to start operations. A shareholder's loan was made to Northern Emak by Jerome and Bill to cover expenses. This was paid back from the next year's revenues. In the first year, there was approximately a $10,000 loss but since then the business has broken even. This means that all expenses were paid from the revenues. Revenues have quadrupled since the first year of operation. Bill expects a 25% increase in the number of customers in 1991, which should put the company into the black, so that the partners can earn a return on their investment.

No dividends have been paid to the partners, but George and Gary take a salary from the company's revenues to operate the outfit. Every year they have invested in more equipment using earnings that otherwise would have been profit. As Bill says, "We don't formalize a lot of our dealings with regular meetings or whatever. We do a lot of sports hunts with George and we come up from time to time. The bottom line is trust."

Reasons for Success

The Northern Emak partnership is successful for a variety of reasons. Each partner brings complementary skills to the company, with George and Gary running the camp and Bill handling marketing, bookings, and accounting. The absence of serious debt reduces the impact of any slowdown in demand for fishing trips. For George, the company allows him to earn a living at something he loves. George and Gary offer friendly service to their customers and provide employment opportunities for local young people.

Bill states, "The partnership has worked because we knew that George is a solid kind of person who is reliable and smart. There are lots of proposals for joint ventures in the North right now. The idea of a joint venture usually means mixing, for example, Native people, who are excellent guides and hosts, with partners who have the marketing expertise. Many Natives lack public relation skills or business skills to do the marketing, so it's a mutually beneficial arrangement. Tourism and many other businesses would benefit from a joint venture situation."

There is a conscious effort in Northern Emak to share the marketing expertise among partners. Bill says, "I've taken George down to a couple of shows in the States so he can understand the concept of marketing and have a chance to sell. I've never seen a guy from the North with no previous experience who's been able to facilitate a booking from greeting the potential customer to the point of taking a deposit. He's been fantastic."

George likes the opportunity to combine his chosen lifestyle with a business. He says, "You can't last in this business if you don't enjoy it. This is something I enjoy very much even if I'm not the one catching the fish. It's quite exciting just to see the fish caught, especially with this new type of fishing called 'fly fishing.' It's very exciting."

Bill thinks that the natural hospitality that clients are exposed to in the North contributes to the success of any venture. People feel welcomed by the local partners and their staff and many are already providing repeat business to Northern Emak.

Another important reason for the success of the fishing camp was the policy of minimizing the initial outlay for expenses. Bill points out, "We don't believe in high capital expense. When we started we bought all the equipment at a minimum cost so what we have there is ours. We didn't want to invest a lot of money in the thing so if the fishing business goes downhill we've cut the risks. It's not as good a business as it was twenty or thirty years ago but it's still a good investment. The government would like us to invest a million dollars in a business and have a big opening – cut ribbons and have ministers there. What we have here is a bare-bones operation that just tries to make money and hopefully will survive."

In addition to minimizing expenses, another successful element in the start-up phase was the pilot project. It was a way to assess at little cost whether or not the demand for a fishing camp existed and could be met properly. Bill states, "The main thing is that if you've got to walk a thousand miles, the first mile is the hardest. With the pilot project George and Gary travelled the first mile, just to get the kinks out, and then we let it roll."

Northern Emak plays an active role in providing training and employment opportunities for people in the community. The young people are able to develop invaluable skills in dealing with people. Since Northern Emak is still a new business George and Gary are unable to support local charities to any great extent but they plan to do so in the future. Bill notes, "There's a multiplier effect with a business. Skills and dollars stay in the community and multiply. I believe in letting people do their own thing. Governments have introduced all kinds of foreign activities through their bureaucracies and it hasn't worked very well."

In the summer months, George operates the fishing camp, and

in the winter months he is a guide for big-game hunters. He still does repair work on Yamaha equipment on a part-time basis in the winter and he hunts on the land and provides meat for his family. He appreciates the blend of a traditional lifestyle with a modern way of earning a living. Bill also sees this mix of opportunities as crucial. He states, "The answer to making tourism work here is not to offer jobs as chambermaids. Opportunities should combine more naturally with the cultural interests of the people."

George and Mabel's family life is busier with the fishing camp and the tours. George says, "Mabel knows as well as anybody else that I like being out on the land and there's nothing that I would rather do. Gary and I sit and chat about the things that we could do and it looks good for the future."

Environmental Responsibility and Sustainability

It is in Northern Emak's interests to follow procedures that minimize the impact of operations on the environment because nature is the source of their revenue. If the environment is destroyed, not only will it close down their business but the quality of life for their children will be adversely affected.

Mabel and George have three children. They hope to pass on a clean environment and a way of life that includes sensitivity to that environment. George takes his sons with him when he is hunting on the land and is passing his knowledge and skills on to them. During tours to Mount Pelly, Mabel makes sure that all garbage from the lunches are brought back into town. The fishing camp is kept clean and the waste is disposed of properly. The limit for char is seven fish, but George has voluntarily set a limit of four so that the stock is not depleted.

Factors that should improve the future of the company include its ability to react quickly to changes in demand, fair prices, and minimal debt. If demand did slow down, George feels that they would be able to tighten up on expenses and survive. However, it is difficult to predict until they experience a drop in demand. Revenues have climbed steadily upwards since the fishing camp opened. George notes, "Our prices are fair for the amount of fishing that our customers get in. We'll continue to get people coming back."

Capital expansion has been slow without incurring bank debt. It was initially financed by two of the partners; now expansion is financed by company revenues. Bill notes, "By minimizing the amount of invested dollars, we have created some immunity to falling demand. If we had invested piles of money, we would not have that immunity. We've also kept debt low."

Future Development

The future looks bright for Northern Emak. Bill predicts a 25% increase in the number of customers next year. George and Gary are always discussing the future and the possibilities that exist. In the short term, plans are in the works for a permanent structure to house the dining room. Other areas for expansion include upgrading the facilities at the camp and expanding into other services. At this point, there are no plans to expand the town tours that Mabel operates.

Bill states, "There's an existing camp on the lake where we're operating. They don't have a lease any more, so negotiations are under way for purchasing that whole outfit." If Northern Emak can't purchase the existing camp, then they may build a permanent structure to house the dining area and kitchen.

Plans to upgrade the amenities in the camp would make it more attractive to large groups. George states, "We're looking at things that would make the camp a little more comfortable, such as different types of heating for the sleeping quarters and adding showers."

Bill would eventually like to develop tourist packages for the fishing camp and have an operator in Cambridge Bay to facilitate the tours. George and Gary have discussed adding hunting packages to the services offered by Northern Emak, but that possibility has not yet been fully explored. The brothers may even try to buy their partners out in the future, depending on the company's profitability. A new business is opening in Cambridge Bay that will offer winter skidooing tours. However George and Gary are more interested in staying with hunting and fishing.

Staffing requirements will increase with any type of expansion, which will benefit the community. As Bill points out, "Planning for the future is just by the seat of the pants. We'd like to get a permanent camp there and we'd like to buy the existing business on the lake, but I think the bottom line with us is market trends. We just have to feel our way and see if things are going to go well before making any further investment."

Advice to New Business

For the new business person, the essential ingredients that will improve the chances for success include planning, operating a pilot project, setting clear policies for clients, and being prepared. There are also certain preconditions that should be considered in entering a partnership agreement.

Once a business concept has been identified and seems to be feasible, then time should be spent planning the venture in detail.

Financial planning in George and Mabel's experience is very important. Determining that the required services are available at a reasonable cost will prevent future problems. In this case, there are unemployed people in Cambridge Bay with the necessary skills to operate a fishing camp and planes are available for charter to take clients to and from the camp.

George states, "I would have liked to have heard somebody pass on a little advice so I'd have had an idea of what to expect. That sort of thing really helps. Dedication to the business is very important, but it hasn't all been easy. There are a lot of headaches sometimes. Opening the camp at the beginning of the season is very hectic. It's a mad rush to get everything in once the ice is out; we have a very limited time to set up."

Planning an inexpensive test of the business is a good idea. George notes, "It worked out well because we didn't know what would happen until after our first try. We went ahead because we found that it could work at our trial run."

It is important to be prepared for problems that might arise. By letting clients know what the policies are and encouraging them to mention any problems, misunderstandings can be avoided. Customer satisfaction is everything. George states, "Right off the bat you should have a schedule of what goes on, posted on one of the tents. It should list what time you have meals and your hours. It makes life a lot easier. If you don't have something like that, you always get guys that want to fish twenty-four hours a day. Also, in the evenings before clients go off to bed, I see how their day was and give them a rundown of plans for the next day."

Partnerships such as Northern Emak can be successful. Bill states, "I like double risk. Double risk is where your partners in the community have part of the risk in getting business, as does the booking agency. Many tour companies have great ideas but they don't materialize. The tour company doesn't have a risk of their own to sell the tour and make money. We have to plug away to get the clients, and from their end, partners in the community have to plug away to make the product work. When a partnership deal is formalized then both parties have that risk. It is not government-funded risk, but business taking a risk. We are very cautious before we form a partnership because we want it to work."

Summary and Conclusions

Northern Emak illustrates a mutually beneficial arrangement for a tour operator and two Inuit living in a small community. It is an opportunity for two partners following a traditional lifestyle to earn a living doing something that is culturally appropriate. They also have a chance to learn new marketing skills.

The partnership was the result of a relationship that Jerome and George cultivated over several years. When Jerome and Bill decided on a new venture, they approached George because of his record for reliability, intelligence, and friendliness. They knew he could handle the operations of a fishing camp. It proved to be an opportunity for Mabel as well, when the local tours were added.

Their arrangement is recorded in a partnership agreement. Risks are shared: Bill has an obligation to market the fishing camp tours to the best of his ability while George and Gary have to offer quality service. A good deal of planning went into the project in the early stages. Appropriate approvals were obtained from the local HTA and town council. Further, the camp adheres to territorial regulations so that all licences are maintained. This includes meeting obligations regarding minimal environmental impact. In fact, George has set a standard for catching fish which is well below the allowable limits.

In offering high-quality service, George and Gary try to make their clients' stay as pleasant as possible. Although the amenities of the camp are basic, they have plans to upgrade them in the future. They train their guides in the appropriate methods of dealing with clients and they encourage warmth and friendliness. Their equipment is kept in peak condition. They offer employment and training opportunities for local residents and especially for young people. They also support local businesses, especially by chartering planes to ferry the clients back and forth from the camp.

Northern Emak's partners have followed a prudent course in developing their business. The idea for the fishing camp was based on a perceived need by two partners with extensive experience in the industry. They minimized their risk by operating a pilot project in the first year to avoid costly mistakes. Debt has been minimized by financing the initial capital investment through shareholders' loans, which were subsequently paid off. Further expansion has been paid for from income and future expansion is based on plans that seem reasonable, given market conditions. This low-risk profile should greatly improve the chances of Northern Emak's survival in any downturn in the economy or in demand for their services.

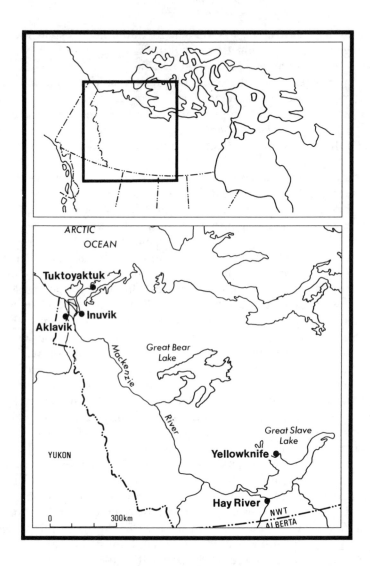

ENTREPRENEURS' ENDORSEMENT

We, the undersigned, acknowledge that we have read our business profile. We approve of the contents of the profile and recognize its accuracy in describing our business.

Dated _MARCH 25 ᵀᴴ._, 1991

Moira Grant

7

RAVEN ENTERPRISES (INUVIK) LTD
Inuvik, Northwest Territories

Moira (Mo) Grant arrived in Canada from Scotland in 1972, planning to stay for six months. More than nineteen years later, Mo is a successful businesswoman in Inuvik, a community of 2,700 people located on the east channel of the Mackenzie River Delta. Raven Enterprises (Inuvik) Ltd is the company name under which she operates a newsstand and gift shop called Mac's News, a restaurant called Road's End Deli, and a boating tour company called Midnight Express Tours.

Through hard work and perseverance, despite various setbacks, Mo has several successful businesses. With Mac's News, she offers a wide variety of items, many of which are not available elsewhere in Inuvik. For example, hers is the only shop to carry newspapers and to provide them on the same day that they are published. The deli is the only one in town and offers an alternative at lunchtime. Midnight Express Tours does have some competition, but Mo offers several unique trips, including tea and bannock at a local camp and a midnight champagne cruise. Her story begins when she came to Canada to visit in 1972.

History

Mo recalls how she came to Canada and ended up in Inuvik.

A friend of mine and I planned to spend about six months in the United States and about six months in Canada. We ended up coming to Canada first and we never did go to the States. We intended to work as we went along, so we went to Prince Edward Island. The only job we could get was at the fish plant. It was hard work. We rented a cabin that cost us $60 a week and we were making only $60 a week each. Then one of the ladies felt sorry for us and she gave us room and board for the summer.

We saw just about all of eastern Canada and then we hitchhiked to Jasper and worked there for awhile. Then we went to Vancouver, but it was tough to get a job and find a place to stay. Then we saw an advertisement for cocktail waitresses in Hay River. We thought that it was just another part of Canada that we hadn't seen yet. So we went to Hay River and just hated it when we first got there. It was springtime and muddy.

Since our employers had paid our way, we had to stay long enough to pay them back and then we planned to leave. But by the time we paid them back, a month had gone by and then we liked it a little bit more and had started to meet people. We ended up staying there for three years. Then we heard a magical word, "Inuvik." I think everybody talked about Inuvik in Hay River because it's at the other end of the Mackenzie River. I had a friend who had moved to Inuvik, so I decided to visit her on my way to Whitehorse.

My first job in Inuvik was in the bar at the Mackenzie Hotel and I worked there for one week. That was enough because it was pretty rough and wild. Then I worked at another bar for a few years but I got tired of drunks and I didn't want to be a barmaid the rest of my life. So another friend and I bought a business.

In 1979, we bought Mac's News, a pool hall, and the two-storey building that housed the businesses. We formed two companies, one for the building and one for the store and the pool hall. We didn't have much money so we had to take out a bank loan. The person we bought the businesses from helped us a lot. He financed a portion of our purchase and gave us security at the bank so that the bank would give us the loan. Without his help, we probably couldn't have done it. However, it was a good investment because the store was successful from day one.

We had a big building with virtually nothing in it except the store and the pool hall, so we leased some space out to a hairdresser and a newspaper office and made three or four apartments. Mac's News was about 2,400 square feet. I added a gift store which took up about 800 square feet. The building was run down so we fixed it up with a grant for business improvement from the government, which made a real big difference. Then we formed another company for a delicatessen, a bakery, and a restaurant.

We were putting in incredible hours but the partnership just wasn't working so we decided that we would split up the businesses in 1982. I kept Mac's News and the pool hall, which was operating under Raven Enterprises. I ended up closing the pool hall soon after so that I could concentrate on running the store.

Then my landlord had problems and the bank foreclosed on him. The whole building was in receivership and I was the only tenant in there. So I made an offer to the bank and they accepted my offer on the land. But the actual signature wasn't on the bottom line. Then about two or three

Mo Grant

days after they accepted my offer, the building burned to the ground, in May 1987.

I talked to my lawyer and he suggested that it would be better to say there was no deal rather than fight it. The bank probably thought the land was worth more without an old broken-down building on it, because they put it up for tender. I bid on it but my competition bid higher and he ended up with the land. He built a grocery store and is competing with me now.

Mo recalls her feelings after the fire.

Lots of times after a period of hard work I had said in passing "I wish this place would burn down." But when it did, the only thing that went through my mind was to get up and get going again. I've got regular customers in this town. One of the things they like is their magazines and their daily newspapers. There's a lot of loyalty and I had a lot of support from everybody in town when the fire happened. My only thought was to get something going for them.

The same day of the fire, a local company offered to sell me a doublewide trailer. I went down and looked at it and decided it would be big enough for the time being. The question was where to put it. The Inuvialuit Development Corporation had a piece of land on the main street that they said I could use temporarily. They charged me very little for using it. I had my doors open in two weeks after the fire with a lot of volunteer help.

I operated Mac's News there for almost a year. Then I had to move and I ended up making a deal to buy six lots on the main road. After I made that deal, the space I'm currently leasing became available. Rather than commit myself to putting up a new building, which I didn't think I was quite ready to do, I ended up moving in there. I still have those lots and I might put up a building and move into it in the future.

Memories of the fire are still painful. Mo recalls, "I can never forget the fire. It was arson, but unfortunately nobody was caught. I got a phone call about 2:00 in the morning saying that there was a fire call at Mac's. I was there in two minutes and I thought I'd need the key to get in to find where the fire was but when I got to the store, there were flames and smoke coming out of the top storey. It destroyed the whole building but it took about three or four hours to reach my part of the building. It was very sad. They were lucky to keep the fire away from the other buildings because it could have easily kept going."

Mo opened Road's End Deli in 1988. It is a restaurant located across the main street from Mac's News. Even though Mo puts in many hours with Mac's News, "I felt it would be good for this town to have a deli. I had a concept of what I wanted the deli to be and several interested partners. We started operations but the partnership broke down because my partners weren't prepared for the requirements of running a business. I was not prepared to close the doors so I ended up running the deli."

The first full summer of operations for Midnight Express Tours was in 1989. Mo recalls why she started the boat tours, "The tourists would come to Inuvik and there was very little for them to do. I had people almost begging to go out on the river in my little speedboat but I didn't really have the time to take them. I started the boat tours because it's something I really enjoy."

Mac's News

Operations

Mac's News
Mac's News is open seven days a week throughout the year. The selection of goods carried has changed over the years. Mo says, "When we first started, we didn't sell groceries. We had magazines, T-shirts and souvenirs. But now I carry fresh flowers and I have a gift section. I've expanded into areas where there seemed to be a demand. I used to get to the store at 8:30 a.m. or 9:00 a.m. and leave around midnight. My schedule hasn't changed much. I don't put in as much time, but I still put in a lot of hours." Generally, customers for Mac's News live in Inuvik, but newspapers are mailed regularly to the surrounding communities.

The suppliers for the goods sold in Mac's News are southern. Mo says, "I use Stanton's for potato chips and North Star for pop and chips. My flowers are shipped in from Edmonton once a week. I carry hundreds of magazines and I get three boxes of novels that come in once a week. Finally, I go to the gift show in Toronto every year in August to order for Christmas. I buy anything that's new, especially brass and wicker items."

With the magazines and novels, Mo says, "I give my buyer a volume for the magazines. He gets new magazines in and sends them. If I get too many of one kind then I ask him to cut back on it. We receive a selection of novels. A customer can place an order for a certain book and it takes about a week to receive it."

Stock for Mac's News and the deli is stored at a warehouse that Mo owns. It is close to both locations and Mo goes back and forth as required during the day. Mo explains, "I have a huge walk-in freezer that is full. Even though it takes time, I feel that it's better to have it out at the warehouse than to give up any retail space." There are three full-time staff for the year and some part-time. During the summer, there are four more full-time staff.

Mo does not do much advertising for Mac's News. She says, "I'll advertise when I have a sale but I haven't done a lot of advertising for Mac's. I feel most people know it by now." Mac's News is not subject to extensive regulation. Mo says, "There's fire and safety [regulations] and you need a business licence."

Mo enjoys being a woman in business in the North. "I don't think I get treated any differently as a woman. I think I might be patting my own back, but because I've worked really hard, I've gotten respect from many business people in town. People's help after the fire proved that there are a lot of people out there who care what happens to me. That made me feel good."

In reviewing her business philosophy, Mo states, "When I started I didn't know the first thing about business, so I was learning all the time. My attitude hasn't really changed very much. The challenge from day one is still a challenge every day, but it has become more familiar."

Road's End Deli

As was mentioned, Mo and two partners started Road's End Deli at the beginning of 1988. One partner left shortly after the deli opened and Mo is in the process of buying out the other partner. The deli is also up for sale. Mo says, "Our hours right now are 10 a.m. until 6 p.m. The people that are thinking of buying it over may add a dinner menu. We're closed on Sundays so that all the staff get a day off. In the summer, we had three full-time staff and a few part-time. For the rest of the year, we've only got one full-time person and a few part-time."

Most of the business comes from people off the street coming in for lunch. They have a few business accounts and cater for meetings. Mo says, "We'll get orders if someone has an open house. For example, CBC had an open house today. They ordered about eighteen dozen pastries for it. The government will also order bag lunches for business meetings."

Mo continues, "My supplier is the Grocery People out of Edmonton. We get most of our bake-off products from the Grocery People, since we don't bake from scratch. We order our produce from Stantons. Then we order cheese and meat from Vancouver; it comes in once a week."

Midnight Express Tours

Mo received government funding for the second time, to purchase boats in 1988. Her first full season began in June 1989. Mo says, "My first season went well. But the season is so short that it's going to take a few years to start making some money and paying off the boats."

Tours included trips to a local bush camp for tea and bannock, a day cruise to Tuktoyaktuk (Tuk), a midnight champagne tour, and a cruise to Aklavik. Mo has three boats to make the boat tours. "I've got a little speedboat that will take six people. I have a cabin cruiser that will take eight people, and I have another boat that will take twelve people. I use the big one most often for the trip up to Tuk. I use the little one for the midnight champagne tours and the tea and bannock tours."

Mo recalls the first tourists of the season.

Many of my first tourists this year were seniors from across Canada, who were involved with the Elder Hostel program. I took a couple of elders to Tuk and they just loved it. They hadn't been that far north before. They were about 80 years old. I took some of them on the midnight champagne tour. We went out about 10:00 o'clock at night and came back at 1:00 in the morning. They thought being out in the sun at midnight in July was the greatest thing.

I did quite a few tea and bannock tours that I charged $35 or $45 for, depending on which boat we used. I went up to a local camp about nine miles away and had tea and bannock with some really good friends of mine. It's great. Both of them have great personalities. I had from two to six customers at one time. On some of the early trips I took only one person at a time. Even though by the time I pay for tea and bannock, I probably only break even with one person, at least I had one happy person. I take them and I don't really count my time. The way I look at it, it gets me out of the store.

We had a trip to Tuk almost every week, priced at $250 a person. We picked Thursday for trips to Tuk and Tuesday for Aklavik. But we never had any trips to Aklavik. I think that if I hadn't specified Thursdays, and just said daily trips or on demand then I could have had a lot more trips to Tuk.

It's a whole day's trip to go to Tuk. We leave at 8:00 in the morning and sometimes we get back at midnight. When the whales are in during July, I find that people don't want to go right into Tuk. They want to go out on the boat and look at the whales. I give them lunches from the deli, sandwiches and potato salad. I tied in with Western Arctic Air, so my tourists can go up to Tuk and back by boat; they can go up by boat and fly back, or vice versa. They can see it from the air or actually be right on the water.

Aklavik doesn't draw people like Tuk does because it's not on the Arctic Ocean. Most people only go on one tour and everybody picks Tuk. They can go and dip their toe in the Arctic Ocean and go back home and tell everyone. The other tour I offered was the midnight champagne tour for $60 per person. I didn't have many of them but my customers really liked it. I barbecued caribou, muskox and arctic char on the lake.

For advertising, Mo has a pamphlet which describes the tours. "I sent them to the tourist bureaus at Dawson and Whitehorse in the Yukon and I sent them to Yellowknife. I also sent some to the town office for people who write in for information then they get the pamphlet in one of the packages."

Mo states, "We get a lot of tourist traffic especially in July. We're getting more people coming to Inuvik because we have more for them to do. At one time they'd come and turn around and go right back, sometimes on the same day. They would come and ask, 'What's there to see? Where do we go?' I would feel terrible, because I couldn't think of anything. There's a lot more for them to do now."

Staff are reliable in the deli and the store, so Mo does most of the tours herself. Mo says, "I may have a friend coming back next summer who will work with me. He's a local person who's had more experience on the river here than I have. I've had my little boat for about five years now and I've done a lot of boating. I used to go to Tuk every year for trips and camping and I've taken a trip down to Norman Wells. I've learned how to follow the buoys and the markers. I've also learned a lot by asking questions of the coastguard."

Safety is important and Mo has not had any accidents in the years she has been boating. "I've had my share of sandbars this year. The river is really wide and there are some shallow spots, and even out on the ocean, it's shallow. In some places, it's only two or three feet deep so you really have to watch the coastguard markers. I've hit about two sandbars when I was carrying tourists."

Mo continues, "I really love boating. I could stay on the river day and night. It's hard to start doing it as a business. A friend said to me, 'You're dumb because now you're turning a hobby that you

Road's End Deli

really enjoy into work.' There is that downside to it. When I go to Tuk with tourists, I have fun but I never totally relax as I would if I went with a bunch of friends. When I'm with a group of tourists, I always have in the back of my mind that I'm responsible for these people. It's not a problem so long as I can decide to take a boat sometimes and relax because I don't take tourists every day."

Staff
Mo finds that the biggest problem she has is staffing her businesses. "It's really hard to compete with the government. If somebody that is good comes to Inuvik, I can't afford to pay them what the government can, so I end up losing them. I've trained a lot of people and gone through so many staff that I could write a book just on staffing alone."

Mo has tried to hire locally but,

Overall, I've had more luck bringing people in from down south. But I have found some really good people that were living in Inuvik that have been with me for a while. Sometimes, I'll advertise for staff in the south or use Canada Manpower. For some reason, Manpower doesn't seem to find anyone that stays.

If I bring them up from the south, I have a staff trailer that they live in and I subsidize them. If I didn't have the trailer I couldn't get anybody up here to come and work for me. I've had some good people from down south, but usually they stay only six months at a time – if I'm lucky. It's not an easy job. So many kids come in to the store that you get tired of them. It's also tough to deal with the general public day in and day out.

Mo's experience with hiring staff locally has been such that she supplements her staff regularly with people brought up from the south. The staff hired by Mo must meet her standards of operation. "It has to be someone with a personality that can deal with the public. We get a lot of people in that store all day long. The people who have worked out well for me, are people that are a little bit like myself. They are really hard workers. I had one person that worked about ten or twelve hours a day for six months at a time and then she took some time off. Then I get some people that work five days a week, eight hours a day, and complain all the time."

Competition
Several stores carry some of the same product lines as Mac's News. Mo says, "I think everybody is a little competition for my store. Everybody is getting into more of the same products. There's room for everyone, if people don't step on each other's toes."

About her philosophy of doing business:

There are ways to do business and there are ways not to as far as I'm concerned. I'm the only one that's ever carried newspapers in Inuvik. Newspapers are a pain and I don't really make any money on them. But it makes my customers happy because I carry them. It also gets customers into the store.

I think that everyone should have a little respect for what other business people are doing. Then you don't step on anyone else's toes. Other businesses have had people work for them and a few months later they are opening a new business and competing with them. In another example, I've had my supplier ask me, "Why don't you carry videos?" I said, "No, I can't do that. A friend sells videos and I won't compete like that." So I went and talked to my friend because I wanted to put videos in, and we worked a deal. I put his videos in my store. I don't make as much money off them as he does but it doesn't cost me a cent to do it. A lot of people wouldn't do that. They'd just carry videos anyway.

Unfortunately, some of Mo's fellow businesspeople do not share her convictions. She recalls, "The day that my place burned down, it was 2:00 in the morning. At noon the next day, it was still smould-

Table 6
Financial Information for Raven Enterprises (Inuvik) Ltd.
Mac's News

	1984	1985	1986	1987	1988
Total Salaries ($)	95,784*	134,357*	133,531	N/A	132,913
Sales per Square Foot ($)	267*	299*	420	567	467

*Includes the pool hall data.

ering. I phoned my magazine supplier and I told him about the fire and asked him not to send any more magazines until I got myself straightened out. He told me that one of my competitors had already called him and wanted to know where he could get the *Edmonton Journal*. That made me all the more determined to get back into business."

As for the boating operation, Midnight Tours is no longer the only company offering boating tours. Mo says, "The Arctic Tour Company and the Dene Band bought a forty-passenger boat and are now my competition. Competition is not bad, but sometimes it makes it hard for everybody to make a dollar in such a small town."

Financial Information

Sales per square foot have generally increased since 1984 and had increased more than 200% by 1987. The magazines and newspaper section generates the greatest amount of revenue. The gift shop is busy at Christmas time, and Valentine's Day is a big day for fresh flowers. Total revenues have fluctated around $1 million over the five-year period. These sales were generated by assets valued at approximately $200,000.

Reasons for Success

For Mo, the challenge of running a business the way she wants to makes the business a success.

It's not just the money, because I actually very rarely think about that. I have money to pay my bills, so I never think about the bottom line. My business provides a needed service to the community. An important part of my business is my good selection of magazines. Many people have told me that they've been in stores in Toronto and all over Canada that don't have the selection that I do.

The other service that I provide is supplying newspapers, although I don't really make any money on them once they are flown in. I always have each day's *Globe and Mail* and the *Journal* in that afternoon. My customers like that and a lot of them come in every day for their newspaper.

Mo had the chance to establish a good reputation because it was the first store of its type when she bought it. Mo recalls, "Mac's News had been in operation for about three or four years when we bought it. It had started from a tiny store that I've expanded many times. There wasn't any competition so that I got a good footing in town. It's taken hard work and determination."

The North has its advantages for business: "Still, it's easier to make a business successful in the North. I would never go south and even try and open a business because there's too much competition. I'd have to be very competitive and I'm not that competitive. When I get an idea, I think about it for long enough and if I think it's going to work then I'll give it a try. It's a lot simpler to do that in the North."

For Mo, the satisfaction of owning her own businesses does not come from money. "Money is secondary to me. It's mainly getting an idea, working on it, and seeing it work that gives me satisfaction. The challenge of starting a business is more exciting for me now in a lot of ways than running a business. I enjoy a challenge. When I worked in bars, I earned money for a reason. I've got a house in Scotland that I paid for when I worked twelve or fourteen hours in the High River bar. So while I was working as a barmaid or bartender, it was a challenge. It wasn't just another job. I used those jobs as stepping stones to something or for something else."

Area for Improvement

Mo identifies one major area that could be improved in her businesses. "I like the day-to-day operations but find that training people sometimes requires more patience than I have. I'm a worker, not a manager and I hate paperwork."

Environmental Responsibility and Sustainability

Mo has a concern for the environment which is reflected in her policies. All garbage produced by the store is taken to the dump. She and her staff try to keep the store as clean as possible, although it is difficult when customers bring mud into the store during the wet season.

When Mo bought Mac's News, it was at the end of the oil boom. She was looking for a small business with good potential for success in any type of economy. She didn't want a business that would suffer without the oil business. Mo recalls, "The person that I worked for owned Mac's News. I was tired of being a barmaid and dealing with the drunks. My partner and I knew Mac's News was for sale and we knew it was a good business. Then the owner sweetened the deal so we were able to buy the business. I don't know if I'd really thought about the decision, if I would have gone ahead with it, but it seemed like a good idea at the time."

As for the place her business has in the community: "I think my business is a necessity. If I close my doors tomorrow then somebody else would probably pick up my business. I do a lot of the work myself and that personal touch sets my store apart. I have people buy magazines that they've tried to get everywhere else and they can't. A lot of new people that have moved into town think they are going to miss a lot living in the North. When they walk into the store, they're just amazed at the selection. I get lots of positive feedback on the gift shop too, especially around Christmas time."

Future Development

Mo would like to sell Mac's News and the Road's End Deli.

Mac's News is up for sale but I haven't had any definite offers on it. I'd like to try to do something different. The challenge with Mac's News is gone because it's off and running. There's not a lot more I can do to it except build my own building with a nice area for a store and a gift shop.

I've thought about selling Mac's for a long time. It's usually after a real bad spell when I haven't had any staff. I'm really frustrated and working hard and I can't do the things that my friends are doing so I think, "Time for a life." If somebody comes along and I get my price then I will sell it. If I don't get my price then I won't sell.

I've run out of energy and overextended myself with Mac's News, the deli, and the tours. So at least one has to go. I've got a couple interested in the deli and we're negotiating right now on a lease-to-purchase arrangement. So if that goes through and if I can find one good person to run the store for the summer, then I would concentrate more on my tours next year. I did as much as I could do with the tours this year. I didn't turn any trips down but I didn't really promote the business too much either.

Eventually, Mo would like to operate only two businesses, Midnight Express Tours and a marina. She says, "I would like to build the docks and lease them out. I would sell fuel, and in a nearby building I would sell fishing tackle, licences, pop, chips, and mosquito dope, things that people who are going out boating might forget."

Mo continues, "Right now, my big boat is parked on the edge of the government dock. That's the only dock in town that I can put that size of boat on. Once the water drops, then it's quite a jump down to the boat for elderly people getting on and off. It's awkward to gas up. Anybody that has a boat in this town knows how badly we need a marina."

Mo has considered different ideas for the marina.

I would like to have a decent-sized building for a club, such as a ski club or a skidoo club. It could open in April and run until the end of October. Then I would travel for the rest of the year. I would also like a museum. I have a fully mounted polar bear, a muskox, a grizzly bear, a couple of ptarmigan, and a caribou for display. I also have a couple of big Inuit carvings. I would collect some old photographs of the area and give a little history.

I'd like to have a coffee shop where you can have a coffee by the water while deciding whether to go on a boat tour or take a flight with Western Arctic Air. It's not just one drawing card that would make the project work. I think it would be all the little different things that go together, just like Mac's News. It's not just our magazines. It's our magazines, our newspapers, our cigarettes and our pop.

In order to get the marina project going, Mo has to line up financing. "The best place to locate the marina is at Twin Lakes. There's a little channel there but virtually no water in it, so I'd have to dredge that so bigger boats could get in. There might be some government funding to do a feasibility study and the dredging part of the project, but it would be costly."

For the rest of the project, Mo would like five or six private investors who would let her run the operation. "I've talked to quite a few people in town and there are about five people who are willing to invest money in the marina. These people know that I'm a hard worker so they would be quite happy to be silent investors. Even if they didn't have the money, they could give some sweat equity by building docks. It would be fun to be down by the water and with the boat during the summer."

If Mo couldn't sell Mac's News, she has the option of walking away from it. She says, "I have another three and a half years on my lease. If worse comes to worse, I could just have a big sale at the end of my term."

Mo has thought about expanding Midnight Express Tours. Whatever shape her future takes, Mo is in Inuvik to stay. She enjoys her cabin at Airport Lake. She owns property in Inuvik and she enjoys the lifestyle. She has made a lot of good friends and she enjoys boating, swimming, and waterskiing with them in the summer. In the winter, she goes skidooing and cross-country skiing. To get ahead in the North, Mo has taken advantage of opportunities that she believes are not as readily available in the south. There is a much smaller labour pool competing for positions so it is quite easy to work up from dishwasher to manager in a relatively short time.

Advice to New Business

In reflecting upon the merits of running her own business, Mo admits that she puts in many hours but she enjoys not having to answer to anyone. "There were many times in the beginning that I had to fire my paycheque back into the company just to keep it going. But now there are times when there are benefits for me."

One big lesson that Mo learned the hard way is that it is best to avoid having a business partner. "My piece of advice for anybody that wants to start a business is, 'If you can, do it on your own.' My first partner and I were really good friends before we went into business together."

Mo has purchased an existing business and has started a new business. She says, "I think the best challenge is starting a business up from scratch. You have to have confidence in your idea, which you get if you think about it for a long time. A lot of people get an idea and they jump on the idea rather than waiting a while and thinking it out. If I was going to start a business, I would probably think about the area and think about what was lacking in the area rather than doing something that somebody else was doing already. There's always more of a challenge to do something that you feel is a benefit or would be a good thing to have in the town."

She has had tough times in her business. " I figure the fire probably put me back two years. But it is worth hanging in there. I had to go with the loan officer from the bank a month ago and point out my properties to her. That outing reminded me of what I do have."

Summary and Conclusions

Moira Grant has persevered through a number of major and minor setbacks, from her business being completely destroyed by fire to the breakup of several partnerships. She has made Inuvik her home and enjoys the challenge and the lifestyle that she earns from operating her own businesses. She sets goals for herself, such as purchasing property or coming up with an idea for a new product or service, and she puts in hard work to accomplish her goals.

Mac's News has an established reputation and provides one-of-a-kind services and product lines to the community. Same-day service for newspapers is provided by air express, and a considerable variety of magazines is available. Fresh-cut flowers are available, and a selection of gifts is popular with tourists and local residents.

Mo's other businesses are Road's End Deli and Midnight Express Tours. These businesses introduced a new service into Inuvik. The investment in the deli began as a partnership, but soon Mo will be the sole owner, once she completes a buy-out. Midnight Express Tours provides an outlet for Mo to enjoy her boating hobby and earn money at the same time.

The major problem is staffing her businesses. Mo finds that her more successful employees come from the south and are hard working. She finds it difficult to delegate any of her responsibilities to her employees because she considers herself a worker and not a manager.

The success she has earned through her businesses is a result of her hard work, perseverance, and personal service for her customers. She offers a good mix of products that get her customers into the store on a regular basis. She has a good reputation that has grown over the years. She provides an essential service to the community through Mac's News.

Eventually, Mo plans to sell Mac's News and the deli. She would like to build a marina to serve boat owners and fishing expeditions. This project would nicely enhance Midnight Express Tours, which would be expanded. She would also like to have a museum as part of her tourist attraction.

Her business experience has revealed the problems with partnerships and her advice is to start a business without anyone else's participation, except as a silent investor. She recommends that effort be put into planning for a new business that will bring a needed service to a community and not duplicate an existing business. Competition need not be tough but can benefit all concerned parties.

Postscript – 1990

The summer went well for Mac's News. Mo left a very good employee in charge and was able to take some time off for the first time since opening her business. She hired someone to operate Midnight Express Tours but that did not work out as well. She sold the deli in October to the people who had been operating the business for a few months before the purchase. This is an excellent way for prospective buyers to evaluate a business for no cost. Several local buyers are interested in purchasing Mac's News.

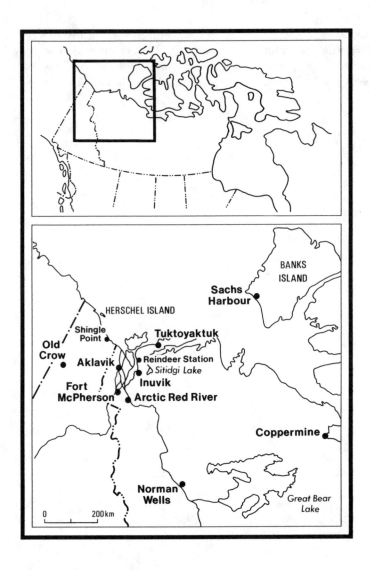

ENTREPRENEUR'S ENDORSEMENT

I, the undersigned, acknowledge that I have read my business profile. I approve of the contents of the profile and recognize its accuracy in describing my business.

Dated *June 27* , 1991

Fred Carmichael

8
WESTERN ARCTIC AIR LTD
Inuvik, Northwest Territories

Fred Carmichael, a Métis Indian from Aklavik, is part owner and general manager of Western Arctic Air Ltd. Western Arctic Air is a connector airline and provides scheduled service to the smaller northern communities around Inuvik for passengers travelling on NWT Air, a connector airline for Air Canada, and for local commuters.

In addition to scheduled services, Western Arctic Air provides an exploration charter service and carries on a very successful tourist charter business which operates as Antler Tours. Miki O'Kane is assistant general manager and manages the business end while Fred flies and coordinates the maintenance work. Sheila O'Kane, Miki's sister, has managed Antler Tours for the past three summers.

Fred has worked in the aviation industry since 1960. Despite several financial setbacks and tragedies, Fred is happy about the success that he has achieved with Western Arctic Air. He agrees with Sheila and Miki that this success derives from the personal service they are able to offer to their customers. Both Sheila and Miki go further and say a large factor in their success must be attributed to Fred's excellent reputation in the community.

History*

Fred's father was Frank Carmichael, a trapper from the south who settled in Aklavik in 1927. Frank married Caroline Kay, a sister of a former chief of the Fort McPherson Dene band, and had two sons,

---

* All quotations from Freddie Carmichael in this section are taken from Watt, "Freddie Carmichael," 19–20.

John and Fred. When Fred was sixteen, he met Don Violette an evangelical missionary with a pilot's licence. Fred fell in love with flying when Violette let him handle the controls of his small aircraft.

Fred saved enough money to go to the Edmonton Bible College in Alberta and to take flying lessons in the fall of 1954. "But it didn't take long for me to realize I was more interested in flying than in becoming a missionary like Don." He was nineteen when he became the first Native in the Northwest Territories to earn his commercial pilot's licence.

An incident in 1958 helped build his reputation as a pilot, although it had an unhappy ending. It was his first rescue mission. He had to fly an Inuit woman, who was bleeding internally, from Reindeer Station to Aklavik. Radio communications were out between the two communities, so there was no way to get flarepots lit on the runway when Fred reached Aklavik. He was finally able to land using only his landing lights, on rough ice in the West Channel, only to learn his passenger had just died.

In 1960, Fred and a partner started a charter company called Reindeer Air Service. His partner sold his interest in 1969 but then returned and bought Fred's smaller airplanes in 1971 and started Ram Air. Fred continued with Reindeer Air Service but had bad luck in 1972. One of his pilots undershot the runway at Sachs Harbour, on Banks Island and wrecked a twin-engined C-46 Curtiss Commando. Then a month later, two pilots were killed when their plane crashed in a sudden storm outside of Norman Wells. "That knocked the dickens out of me," Fred says. "I tried to carry on, but my heart just wasn't in it."

His run of bad luck continued. "By 1975 I'd found a buyer and the documents for the sale were all drawn up when two friends talked me into carrying on. They were going to buy in as partners and run the business end; I'd do the flying. Six months later we were in receivership. It turned out my partners had no money and I was stuck with the bills. The offer I'd had would have paid off my debts and given me $250,000. As things worked out, I finally paid off Reindeer's debts in May 1988."

In 1982, he started a new company called Antler Aviation with three aircraft. By 1987, he merged Antler and Ram Air and formed Western Arctic Air Ltd. It is a fifty-fifty partnership with the Mackenzie Delta Regional Corporation, which is made up of the Métis and Dene bands in Inuvik, Aklavik, Fort McPherson, and Arctic Red River.

When Miki O'Kane started as office manager in 1982, they used two Cessna 185s and two float planes to serve the needs of the

Freddie Carmichael and Miki O'Kane

hunters and trappers in the area. She started Antler Tours in 1985 as a result of visitors seeing their air charter sign and dropping in to ask what they could see. Miki recalls, "We were lucky and can't claim any great innovative thinking behind developing it; the tourists came to our door and knocked. We sat down and thought "How can we put something together that could be economical and affordable for these people and that would bring us some summer business?"

They decided from the beginning that all they would do is fly the tourists to their desired destinations. Miki says, "What we try to do is take people to the communities and let the communities deal with serving the tourists' needs within the community. The minute the tourist steps off the plane, it's up to the community how well they present themselves." Once they put tour packages together, the next thing they needed to do was to fill up their charters.

Miki recalls their aggressive marketing strategy. "It would probably be considered illegal. What we did was literally comb the camp-

grounds knocking on doors and talking to visitors and handing out
our homemade information sheets just inviting them down to our
float base." She would try to fill a charter with at least five people
from the campgrounds, the information centre, and the hotels. After
awhile, the best advertising was word-of-mouth. People travelling
down the Dempster Highway met people travelling up and mentioned Antler Tours favourably.

Operations

Western Arctic Air conducts business year-round. They operate a
fleet of ten aircraft: a single-engine Cessna 177, which can carry
three or four passengers; a Cessna 185 on floats; a Beech 18 on floats;
three seven-passenger Cessna 207s; a six-passenger Cessna 310; and
three twin-engined Britten-Norman Islanders, which can carry nine
passengers.

Miki O'Kane notes that the aviation industry is a tough business
at the best of times. "It's an expensive enterprise. You have expensive equipment that you have in the hands of many different people;
pilots that you are placing your trust in. Aircraft costs are high and
maintenance costs are quite high. Living north of 60°, in Inuvik, you
have the added expense of freight costs. In order to keep your licence
and keep your customers happy, you have to provide year-round
service. In the winter months when you're not flying very much, it
costs more to get your engines going and to keep your aircraft
heated; and to keep your maintenance facility heated you literally
watch your money go up in smoke. It burns away while you're
keeping warm until spring comes again."

Western Arctic Air provides regular service to Aklavik, Fort
McPherson, Old Crow, and Tuktoyaktuk. There are ten pilots, six
maintenance crew, and six office persons in the summer and about
ten employees in the winter. The office staff work five days a week.
The maintenance crew work a forty-hour schedule, putting in rotating twelve-hour shifts, and the pilots work six days a week.

Fred, Miki, and Sheila put in many hours and work seven days
a week in the summer. Sheila notes that the company takes priority
over everything. "You need to be strong enough to do it yourself
or have enough family that can do it with you." This is the first year
in which pilots are regularly getting time off. When they first started,
Western Arctic Air did not turn down any charter. Miki recalls,
"Forty below and getting up in the middle of the night to take
somebody to a party somewhere wasn't beyond us."

Western Arctic Air tried Med-evac in 1988; they had a team on
twenty-four-hour call to answer any medical emergency in the out-

lying communities. It proved to be too hectic, and they dropped that service so that they could streamline their operations and limit flights to the daytime. They may re-examine this service when considering whether or not to expand their business in the future.

The role of government in the business has been positive. Western Arctic Air has received training grants and has an application in for funding an upgrade of their runway; as well, government officials use their schedule service. There were initial misgivings in dealing with the government, as Fred points out:

They have certainly helped us out. They are there and they are willing to help if you let them. A lot of people don't like government interference. In the past the government dictated to us that this is what you'll do and this is how you'll do it. People naturally had a bad reaction to that. They are sick and tired of government telling them what to do. I'm talking about Native people. Since the territorial government has taken over, they've got quite a different attitude, in that they want to try and help. It's taken people a while, including myself, to realize that they're not there sticking their nose in your business. They are there trying to help you. If you allow it they will help. Not only just in loaning money or grants; they'll provide you with assistance in monitoring your business.

I really believe that they should be doing more. There should be some service where they are there, monitoring your business with a qualified accountant or business person, and can do something for the business before you get into trouble. Now it seems they come in there and spend all kinds of money after the business is in trouble trying to bail it out. Do it earlier and they'd save a lot of money and businesses.

Staffing

Staffing is always a problem. Miki says, "We bring up our pilots from the south and most of the time they are here for a short time only. We are a stepping stone to the airline industry." In order to combat the turnover in pilots, Western Arctic Air has followed the lead of other companies in the industry, and now enters into an employment contract with each pilot.

Fred explains,

It has come to the point where now it's very expensive. Even though they are qualified pilots, we have to go through a training program in our own company to get them on line. It's really costly. We've found that as soon as they get experience then they are gone.

Now we contract with them and if we do put them through the training program, especially if they go into twin-engine, then they have to give us a commitment that they will stay for a year. If they leave before then, we prorate the cost of their training. Hopefully, if they have to sign on the dotted line and it's going to cost them out of their pocket, it will be harder to leave.

In addition, Miki states, "Fred's trying to work with the local Community Futures program trying to get some aviation programs in the North to encourage local people to get involved. We'll always have people coming and going until that happens."
Miki points out another problem they face with staffing.

This is very much a government town and a lot of the good jobs are the government jobs because the pay is high. It makes it really hard for private enterprise to hire because we have a very large turnover in the office. Some of our workers want the experience and then when the first government job comes along, they go, and I don't blame them for doing it. The benefits are better – they get northern allowance and travel allowances. They get hourly wages that are higher than anywhere else in Canada, I'm sure, for the kind of work done. But it certainly makes it a lot more difficult for the small business person trying to employ and keep staff.

In order to foster loyalty and attract people to the company who will stay, Miki and Fred look for personal commitment and an awareness of what it is like to work for a small company. Miki explains, "It takes somebody that is a bit aware of the hard work that's associated with a small business. I think it's important to stay small enough that the people feel that they are contributing something. It's important for our employees to have some sort of input into the jobs, so that they feel like they are an important part of this little business. We have staff meetings that kind of go in fits and starts although we haven't had one now for several months. Mostly I think, if there's any extra time, everybody just wants to sleep."
Fred adds, "I'm looking for people who are interested in maintenance, flying, or the office. I want them to have a real genuine interest right from the heart. I tell them, especially trainees coming in, 'I don't want to hire you or bring you in here just because you think I want you, or your Mom and Dad want you, or your friends want you to be a pilot, or to be an engineer. It's got to be you. You've got to feel it from inside.'"

Antler Tours
Antler Tours is not a separate company but a service Western Artic Air provides in the summertime for its customers. Tourist business starts in late May and goes until September. In 1989, there were about three to six trips per day – almost double the two to three

Sheila O'Kane

trips per day completed in 1988. The most popular trip offered by Antler Tours is up the Arctic Coast to Tuktoyaktuk for $99. Visitors have a chance to dip their toes in the Arctic Ocean and receive a one-hour tour of the community from Randall Pokiak, a local resident, or from his family.

Other tours take visitors to see traditional Inuit life at Tom Arey's summer whaling camp located at Shingle Point. They may see pods of belugas or bowhead whales near the mouth of the Mackenzie River. The trip is priced from $399. Lake trout and arctic grayling abound at Andrew and Margaret McInnes' lodge on Sitidgi Lake, where fishermen are invited to spend a day or more, starting at $149.

Another possibility is Herschel Island, which is located on the Alaska and Yukon borders; wildlife enthusiasts may view more than twenty-five species of nesting birds and more than 125 species of wildflowers in one location. A day tour starts at $279 and a two- or three-night stay starts at $699. Another trip combines tours of the northern communities of Aklavik and Tuktoyaktuk from $169. Customized tours and charters are also available.

Sheila O'Kane says, "It's not economical to send a tour with under five people. We can do it, but then we have to charge more per person. So in order to stay within our limit we need at least five people, and then we can handle anything above that in combination. For example, today's tours started out with five people wanting to go to Tuk and within a couple of hours it built up to thirteen. So then we split it up, with six gone already and seven more to go. Maybe there will be a few more and then we'll send nine next."

This juggling of passengers can result in some funny situations. Sheila recalls:

We had one group of nine this summer who came in prepaid down at our office. They all had their own transportation down to the airport. No problem. Except the last guy. He was late and didn't have his own transportation so I drove him at breakneck speed so as not to hold the others up.

I expected to walk in and find the other eight there. But I walked in to find four. This is strange, because the other four had paid. I couldn't find them and decided to wait. Finally I decided that we can't send a nine-passenger plane with five passengers. We'd just lose money, which is part of our confusion. We're always playing the numbers game, so we're switching sizes of aircraft at the last minute and they're delayed. But at least you run financially a tighter ship and you make a profit. So we downsized.

This meant that another pilot had to be assigned and another aircraft had to be prepared. Off they went finally, five of them in a six-seater plane. While I was driving back to home base, my sister got a phone call from four very upset tourists in Tuk. They'd walked into the airport terminal to our counter where our young dispatcher had said "Your pilot is refueling; he'll be with you in a moment." At the same time, the competition, Aklak Air, was calling a scheduled flight to Tuk. So the pilot announced the flight. These people walked up and mumbled something about Antler Tours and he acknowledged it. Quite by coincidence, four of his people on his manifest didn't show. But the head count was right. So without tickets and without checking names, he took them to Tuk.

Part of our sales job is the plane waits for you and someone comes to meet you at the airport. Well, they get dumped, the plane takes off and nobody meets them. So they're beginning to wonder if they've been had or something. So they phone for an explanation. Now we have a six-seater on the way. So I phoned the competition to see if they'd bring them home free, too. He declined. We ended up sending up the larger plane to bring the nine tourists back.

Financial Information

Table 7 sets out financial information for Western Arctic Air and Antler Tours for the five-year period, from 1984 to 1988 inclusive. By 1989, Antler Tours provided about 10% to 15% of total revenues.

Table 7
Financial Information for Western Arctic Air Ltd.

	1984	1985	1986	1987	1988
Return on Equity (%)	9	12	0	0	48
Sales/Assets (times)	1.01	1.3	1.16	1.32	1.9
Total Salaries ($000)	119	159	180	407	658

The return-on-equity ratio is calculated using earnings before interest and taxes, divided by owner's equity. The results of the ratio analysis, shows a fluctuation over the period from 12% in 1985 to 0% in 1987, but then a strong recovery in 1988 of 48%. This is a very good result; for every $1.00 of the owner's capital invested in the company, 48¢ was earned in net revenues. This is excellent compared to the 10% yield on regular bank savings accounts.

The sales-to-asset ratio shows an almost steady upward climb from a sales-to-asset ratio of one in 1984 to almost two in 1988. This indicates that the investment in assets generated almost twice as much revenue in 1988 as it did in 1984. The earning capacity of the company, based on its investment in assets, doubled over the five-year period.

The total salaries increased over the period from $119,000 in 1984 to $658,000 in 1988. This reflects the increased staffing needs as the company's operations grew over this period.

Competition

In 1982, there were five other aviation businesses operating in Inuvik. However, the great stress of operating in a boom-bust economy took its toll, as Miki indicates, "The other companies have sold out or gone by-the-by. Now it's them and us. Aklak Air are our competition now. They serve a different market, so they are in a different niche. We're both working at a little different angle. They definitely have bigger equipment but we're two different types of operations. We work pretty well together. We always have really, although there's been a lot of heavy competition between us."

There is cooperation as well as competition. "When it comes to joint aviation concerns we work together. If there is something that is a common threat to us then we lobby together. Our maintenance people and their maintenance people help each other back and forth, so it's good, stiff competition but there is also a lot of friendliness as well. That's a good thing."

Western Arctic Air

Antler Tours has direct competition with Arctic Tour Company, an actual tour brokerage operation. Sheila states, "There are other people who offer tours. There's a boat tour starting up. Arctic Tour Company has some boating services that they offer. Midnight Express Tours has just started this summer."

Sheila continues, "In some respects, Arctic Tour Company is our competition. In other respects, they fly with us. We discount some of the fares to them. It's interesting because both tour companies were spearheaded by two women, Miki with Antler Tours, and Kim Staples in the case of Arctic Tour Company. I'm Miki's sister and I work with Antler. Karen, Kim's sister, comes up in the summer and works with Kim."

Again, the competition is friendly. "Karen and I are the ones that have the most contact on a daily basis. We've done things where one of us is short of a van and the other one lends it. She'll be taking a group to the airport but they're flying with us so she'll take them one way and I'll drive them the other. There's one thing that I think about the North: you're too small to be seriously competitive. You've got to share resources a lot more. You never know when you're actually going to need the other person. It's important to have a good working relationship."

She also co-operates with Moira Grant.

Another example where again it's better to work together is our relationship with Midnight Express. One of the things that Midnight Express does is boat people to Tuk. It's a five-hour boat ride. If you go up and spend any time up there, you are looking at a long haul. So the owner preferred to boat people the one way and fly them the other. So then if we work together, everybody gets the benefit a bit more. Usually in some of those social science classes they'll get you to play the Competition Game. Those who really try to compete always score less than those who intuitively, without talking about it, decide to just cooperate and not worry about outdoing the other. They always score more highly as a team. I think that works in real life too.

Reasons for Success

The business is a success, according to Fred Carmichael, because it is meeting a real demand and it is continuing to expand. Fred's reputation in the community and Western Arctic Air's ability to provide personal service are the factors that Fred, Miki, and Sheila feel have contributed to the company's success.

Fred's reputation in the community is excellent. Sheila states, "Fred has a wealth of expertise. He has flown the Arctic for over thirty-five years. I think that he has a lot of his own wisdom that he brings to the business."

He knows the terrain. Sheila recalls, "It was about two summers ago that one of the sons of a local family went missing in a boat on the Delta. The Mounties looked for a couple of days and then called the search off. The mother came in and asked Freddie, 'Please, please, just go look for him.' Freddie did and found the son. He knows the land, the conditions and he knows the people."

Miki adds, "He's the first local guy to get into this type of business and to prove himself. I think that most people know that he's not just here today and gone tomorrow. He's here to stay, and he cares about them. He really has some ethical viewpoints about the business and serving people here. I think that they appreciate that. A lot of people deal with him individually, so I think that he is a big part of our success."

Western Arctic Air's operating policies indicate that personal service is an integral part of the business. Miki O'Kane notes:

A big part of business is our customers. They seem to like the style we have. We're not always punctual. We're not airlines. People roll up from the Hudson's Bay or the bar and we're here usually, and if they phone we'll wait the five or ten minutes. We're not always on time. But most of the time, people understand it, because we've waited for them at some point. Just a lot of customer support has made us successful. That's something I just hope we never forget.

The reason we're here year-round at an expensive time – we earn money for seven or eight months, and probably lose money for three to four months of the year anyway – is because Freddie feels he has to provide a year-round service. The people in the area are the ones who really count. They are the ones who are here twelve months a year. They are the ones who supported us when we got started. They are the ones who have seen us through in tough times as well as the better ones. So we can't ever forget that. That means we've got to hang in here when it might be more lucrative to close the door and go bask on a beach somewhere for the winter months and come back in the spring when it's warm again. That's not our style at all.

Antler Tours

Antler Tours provides an excellent supplement to the summer's revenues for Western Arctic Air. Miki says, "Being connected to the airline doesn't hurt. Being part of the airline, we are not dependent on living solely off commissions, and I can flog the empty seats on Arctic Air. If there's a flight going with empty seats and there is somebody who wants to go on a tour but can't because of time restrictions, sometimes I can just send them on a round trip so at least they fly over the land even though they don't get to go on the tour."

Sheila continues:

It's been nice serving end-of-the-road customers, so we don't have to deal with tour company upon tour company further south and add commissions to every one, which means it is a better deal for the consumer. It's been an uncomfortable adjustment, in a way, with [Arctic Tour Company] starting off as a regular tour company. There's the need to find a balance between working with them and with their need to have commission and continuing in our own way, which is providing direct end-of-the-road service so that we don't have to add commissions.

Some of the other tour companies are beginning to come to us. A couple of our tours are priced so that we can afford a small commission, but our most popular is a bare-bones special. And that is what the customers want.

Challenges

Western Arctic faces limited financial resources for expansion or reinvesting in equipment. It is also difficult to expand Antler Tours when there are limited options for tourists in the communities.

The partnership with the Mackenzie Delta Regional Corporation has been beneficial in many ways, but beyond the initial financial contribution and some contribution since then, the corporation has no cash available to invest in the company until a land claims settlement. Miki recalls:

When we started in 1982 and interest rates were up at 22% or 23%, there were five operators at the time. There was a lot of stiff, heavy competition. We were the poor kid on the block; we had the least operating capital. Our partners didn't have their land claims settlement, so we just didn't have the money to invest. But I must say, they have always been very, very supportive of us, as much as they can be. If we go to them and say "We need a little bit of clout here; we need you to help us sort this out there," they've been very good. They direct business our way whenever they can.

Our partners made half of the initial capital investment and there has been some since, but certainly not to the extent of our competition. So that's definitely been a drawback with us, because we've had to compete with a lot of big bucks. That has made a difference, because we just can't go out and buy two or three Twin Otters and have them sitting out there. We have to be very careful and grow gradually and slowly.

That's had its drawbacks, but maybe things have been okay in the long run because we have been very careful. We don't move unless we're sure we'll be able to handle it pretty well. Whether it's buying another airplane or taking on another contract, we're very careful that we don't overextend. There's been a silver lining there too.

Antler Tours has had problems with connecting with outfitters or guides in the community. Through Fred's contacts, they were able to find their initial tour guides but it has been difficult to expand. Sheila explains:

A subsistence lifestyle is still important. So there are seasons when people aren't as available. Starting in a day or two, Randy Pokiak and his family will be off to their cabin to do berry-picking and probably some fishing. Someone has to substitute for them. They've arranged it for the one-hour tour. But the day tour, which is their specialty, they don't like to farm out. So that's cancelled while they are on leave. It's for a week which will take us pretty close to the end of the season. It doesn't affect us but it affects Arctic Tour Company, which does more business in the longer tour.

Another one of our outfitters we take people to is now at a second camp. The season has changed. It's in a different land claim settlement area, so he has to go through the whole approval process again. Until then, he isn't in a position to take people although people want to go and he wants to have them.

Social Responsibility

Fred Carmichael's goal is to encourage local people to train as flight pilots or maintenance engineers. "Local people make the best engineers and they make the best pilots, as far as I am concerned. They are working in their own environment. They understand it and they know it." Miki adds, "Fred has a real strong feeling that he'd like to see more Native local people involved as pilots or engineers, because it was somebody here that gave him a break and got him going. If we want to be more efficient, it's easier to hire someone from the south because they've had the exposure and the training. Although it costs more to hire Native employees, it's worth it."

Some of their employees are Natives. Miki notes that "Right now in our maintenance facility we have six full-time staff and four of the six are local Native guys. It's different with pilots because it's so hard to get through the training. But in our office again we have local people hired. Our ramp foreman is Native. The kids we hired this summer, 50% of them are Native."

One of the maintenance people, an Inuvialuk, is a good friend of Fred's. "Richard has been with me for over twenty years. I would say he's one of the top maintenance people we have. Those are the kind of people I'm looking for that have a commitment to themselves and to the job and to the company."

Fred tries to accommodate his employees regarding vacation time, whether or not it is related to their traditional lifestyle. "If you want time off, it doesn't matter who you are. If the guys from the south want to go home for a couple of weeks, they take their annual holiday. If at all possible we accommodate them regarding timing."

As for local people, "We try whenever possible to give them time off when they want it. It's difficult because we start getting things ready for the summer about May and a lot of them like to be out on the land, hunting and trapping. It's just to be out there in the spring. It's tough when they want to go then. It's busy but we've been allowing it. Especially with Richard, we let him go every spring. We schedule him for that. We try to accommodate everyone as much as possible. That's what makes a company, it's the people around you. Happy workers."

Environmental Responsibility

Fred is still close to the land and respects it. He states, "We don't allow people to abuse the environment. It's never been a problem and certainly if it was then we'd deal with it. For example, you come here in the winter and the town's sewage lagoon overflows into the river and into the ponds right by our hanger and the kids go and skate there and play in the water in the spring. I've personally taken environment people down there and shown them, but nothing ever happens. If that was private industry you can bet something would be done. That's politics for you."

Sustainability of the Business

The oil business, and the megaprojects associated with it, has had little effect on Western Arctic Air. Fred feels they have survived for that very reason. "You can't build a business on boom-and-bust. The business is there and it's a great help when it does come. But you don't want to depend on it."

Fred admits that the company did try for some oil industry work when they first started in 1982 but was unable to secure it.

Being a northern Native person, people from the south, especially oil companies, have a lot of skepticism somehow. "Wonder what kind of an operation this guy is running?" although you're inspected by the government and you meet the same standards as any other operator throughout Canada. But I find that really the oil companies are hypocritical. It's all politics. I tried my best to work with them and get their business and give them service. But I got to the point I started to say, "To hell with them. I don't need them. I was here before they ever showed up and I'll be here a long time after." I survived. That's the way it stands today. They come in and want to use the shippers. Fine. But I won't go begging to them because they're here today, gone tomorrow. They've ruined a lot of people and they've ruined a lot of businesses because of the boom-bust situation.

At first I found that really tough to take. Just a little example. We wanted to get the oil patch business pretty badly. It was fairly lucrative at the time when we were first starting out. My airplanes had to have a certain type of equipment so I looked and there was an aircraft in Norman Wells, a twin engine, that met all the requirements of oil companies in the Wells. This plane was up for lease, so I decided to lease it. The oil company came in and did their inspection. Then they sent us a letter saying their policy is not to use light twin piston-engine airplanes since the capability of the aircraft was insufficient. Minimum altitude between here and Tuk is about 2,300 feet. The oil company had approved that same airplane to do crew changes between Norman Wells and Whitehorse. The mountains are 10,000 feet. So the same aircraft was suitable for those crew changes, but they told us that the capability of that same airplane wasn't suitable for the Inuvik-

Tuk run. They did not want to use us. So a lot of it is politics and corruption fostered by the oil industry.

Future Development

Although there is good potential for growth, Fred has decided he would like to get out of the business. One option is to train someone to take over; another is to sell the business. He says, "I think that I'll step aside. I'm putting young people in here, Native people, to take my place eventually. They're quite capable of taking over and they will take over one way or another. The Métis are looking at taking over my shares, and whether they do or whether I stay, I think it's time for me to sit on a board with some other people and let the younger generation take over. They have the drive and the desire to make things go and I'm getting a little tired."

In the meantime, Fred and Miki want to maintain a viable business and expand in a thoughtful and organized way. Miki says, "Right now we're having problems harnessing and directing our growth. We have to direct our energies in the right way and decide where to channel our energy. When we started we didn't turn away any trip, ever. It's not that we want to now, it's just that if we don't channel our energy we won't be providing good service to anyone."

Fred continues:

If we don't sell immediately I'd look at major expansion. It's almost a sure thing that the pipelines are going to go ahead and it's just a matter of time that our people – Dene-Métis people – will get their land claims. We'll have a good solid financial backing and will continue to operate as a viable business. What happens now is we're hampered by borrowing power. If an opportunity comes up, supposing the pipeline starts tomorrow, we're limited in the amount of money we can borrow to get contracts and to get other equipment to serve the new customers.

When our partners get their land claim, they hopefully will make a commitment to have funds for this company to upgrade. They want to see this airline go because it's their airline. They want to see new equipment out there that's right up-to-date with all company colours. But they want to see us make money as well, and they will. Once that happens, then there's no stopping this company. Also we're looking at some point of going regional right down the valley.

If Fred sells the business, he will probably go back to a small float operation in which he would fly tourists in the summer to Herschel Island for wildlife tours. As he looks back on his experience in the business, Fred says, "There have been a lot of good times and bad times. I often think of how flying's changed and how I don't find much fun in it any more. My good memories are jumping in my 185 and flying trappers out to their cabins and being able to sit and have tea and a good meal with them. I got satisfaction from taking them home and knowing they were happy when they thanked me. It's a totally different business now. The nature trips would put me back with people enjoying the land."

Opportunities in the Aviation Industry

Being in the aviation business can bring satisfaction, but Fred has some advice for anyone thinking of starting up a business. "The day of getting yourself a little four-seater airplane and working out of the house or working out of a snowbank is gone. It's getting to be a lot more sophisticated. Government and industry won't go anywhere without twin-engine airplanes and two pilots. So you've got to go into it in a fairly big way, which is expensive."

With the high cost of entering the aviation industry, Fred points out that more companies are aligning themselves with Native organizations that expect land claims money. Another issue to consider is determining what market to serve. Miki says, "In the North, it's smarter to find a smaller niche and not try to get too big. A smaller niche is important, one in which customer service is your biggest priority and you are prepared to put enough sweat equity into it so that it works. You can do that best if you stay small and efficient."

A small local service could provide a viable source of income, but not in the area surrounding Inuvik. Fred says, "I don't think that there is much of an opportunity around here. They tried over in Old Crow with the band and that failed because it's a very small community. It probably could have succeeded if they were happy to stay very small. It served their own needs. But how do you get a pilot that is happy to stay there on a year-round basis, unless you train one from the community? You also need maintenance people."

Finally, Fred adds, "You have to certainly do good market research before you start to make sure that there is a need for your business. Be prepared to work damn hard. You have to have good management and have good people looking after your money."

Summary and Conclusions

Western Arctic Air is a successful small airline in a highly competitive and risky industry. Fred's reputation and philosophy for serving customers' needs has contributed to the firm's success and earned it the support of the community. It is a family business that is able to provide personalized service to their customers, whether it is holding a flight for a few minutes or looking after a dog left in the car while its owners take a flight with Antler Tours.

The company provides service to the smaller communities on a year-round basis, despite the high costs of operating in winter. Antler Tours' summer tourist business contributes increasingly to the company's total revenues.

Both Western Arctic Air and Antler Tours cooperate with their competition, and so everyone benefits to some degree. They may share tools, or discount fares, or split transportation requirements with their competitors. It is not the cutthroat business environment common in large centres in the rest of Canada. It is more typical of business done in small or rural communities.

This cooperative relationship with their competitors also reflects their relationship with the community. Friendliness and giving the extra service needed to provide customer satisfaction has earned the company its excellent reputation in the community. Further, Fred willingly accepts the extra costs associated with training local people as maintenance engineers or encouraging them to take pilot training, as someone once encouraged him. He is actively working toward a northern-based pilot training program so that more young people will be part of the industry.

Finally, the company is committed to preventing damage to the environment and drawing attention to environmental problems in their own community. It would rather offer tourists a chance to enjoy nature and to see a way of life that is disappearing than to fly big-game hunters, although Fred did grow up on the trapline and supports traditional hunting and trapping.

Their message is that more people in the North need to be encouraged to go into business. Friendly bankers and the expertise to help people get set up and get moving will capitalize on the potential that exists in the North.

Postscript – 1990

Freddie sold his 50% share in Western Arctic Air to the Inuvialuit Development Corporation (IDC) in early 1990. It is the first partnership between the Inuvialuit and the Dene-Métis people. Freddie comments:

Aklak was my competition for years. Pressure was put on local people to support the Inuvialuit-owned airline, Aklak Air. It started to divide the people. I grew up in Aklavik, which is a mixture of all peoples including Inuvialuit, Dene, and Métis people. I feel as much at home with Inuvialuit people as I do with my own people. They approached me last year but we couldn't work anything out. Then we started negotiating again and eventually they bought me out. They told me they hoped this will be the first of many joint ventures with the Dene-Métis people. That made me very happy, but unfortunately it looks to me like they bought my share of the company just to eliminate competition.

They have never operated the company. The last year we operated it made a very healthy profit. It provided an essential service for the people of the area because it served needs of the local people. After the sale, they actually cut back their routes and raised the rates. They knew they had a monopoly and that's what they did.

Freddie kept a couple of planes and started a small tour operation called Western Arctic Nature Tours. He had several trips in 1990 and will try it again next summer. He is offering nature trips to Herschel Island and various attractions in the Mackenzie region including Summit Lake, Horn Lake, Peter Lake, and Reindeer Station. He does admit to needing a change, though, and he may decide to live somewhere else for awhile. He notes, "There is one little sweet revenge. My son Frank has started his own air service out of Inuvik. The people in this town and the surrounding area are so fed up with Aklak Air, he can't help but do well. He's a real go-getter."

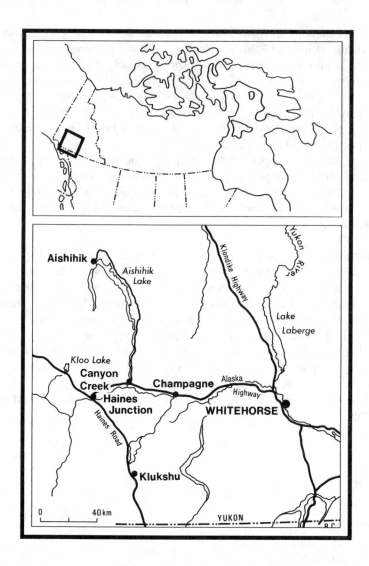

ENTREPRENEUR'S ENDORSEMENT

I, the undersigned, acknowledge that I have read the band business profile. I approve of the contents of the profile and recognize its accuracy in describing the business.

Dated _June 21_, 1991

Paul Birckel

Chief Paul Birckel

9

CHAMPAGNE - AISHIHIK ENTERPRISES LTD
Haines Junction, Yukon Territory

Chief Paul Birckel heads the Champagne-Aishihik band and oversees all social programs and economic development initiatives, including one of their successful business ventures, a construction company called Champagne-Aishihik Enterprises Ltd. Based in Haines Junction, the company employs a number of band members on a permanent basis and provides seasonal training opportunities for other band members.

The company's revenues have grown steadily under Paul's stewardship. It has successfully trained and given jobs to many band members, thus fulfilling its original purpose. The company's reputation has spread in the community and its client base has expanded beyond the territorial government.

Despite the problems of running a band-owned business, Champagne-Aishihik Enterprises has survived. Critics have scrutinized the company's performance and have sometimes made it a political issue. These pressures will likely shape the future of the company, but Paul and his employees are pleased with the company and its potential to improve the lives of band members. The following section outlines the history of the construction company.

History

The Champagne-Aishihik band is made up of over 700 members descended from two aboriginal groups, the Southern Tutchone and the Coastal Tlingit, which merged. There are close to 300 band members living in Haines Junction; the majority of the remaining members live in Whitehorse. Band members also live in communities throughout the southwestern section of the Yukon, including Champagne, Aishihik, Canyon Creek, Kloo Lake, and Klukshu. The band conducts economic development initiatives under two main companies: Dakwakada Development Corp. and Champagne-Aishihik Enterprises Ltd.

Champagne-Aishihik Enterprises Ltd began operations in the summer of 1976. Unemployment among band members was high. Harold Kane, the company's general manager recalls, "One of the principal reasons the construction company was started was to create employment for our people." Paul was elected chief of the band in 1980 and has been re-elected for every term since. He has taken steps to expand the company in his role as company president.

Paul recalls, "In 1980 when I started, all we were doing was hauling garbage, wood, water, and sewage. Since then we've expanded quite a bit. We bought some heavy equipment, including a grader and a loader, and started doing our own roads. Construction of band members' houses was contracted out at that time. We started doing most of that ourselves, although we contracted some of the houses out, depending on our manpower."

Paul is a driving force behind many of the changes that address the social and economic problems faced by his people. Before becoming chief, he worked for a utility company for fifteen years as a self-taught mechanic. Then he went to work for the Council of Yukon Indians, a political organization, for six years. At the same time, he took night courses on bookkeeping and general management. Paul notes, "Whatever I learned I picked up on my own. I've been through a lot of courses at night school but basically I've done it on my own." He is a successful entrepreneur in his own right and operates a business services company.

Paul recalls some of the activities undertaken by the band since he became chief.

One of the first things that we did was to reorganize the band. We developed a new band constitution and we were the first band to set a membership code. We were also the first band to sign an Alternate Funding Arrangement (AFA) with Department of Indian Affairs. An AFA is almost like block funding.

We handle our own child welfare program, which is a first again for the Yukon and almost first across Canada. We've developed our own operations manual and it's fairly successful. We place some of the kids that were in the territorial child welfare system back with their parents. Finally those parents are beginning to look after their kids. This contrasts with the way the Yukon Government handled our kids. They were taken completely away from the band and were institutionalized.

Chief Paul Birckel

Most band funds are channeled into social programs. Paul comments on his band's social problems: "In a way, our band is probably better off than other bands, although we feel our problems are horrible. In some places I have visited, young kids were drunk in the middle of the day. I go to some bands and I see members sleeping under a table or passed out somewhere."

His people are doing better. "It's unusual to see somebody in our band staggering around in the middle of the day. We have a couple of guys that don't have any skills or tools and they get drunk once in a while, but not like that. We're trying to find ways to solve our problems, but we sometimes don't realize how lucky we are until we visit somewhere else."

Unemployment is a major problem. However, more young people are wanting to work because they see what their friends can buy when they are employed.

They're buying cars and skidoos and getting into debt and they have to service those debts. They're more mobile and they buy good clothes and good houses. It all builds up their self-confidence and they want to stay sober.

We still have a few young guys who haven't found their way, but they're just being young and I'm not sure how you're going to change that. I'm not going to preach to them. They've got to get that energy out of their system before they settle down. One of the things that we've tried in the past that has worked fairly well is … to hire students right out of school in the summer with funds from the government. We put them to work in the construction company and they have to work so many hours a day.

It was a bit of a failure in the summer of 1989 because some of the kids were just too lazy to work but I think it's worked in the past and will work in the future. It's tough. Things happen all around here which makes it tough on everybody. For example, sometimes street drugs come in from somewhere and everybody gets high on them. It's something that I'm not sure we can get away from.

Operations

Champagne-Aishihik Enterprises Ltd generated total revenues of $1.7 million in 1989.

We build houses and roof trusses and do road construction. We're putting in water and sewer right now in Haines Junction. We put in a chip boiler last year, so we'll be selling heat mainly to the band. We do much of the mechanical work on the water and sewer system but we do bring in people for specific jobs on our projects, such as on the chip boiler.

We've built houses and done road construction all over the Yukon for the territorial government. The majority of our revenue comes from contracts for housing, roof work, and preparation of construction sites, and for hauling water and sewage. In the winter, we build roof trusses. Our biggest customer is Beaver Lumber. We also run the boiler system for the band. With the revenue, we employ people to cut wood as a job creation project. Ninety percent of our employees are band members.

The organization is headed by Harold Kane the general manager and a band member. The housing superintendent, Phil Zaitsoff, is a non-band member who handles the housing and truss plant. He handles all design work for the trusses. Paul notes, "We build roof trusses that support the roof covering. The design is quite technical because the truss handles different stresses. Since they are used in the North, the truss has to be higher up than normal so we can get proper air function. We work with an engineering firm who puts their engineer's stamp on our truss plate designs."

Harold Kane has been general manager for the past eight years. He came to the position with extensive experience in the road-building industry in the Yukon and British Columbia. When he started, Harold recalls, "We had only two permanent employees and now we have about five. My job is not really clearly or perfectly defined. I do what needs to be done. Sometimes I'll run equipment or do mechanical work or welding. I'll even cook in camp if necessary."

The band and the government are the major customers of the company. Bids are submitted for government projects, as well as to private corporations. As Harold notes, "Notice of project bids are watched for by people in the band office and we rely on the mailing list from the government. Bonding has been a major problem because operational dollars were a long time coming. We couldn't bid on the bigger jobs because we didn't have the money to meet the bonding requirements. We only owned one or two trucks to start with, but now we must have a million dollars in trucks and tools."

In the construction industry, a general contractor such as Champagne-Aishihik Enterprises must put up a bond when submitting a bid for large contracts. This bond shows the client that the company will not fold before completion of the project and acts as a guarantee that the successful bidder is financially capable of carrying on the project. It is usually a percentage of the total value of the project. It can be very difficult for new companies with little operating capital to meet the bond requirements.

Another non-band member prepares all the bids and designs software to handle the company's computer needs. Paul notes, "We're computerized to some extent. Accounting and payroll are on computer and Larry Jacobson uses it to prepare all the estimates and bids. We're working on developing a software job-costing program because we can't find a program that will fit our needs. There are some programs on the market, but they're expensive. We would have to buy their hardware and not use ours. We're still looking for something, but we don't have the money to go ahead. If we did have, then we would hire our own people to design the program for us."

Staff

There are five permanent staff in addition to the managerial staff. There are approximately fifty or sixty seasonal positions, including trainee positions, in the peak summer period. The hiring policy is to offer jobs to qualified band members first and then seek non-band members for any vacant positions. Training positions are only for band members. If employees want to take time to hunt or fish, then it is taken as regular vacation time any time other than during the peak summer months.

Champagne-Aishihik Enterprises

Paul says, "We do have five or six guys who stay on almost all winter. We try to find projects to involve the rest of the employees in the winter, but houses are taking so long to build that we're either into December and January anyway. In the 1989–90 season we're going to try to make it year-round, so that we can keep the good employees working. We'll do the majority of the houses and hopefully be ready to start the last house around January or February. By the time that's finished, we'll be starting a new year again."

As Harold notes, "Most of the good workers do stay but everything is governed by the contracts that are in the public sector. It is all seasonal work which means that you can't plan your life around it."

The company faces some staffing problems, including high turnover among trainees, a shortage of skilled manpower, absenteeism, and few management trainees. Policies have been undertaken in order to address some of these issues, while other issues are accepted as inevitable in band-operated businesses. The following discussion addresses these issues.

As mentioned earlier, the mandate of the company is to provide training opportunities for band members. However, there are drawbacks to the training program. "We've been doing training programs but that is our downfall right now. The people we've trained have moved somewhere else, so we're continually having to pay for new training programs. We've applied for training dollars and we've received a little bit here and there, but not enough to meet our needs. The biggest obstacle that is stalling the expansion of our operation is mainly lack of skilled manpower."

Other problems arise with trainees, as Paul notes, "The abuse of the equipment is high and the cost of maintaining that equipment is very expensive. Some of our trainees are very careless with the equipment. A truck was burned up once, and it adds up. There are a lot of little things that happen and we can't keep track of it all. Lately we're training a number of young guys who are coming along well so this problem should be minimized."

In the summer of 1989 there were ten to fifteen trainees working on construction projects. "We've got a few seasoned operators who are very good. At our carpentry site, most of the guys who were running equipment want to be carpenters now, so we're lining up their training. We did manage to build our band hall extension with almost all trainees except for a couple of journeymen carpenters. The training programs are an investment for us in the long run, but it's still kind of painful."

Planning for new projects is difficult, given seasonal work and the employee turnover.

It's a hard thing to get a handle on because you never know if the skilled people are going to be available for work. Then some people only work for a week or two weeks and then they're gone. They've decided to quit, go work somewhere else, or they have problems with their girlfriends and they decide to give it up for awhile. However, I do find that people are willing to work more and we're finding that more and more people in the community are willing to stay on longer all the time.

I think attitudes are changing because everybody is working. There are people with drinking problems still but it's not as bad because it's only on the weekend. In the summer, the majority of guys worked seven days a week so any drinking problems were at a minimum. One technique that has worked well in the past is if someone didn't come in until Monday or Tuesday because they got drunk on the weekend, we would tell him to take the rest of the week off. He can come back the week after and work.

It's worked to a certain extent with some people because they've sobered up or run out of money and they want to get back to work. However some guys only work for a month or two months every year, then they fall off the wagon and they don't come back until the next year. Sometimes we might give too many chances to people but we're under a lot of pressure from the community to do that.

It can be difficult to take disciplinary action due to these community pressures. Paul states, "It seems to make a big difference if it's a non-band member that is the boss and fired them. If it is Harold who fires somebody, then a lot of people are after him, so he feels the pressures quite a bit more than I do. Sometimes he hurts and last year he quit for a while because of the conflict. We got him back finally."

From Harold's perspective there are pros and cons to being the general manager and a band member. He says, "On one hand their loyalty is there. On the other hand, it's hard to discipline some of the people that you grew up with. You end up left out in the cold in the community for awhile. It's a chain reaction that spreads through families. However, it's probably going to be common in just about any band-owned corporation."

Some difficulties have been encountered with attracting employees who can handle middle or upper management responsibilities from within the band.

When Harold left last year we couldn't find anyone else to take his place. It's hard attracting people when other employers can offer a better salary. We've tried promoting people in the past, but it didn't work out. One person decided being boss meant sitting in the truck and doing nothing. Last winter, we put in management courses, but it was hard for people to do it. We either get people whose heads get bigger and they float two feet off the ground but don't get anything done, or people who are just scared of doing it.

We do have a couple of guys that have developed and are happy. One fellow worked one summer, but he got drunk and never came back that year. Then the next year we got him back and tried him out as the foreman. He changed totally. He comes to work early in the morning until late at night, working at keeping all the guys busy. Where we're lacking trainees is in the middle and top management area. We do have some good people; unfortunately they work with other organizations.

Financial Information

Champagne-Aishihik Enterprises Ltd generates enough revenue to support its operations. Paul says, "We do get government grants or loans for the purchase of equipment and some training programs,

Table 8
Financial Information for Champagne-Aishihik Enterprises Ltd

	1985	1986	1987	1988	1989
Return on equity (%)	0	0	0	0	36
Sales/Assets (times)	3.61	3.12	0.77	1.07	1.38
Total Salaries ($)	254,597	281,783	254,597	335,196	500,631

but not to meet operating expenses. We're proud of the balance sheet."

The accounting system is computerized and the bookkeeper is a band member. Paul notes, "We had a tough time finding someone but our bookkeeper was living in Vancouver and decided that she wanted to come back home. She had worked for me when I was with the Council for Yukon Indians."

Over the five-year period from 1985 to 1989, revenues doubled and then tripled. Net profit was negative in 1985, 1987, and 1988 but it was 20% of net revenues in 1989. These facts are reflected in the return-on-equity ratios displayed in Table 8. Owner's equity was negative for the first three years of the period, and then was close to $1 million in 1988 and 1989.

The low net profit figures can be attributed to the high costs associated with training. Other construction companies operating in the private sector have fully trained employees and can concentrate on the bottom line. Their net profits would likely be higher. However, it must be kept in mind that the company is covering its operating expenses and meeting its major goal of providing employment and training for band members.

In examining the asset utilization ratio, every $1.00 invested in assets generated sales revenue ranging from a rate of .77 times to 3.61 times over the five-year period. The decrease in the ratio in 1988–1989 from the 1985–1986 ratios reflects a period of increased investment in company assets. In any case, sales revenues more than matched the increase in asset value in this two-year period. Total salaries doubled during the period matching the doubling of permanent staff.

Reasons for Success

As discussed, Champagne-Aishihik Enterprises is successfully operating as a training and employment centre for band members. The growth in sales and profits can be attributed to various factors, including Paul's continuing influence and his philosophy in decision making. Promoting a team spirit and cultivating a good reputation in the business community have also contributed to the company's growth.

An important influence on any company's operations is the vision held by the management team for guidance of company operations. When that vision is working satisfactorily for the company and its shareholders, then the continuing influence of the management team can be critical to the company's success. Bringing in new management or a board of directors, as commonly happens with band elections, can be very disruptive to a company. Champagne-Aishihik Enterprises has probably benefited from Paul's re-election as band chief since 1980, as reflected by the growth in permanent employees and company revenues.

Paul equates the pressures of running a band-operated business with that of running a family business.

Everybody wants to make sure that they are hired or that you hire this person or that person. It's hard to work sometimes, because there is a lot of conflict and you're caught in the middle. It's a real juggling act, although we do fairly well. I know other bands have a real struggle. It can be very difficult if a new chief gets elected and he brings all his family and his people with him. Current employees are pushed out.

I don't operate that way. We want to act consistently and we try to promote a team spirit. A key element for that team attitude is that they have to respect the people that they work for. I also promote working together so that there is no conflict between Aishihik members and Champagne members. The two bands have been working together for quite a few years so it's not a big problem. It's just that once in a while a conflict occurs between personalities so that issue crops up every now and then.

Paul's management philosophy for all of the band's operations is to move forward decisively. He says, "I've had meetings where it is hard to deal with anything because people are so scared to take a step. The way I look at it, if I make a decision then I'll be right at least 50% of the time."

Paul is for taking action, "There are going to be mistakes but at least we're moving forwards and not going backwards. Some bands take a wait-and-see attitude while others want to fight the system. It slows everything down. Some guys just raise hell at every meeting. Then everybody gets jittery and upset. It's hard to work in that type of environment. I like to get things done."

Champagne-Aishihik Enterprises

A growing source of revenue is from the private sector because of the company's successful bids and growing reputation in the industry. In the beginning, it was difficult to be a new company with no track record. According to Paul, another obstacle to overcome was the negative perception by some of the industry regarding a Native-owned business. Paul states, "Most times, being a Native business closes doors. We have to work twice as hard for contracts. For that reason, people don't give us work like a regular company or phone us regularly for jobs to bid on. The government has been good for us because we can bid in the open market and outbid anybody else. We outbid the competition rather consistently . But I think we don't get as many private contracts as we would if we were a white business. We're building our reputation and credibility but there's still that prejudice out there. It's going to take a long time for people to get over that but it will come."

Areas for Improvement

Several areas which could be improved are further computerization of the company's operations, a better apprenticeship program, and lower bonding costs. Completing the computerization of the company operations depends on funding for regular or customized computer programs and computer training for employees.

Generally, band members who receive technical training at a college plan to apprentice and then become journeymen. In order to pass through the apprenticeship, the apprentice has to be trained by an accredited journeyman. Harold states, "Since the local college opened, I think it's making quite a difference for us. Students get the post-secondary training in the college rather than trying to get on-the-job training with us. It is good, but the only trouble we have is that we don't have very many journeymen who can supplement the apprenticeship programs because journeymen are very expensive. We don't turn people away but I give them the option. One of the mechanics just graduated and he can't get his ticket from here but he still prefers to work here. He's not going to be certified, which is a shame."

The bonding problem is a situation that Champagne-Aishihik Enterprises has faced for most of its operating history. Since they have had more losses than profits, bonding companies and banks are very cautious in any financial dealings. Paul hopes that several more profitable years will ease this situation.

Paul explains the way they currently meet bonding requirements. "We have a new company called Denendeh Ventures. We buy bonding insurance from them. This year it cost us $4,000 to have a sum of money that we can use whenever we want to bid on a job. That's expensive. Once we get a job and we need the money, we have to pay the regular interest rate on it."

Environmental Friendliness

Paul is proud of the company's record for minimizing the impact of their operations on the environment. He states, "It is part of our tradition as Native people that Mother Earth should be protected. For example, we try to eliminate any unnecessary tree cutting and if we are building a road then we will try to get gravel from gravel pits that have already been created. This philosophy is hard to put into words because it is an integral part of our way of life." Harold adds, "We are the guardians of the land and if we ruin it, then that is our heritage that is affected." Environmentally safe practices are commonly part of the terms of all government contracts and must be followed by all successful contract bidders. This process is monitored regularly by government officials.

Future Development

The short-term plan for the construction company is to maintain the current level of revenue, hire a president, continue funding education, and promote development of a practical component in the college training programs. There may be a move towards subcontracting more work out to band members or privatizing the company. Once a positive cash flow is established from the construction company and other band investments, then additional economic development is planned.

Given the number of investments and programs that the band is currently involved in, Paul does not want to stretch his resources by expanding the construction company at this time. He says, "I don't want the company to get any bigger right now because the bigger you get, the more headaches that come. The next step is to hire someone to oversee all our operations." This person would relieve Paul from some of his duties and allow him to concentrate on planning the band's future development.

The training of band members remains a major objective. Paul plans to encourage Yukon College to incorporate actual work experience into the training programs. He states, "We need to develop a good training program with on-the-job training. It's okay for somebody to go to school and train to be a mechanic, but it's very different when you put them on the job. They learn the theory, but they need to learn the practical side also." This program improvement would ease the supervisory burden that is placed on the construction company when a new graduate begins work.

Paul states, "If we were as big as the Yukon Territorial Government Maintenance Yard where they have their equipment and lots of mechanics, then new guys could work along with other mechanics. They would learn faster and learn the right way to do things. But we're not that big and we don't have as many people with the experience to supervise the new fellows."

In order to get around this problem, they plan to encourage graduates to get experience elsewhere and then come back and work for the band. It will be difficult because they need all their manpower for current projects. There is also the risk that these band members will choose to stay away rather than return to the band.

The band plans to continue to encourage band members to take training to alleviate the shortage of skilled labor. The band does not offer scholarships, but according to Paul, "We tell them to go to school. We can't provide everything, but we'll help them. We only

fund short programs even though some of our people want to go
for a longer term. We can't afford to let them go because we need
them. We can't bid on projects if we don't have skilled people to
hire."

One of Harold's major objectives for the construction company is
to increase the level of subcontracts let to band member companies
and to investigate the implications of privatizing the company.

I try as much as possible to use as many band members as subcontractors
that are available. However, the general feeling I get from people is that
there should be more privatization of the company. People want to increase
personal benefits. This could mean that band members contribute equipment to the company which continues as the principal contractor. Then all
the band members have their own incentive to bring projects in and they
contribute and benefit from operations. The band won't be the principal
source of economic development in the community. The downside of privatization is, if there is a certain amount of money to be made, they're not
going to waste time to train anybody.

Any further economic development must be financed through
the land claims settlement or through increased revenues from
current band investments and operations. Harold sees his biggest
challenge as making the construction company more profitable. "We
can't train people at our current level, compete in the private sector,
and expect to show large profit margins. Private contractors just hire
the best people and get the job done. Eventually we'll have enough
trained people; that will decrease our training expenses and contribute to our profits. We'll still be training, but on a smaller
scale."

Once more capital is available, then current joint-venture projects
will be expanded and more economic development investments will
be made. The band is 50% owner of a company that digitizes maps
and puts them on computer. There are six employees trained to
handle the digitizing and the company holds the franchise for the
Yukon. An Edmonton survey company handles the marketing for
them. Paul says, "We plan to get other bands involved. We would
advise them on equipment purchase and help train them. We would
own a share of their business."

The band is also partners in a company which is experimenting
with technology to grow vegetables. Paul states, "Once the special
growth chamber is perfected, we'll supply fresh vegetables year-
round for Whitehorse and up and down the Alaska Highway."

Profile in the Community

Alleviating the unemployment problem among band members remains a priority for Paul. The employment opportunities provided by Champagne-Aishihik Enterprises have been augmented by other projects. Putting people to work on the land working for Parks Canada or conducting tours has been successful. Paul explains, "It's surprising that even people with drinking problems who are sent out in the bush to do slashing work for Parks Canada are doing well. They are in their environment and have some responsibility. I think we're winning some of the battles that way. But it's hard and painful and sometimes it wears me down."

For people who follow a more traditional lifestyle, "We set up a tour company so that we can get our band members who have horses to take tours out. It's gradually working, since it's more of a traditional style where they feel comfortable in the bush anyway. They know horses and there's not too much else to do. We help them with their books or do their bookkeeping for them and just pay them for their time. It cuts down on their paperwork and they don't have to look at the marketing side, which we can look after."

Advice to New Business

A band-owned business can be the best choice to accomplish the objectives of chief, council, and the band membership. It can serve as a vehicle for acquiring funding that individuals might not be able to get. It can provide a way to deliver training programs that individual businesses cannot afford. Spin-off benefits occur for local small business owners, who subcontract for work with band businesses.

Opportunities can be provided to band members that they might otherwise not receive. For example, if an employee is consistently late or unreliable due to a drinking problem, a band-owned business is flexible enough to make a difference in that person's life by encouraging better work habits. Many small businesses would have to fire the employee because they could not afford to give a second chance. The quality of work on band projects could be better because the employees care that fellow band members receive their best efforts.

Paul and Harold have a number of insights into the pitfalls of running a band-owned company. Besides losing trained band members to other companies, it is difficult to juggle training with turning a profit. In addition, political pressures come from the community because the board of directors and the chief executive officer are elected band representatives as well as company officials. Many times a business decision has political ramifications that must be dealt with.These are problems that individuals in private businesses do not face as often, if at all.

Paul laments, "One large construction company has half our people working there. They're all good carpenters and some have their journeymen papers. It's all we've been doing for the last eight years is training all these bloody carpenters and then they're gone. Many young men want to work in the city because it's more exciting."

With the high costs associated with training employees, it is very difficult to make competitive bids and earn a profit. The training costs increase operating expenses: "We bid on some of these jobs and we might break even or make a little bit of a profit. Most of our competitors can go to Canada Manpower and get all the skilled people they want. Then they do the job and lay the guys off because they've got no further responsibility. Whereas we have a responsibility not only to get the projects but to house and feed our people and find work for them."

While it makes sense to have a policy of hiring qualified band members to run band-owned businesses, sometimes it is difficult to find a band member who can also handle the political pressure. One option is to consider hiring non-band members for management positions. "It's better to get somebody totally outside of the picture to manage the company rather than have somebody from inside who is related to other band members." A band member who is manager is on the front line when hiring or firing a fellow member.

It is a hard position to be in, Harold acknowledges, "If I look at the long term, then I figure I'm doing something but sometimes it gets pretty rocky. The biggest thing to handle is the family conflicts. Actually it shouldn't be, but in any band operation there is always a high degree of politics. It's probably the hardest part of being the general manager in a band-owned company, because everybody's got their fingers in the pie, so to speak."

It's hard to give advice to other people on how to handle the political problem. "After eight years, I haven't even learned to handle it. I don't have a problem so much with my employees but when certain factions in the membership make a political issue of a specific decision then it becomes very hard to be in my position. A few young people come and give me encouragement when I feel a little bit down. It's nice to see that they see what I'm trying to do and it is appreciated."

Harold has advice before starting a band-operated business. "I think other bands should do an in-depth feasibility study. Band-owned businesses are very hard to get off the ground and keep running. The political issues are a large part of the problem. It's really hard, and there are going to be a lot of downfalls. I've seen a few band-operated corporations that never made it, despite all their fantastic ideas and government funding."

Summary and Conclusions

Champagne-Aishihik Enterprises Ltd has successfully provided employment and training opportunities for band members. It is becoming more profitable under the guidance of Chief Paul Birckel and general manager Harold Kane. Despite the political pressures that appear to be integral to a band-owned operation, business continues and is beginning to thrive. The number of trainees that have worked on projects over the years continues to grow, as does the number of permanent employees.

Paul has been the leading strategist for the band's economic and social initiatives since he was first elected chief in 1980. In this time he has been able to implement a number of major projects and set the stage for additional programs to meet the need for further education and more employment opportunities and to address the addiction problems faced by some of his constituents. He recognizes that there are no instant cures or miracles but knows that problems can be overcome and gains made over time. Paul takes an aggressive but well-reasoned approach to decision making.

With Harold's help Paul promotes a team atmosphere among construction company employees. Employment opportunities are given to students and recent graduates. Some assistance is provided to apprentices, but the company has limited resources for those employees seeking their journeymen papers. Attitudes seem to be changing in the community in favour of employment. More people want to work as they see what other employed band members can afford to purchase or as they gain the self-assurance to stay sober and employed. Harold's main challenge is to keep the projects coming in so that these people are steadily employed.

As general manager, Harold is on the front line if any conflicts arise in the community due to his decisions. Those pressures are not easy to handle, but the appreciation that he receives from young people encourages him to continue. He is a skilled general manager who takes pride in the company's accomplishments. He tries to solve problems such as employee turnover and absenteeism by working closely with his employees. It is difficult to match the wages and benefits that are offered by larger companies, but the company's accomplishments foster a sense of pride and loyalty in band member employees.

Revenues have grown dramatically over the last ten years. The next challenge facing the company is to continue to make a profit so that further investments can be made in economic development projects. As more band members are trained and join Champagne-Aishihik Enterprises, training costs will decrease and this should be reflected in greater profit margins.

Increased profitability will mean that the company can qualify for bonding insurance and bid on larger projects. This will promote the company's growing reputation and credibility in the industry, which should lead to more projects, and a continuing cycle of growth and profitability will be set into motion. Operations will continue to reflect a respect for Mother Earth that matches the beliefs of their band members.

The Champagne-Aishihik band has a reputation of being progressive and achieving many of its goals, in part because of the success of a number of the band's undertakings, including its construction company. It is the birthplace of a number of leaders in territorial and national native political organizations.

Postscript – 1990

The truss plant was very busy in 1990, with equipment rental by the government another major source of income. The major new project for Dakwakada Development Corporation, the band's corporate arm, was the approval for development of a $42-million first-class hotel, convention centre, and office centre complex in Whitehorse. A Yellowknife construction company will act as the construction manager while Dakwakada will be the management team overseeing the project. The scheduled completion date is early in 1992.

Qualified band members will have an opportunity to work on the project, but they will have to be reliable or they will be taken off the project. Paul notes, "We would like to have an apprenticeship program instituted so that more of our people can be trained." The band will manage the whole property as the developer and will hire a hotel chain to manage the hotel and train employees.

The complex will meet a pressing need for a large project that would generate employment opportunities and profits for the band over the long term. It is hoped that this project will have a direct impact for the band-owned tour company and for new businesses operated by band members. The project should have major economic benefits for other Whitehorse businesses through increased international marketing and tourism throughout the year.

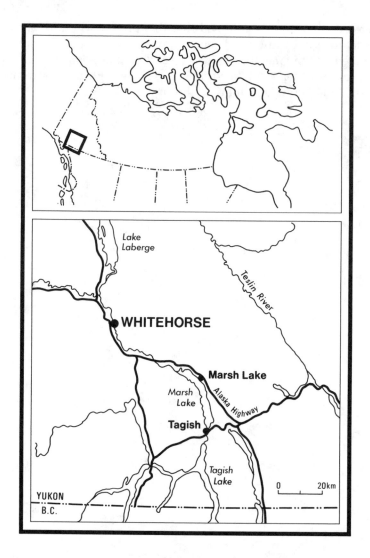

ENTREPRENEURS' ENDORSEMENT

We, the undersigned, acknowledge that we have read our business profile. We approve of the contents of the profile and recognize its accuracy in describing our business.

Dated _MARCH 7ᵗʰ_, 1991

Bill Doehle
Bill Doehle

Gary Putland
Gary Putland

M Doehle
Melody Doehle

S Putland
Laurie Putland

10

LAKEVIEW RESORT AND MARINA MARSH LAKE, YUKON

Located one hour south of Whitehorse, Lakeview Resort and Marina overlooks Marsh Lake. Attracting tourists from the south, visitors from Whitehorse, and the local residents, the resort has developed a reputation for good food and friendly service in a beautiful location. Many of the local residents call it their second home.

The unincorporated family business sits on eleven acres. The main building houses a restaurant, a lounge, ten motel rooms, a laundromat, public showers, a small general store, a beer garden, and conference rooms. In addition, there are ten cabins, tennis courts, an RV park with full hook-ups, and a marina where boats can be rented or docked.

Bill Doehle and his sister Laurie Putland are equal partners in the resort with Bill's wife Melody and Laurie's husband Gary. When they originally purchased the resort, everyone put in fourteen- to sixteen-hour days for the first three or four months. Now both couples work ten- or eleven-hour days seven days a week, all year round, with each couple taking three days off every two weeks. They say the partnership has helped make it work.

History

In 1977, Bill and Laurie's dad, Fred Doehle, built the original house where the resort now stands. Fred had sold his plumbing business in Whitehorse and started building a cabin in Old Constabulary, a district near Marsh Lake. He staked out the area for the resort at the same time. In his words: "To get a bigger piece of ground, you had to do something commercial. And that's how come I said well, okay, I'll start a marina, since there is none in the Yukon. I started the marina and built the cabins and built a big house right up here where this [main building] sits now." He intended running a summer operation serving boaters on the Marsh and Tagish Lake chains.

Fred used his own money to build the original resort and marina. His son Bill helped him clear the site and build the cabins. Fred operated the resort successfully for several years with his daughter Laurie's help in the summers. Then in February 1982, the main house burned down. It was uninsured.

At that point, Fred tried to sell the marina. He was unsuccessful because of the general economic slump. On reflection, Fred notes: "If you can't sell it then you've got to do something else. I had built an RV park, and when the house burned down I lost the showers and the little store and laundromat. So I rebuilt that right away, so it was serviceable for that following summer."

Fred decided that his little operation was not lucrative enough and elected to build additional facilities including the dining room and lounge. He had built ten motel rooms and framed them in, rebuilt the store and the washrooms, and added the floor for the dining room and the lounge when his money ran out. He needed additional funds to buy equipment for the kitchen and furnish the motel rooms, the dining room, and the lounge. He sold a number of properties that he had invested in for his retirement but that was not enough. Fred ended up borrowing $100,000 from the bank and applying for a grant from the Yukon Department of Tourism. There were no repayment provisions for the grant.

Fred states: "You're forced to take grants. I don't believe in them. But when your opposition down the road that way and the one this way are both getting grants, you've got to be stupid if you don't go for it yourself. I don't agree with it at all. Nobody should get a grant." Fred qualified for a grant of $61,000 or 32% of what he was going to have to spend to finish the lodge. The surprising twist in the grant application was that if he had applied before starting to rebuild, he would have likely qualified for almost $200,000. The tourism department did not take into consideration the amount already invested prior to the date of the grant application. It would seem the government discouraged the initiative of the entrepreneur in using his own financial resources under this particular program. Although Fred qualified for the grant, he needed bridge financing, which he obtained from private individuals, because he was required to pay his bills first and then submit them for reimbursement from the tourism department. Again, the government program assistance was not relevant to his needs.

Reopening the resort in 1984, Fred put the lodge up for sale immediately because of the problems with hiring staff and running

Gary and Laurie Putland, Melody and Bill Doehle

such a big operation by himself. He managed the lodge for two years and then sold it to Bill, Laurie, and their spouses. Gary, Laurie's husband, was the first one to suggest the purchase. He contacted Bill, but Bill's initial reaction was that there was no way they could afford to do it. Then Bill started thinking about it and made some inquiries. His investigation revealed that it might be possible to raise the money to purchase the property.

Both Bill and Gary were dissatisfied with their jobs. Gary said: "I was doing surveying work for the government and I was distraught with my job. I was fairly well up and I was making a good salary but it was a dead-end job. I really had no challenge in the job." At that time, Bill was involved in a three-year-old surveying partnership. He recalls: "I was tired of surveying. You work hard all summer, but by Christmas you don't have any money left and you're left scrounging around trying to find some work. I was planning on marrying Melody and I wanted to settle down."

Melody had been working as an X-ray technician in British Columbia. She had no previous experience in the hospitality industry but she remembers: " I walked right into this business and then got married. I didn't really think too much about it. When the

Lakeview Resort

opportunity to buy the resort came up I went into it very quickly and it wasn't really thought out. I never even talked to Laurie and Gary, except once on the telephone to Laurie." Laurie was raising their two children at home. She supported Gary's idea of buying the resort because she was close to her brother Bill and thought she could work well with Melody.

The group hired a consultant to prepare a report for presentation to various financial institutions in order to raise $200,000. One bank was willing to loan them $150,000 on the basis of the financial statements, but this was not enough. Gary insists that being turned down by the banks was the best thing that could have happened. They found a willing lender in Bill and Laurie's uncle. He holds the first mortgage on the resort and Fred took back a second mortgage. Gary favours this financing method because there is some flexibility when times are slow – something he does not think would have worked with the bank. In addition, the interest rate on the loan has remained constant.

Of the four partners, only Laurie had a little experience working in the hospitality industry before they purchased the resort. When asked about their prior expectations for the business, Gary recalls:

"We decided when we took over that we could work seven days a week all summer long and it wouldn't bother us not to hire any staff. It was terrible, confusing, tiring." Laurie comments: "We did it but we were almost dead after two and a half months. Until you start, you don't realize the hours." Melody thought the business would be much quieter and slower so they could really put their energy into it. She says: "We're putting our energy into it 100% now but it's so busy that I don't feel like I've got control of it. It's big business to me."

Operations

The marina opens as soon as the ice goes out, which is normally the end of May. There are fifty-nine stalls for boats and float planes, rented by the day, the month, or the season. Visitors have their choice of six rental boats, a canoe, or a windsurfer. The busy period for cabin rentals, and the lounge and restaurant business are the summer months of June, July, and August, as guests come to enjoy fishing, boating, hiking or a good meal.

September marks the beginning of the off-season when conference bookings from government departments begin in earnest. Conferences are usually for ten to fifteen people and may last for several days. This is an important but busy part of the business. Gary states: "It is surprising how much time it takes, especially if you have all those people staying over. You've got to supply them with their rooms, you've got to be there with their breakfast, lunch, and dinner every day, keep the conference room cleaned up and coffee on the go. You get that many people on a regular basis, for twenty-four hours, it does take a lot of time."

The partners have relied on word-of-mouth advertising for the conference facilities. This seems to be working well since, when interviewed in August 1989, they were almost fully booked in September and October and partially booked for November. They do some radio advertising in the summer for the resort and take a couple of ads out in tourist magazines.

In the wintertime, Gary states: "It's mainly local business when you get into the off-season. It's the people who live around here. You rent a lot of movies from the store, and people will come into the restaurant for dinner. Weekends, there are a lot of people from Whitehorse for skidooing, skiing, or for a drive out of town." In addition, conference bookings continue until May.

Under a new policy, the partners have entered into a five-year purchase agreement with the government to purchase their land.

This not only increases their assets substantially but it will make it more attractive to potential buyers. They are subject to territorial regulations regarding land use and fire control and pay annual fees for business, liquor, and sign licences. Federal regulations must be met regarding sanitation for the restaurant, bar and the hotel.

A large part of the business is the lounge and restaurant, which generate about 75% of total annual revenues. Cabin and motel rentals do not operate near capacity but bookings do increase in the summertime. The large cabins, which contain a full kitchen and bath, a double bed, and a double hide-a-bed cost $75 per night, while the smaller cabins cost $60. Motel rooms are $42 per night for a double and $37 per night for a single. RVs are charged $7.50 per night and tents are charged $3.50.

Staffing

Each partner sees staffing as a problem. In the summer season, the resort hires full-time staff: two cooks, five waiters or waitresses, one kitchen help, one storekeeper, and two bartenders. In the winter, they require one full- and one part-time cook, one bartender, and a part-time waitress. They have a part-time bookkeeper year-round.

In their second year, they hired a cook with an alcohol problem. This situation created problems in other areas of their business. In their third year, a cook quit at the beginning of the summer, but overall the staff were much better. They try to maintain a cheerful atmosphere and to treat employees fairly. They look for responsible and hard-working individuals who are willing to move when business is hectic. The staff that worked out so well included four students, several of whom had worked at the resort before. Gary comments: "The girls, who work in the kitchen where they're under pressure, are fairly light-hearted. They're very easy to get along with and they work hard, so it improves everybody's attitude."

The partners try to hire staff from the community so they do not have to provide accommodations for them. This sometimes puts them in the position of having to hire mediocre people rather than no one at all if they have positions to be filled. Melody describes several dilemmas when it comes to staff discipline. "We have very limited resources for staff and if there is a problem, we don't go to them very often because we have to be thankful for what we've got. Not everybody's perfect and we've got really good staff right now. Another thing, I'm twenty-nine years old and a lot of people that work for me are older than me and have a lot more experience than me in a kitchen. I find it really difficult to tell them what to do and how to do it. Consequently, now when I do say something they

Table 9
Financial Information for Lakeview Resort and Marina

	1986*	1987	1988	1989
Return on Equity (%)	0	0	0	0
Sales/Assets (times)	4.65	5.33	7.87	5.71
Wages ($)	26,944	31,824	47,320	63,781

* six months only

don't like it because I've always tiptoed around. That's a big, big problem."

Furthermore, "We'll discuss problems between the four of us, and a lot of times we decide that a problem has to be overlooked. Or we try little things to solve the problem and if they don't work, a lot of times we just let it go. We live with the people that work for us. They know our friends, we know their friends, and that makes it difficult to be a boss." Laurie points out that anyone thinking of going into this business has to learn to be flexible when dealing with staff and customers. That knowledge can only be acquired by actually doing the work.

Financial Statistics

On the advice on an accountant, a limited company was incorporated to hold the assets of the company. The company hired the Doehles and the Putlands to operate the resort. This structure allowed tax benefits to be passed on to the partners on an individual basis. Losses, which were recorded in partnership equity, were also passed on to each partner. Partnership drawings were taken in each year, but a loss was shown in partnership equity, which accounts for the zero return on equity recorded in Table 10.

The sales-to-assets ratio indicates the company's capacity for generating revenue. For every $1.00 invested in assets, the resort earned 4.65 times to a high of 7.87 times in 1988. This amount would seem to indicate a very efficient use of assets to generate revenue, since the investment in assets remained relatively stable over this period. Salaries do not include partnership drawings, but this figure does increase steadily over the four-year period.

Reasons for Success

The resort is successful because of the quality of the partnership and the owners' high standards for food and service. These standards, and reasonable prices, have contributed to the customer loyalty that their business enjoys. Further, the business is an important focal point for the community of Marsh Lake.

The partnership itself is a major reason for the success of the business. Each partner brings a unique set of strengths which complements the group's dynamics. Gary notes: "We don't see eye to eye on everything but instead of just having one or two lines of thought, you have four." The areas of responsibility shift among the partners as needs dictate. Melody and Laurie tend to handle the restaurant and staff, while Bill and Gary normally look after most of the maintenance, the marina, and the bar.

The fact that the partners are related by marriage and by blood influences the way they work together. Bill recalls that they enjoyed spending time together before they entered the partnership because they liked each other's company. Gary feels that in working with relatives, he has learned to put up with things that he might not with anyone else because of the close bond that exists between the partners.

Each couple tends to work together, with the men switching day and evening shifts once a week. Each partner gets three days off every two weeks and each couple takes a month off in the fall. Laurie feels that another reason that the partnership works well is that the four partners rarely work all together at the same time. When decisions have to be made, it's usually a husband-and-wife discussion. If it is a major decision, then it is saved for discussion with all four partners. There are no regular partners meetings because they do not have time.

Gary recalls their early years: "When we started off, one might do something without the other partners' knowledge. But after a few times, you learn it's not just one person, so that when there's a major decision of some sort to be made then we discuss it among ourselves. Everybody gets their say and three is a quorum. If it's a stalemate with two on each side then you come to a happy medium."

Each partner acknowledges the hard work and long hours, but they still have time for a good laugh. Melody recalls when Gary (who is very reserved, cool, and hard-working) accidently dropped a can of pop on the corner of a table. The can punctured and sprayed the whole restaurant, walls and patrons included, as Gary unsuccessfully attempted to corral the wild can. He still gets teased about it.

Another factor that Melody identifies in the success of their partnership is that they share similar standards. "We would rather go the other way than rip anyone off. If I just wanted money I would

Lakeview Marina

skip on the quality of this or that, but none of us is like that. We treat the customers the same; we all want the same things."

What attracts tourists and the local residents to the resort? According to the partners, their reputation for good food and friendly service brings customers in the door and keeps them coming back. There are a group of local residents that visit the restaurant regularly on Friday evenings. Fred started the tradition of serving large portions, and his children and their spouses continued it, adding high-quality meats and fresh produce. Gary proudly states: "There are very few places which actually give you a real home-cooked meal where everything is made from scratch. For example, we buy a whole veal roast, then we cut, tenderize, and bread veal cutlets. We get very little in the way of prepared foods. Our hamburger we buy by the big blocks, we mix it all up and we make our own patties. Vegetables are fresh ... Nothing is frozen. All the fruit pies are either made from fresh fruit or frozen fruit." They also have a greenhouse where they grow tomatoes, cucumbers, and lettuce.

Kelly Douglas is their wholesale supplier in the summertime. In the off-season, they purchase a week's supply of groceries from a

supermarket in Whitehorse because there would be too much spoil-
age if they purchased case lots of produce.

Prices of menu items have risen with the cost of ingredients but
the partners do not set a specific mark-up. In pricing the daily meal
specials, for example, Laurie and Melody will consider what ingredients have gone into the dish and what they think the customers
will pay for it. Gary points out: "We've found that people will pay
almost anything you ask them to as long as you're serving them a
quality meal. If you want them to pay $15 for a veal cutlet and it
comes out tough and the vegetables are lousy and so on, it doesn't
take long before you'll lose that customer. But with so many of them
being return customers, they get used to quality and they don't
mind paying a little more for a meal than they would in town."
They charge what the market will bear, but margins are still very
slim.

The resort is the only business in the Marsh Lake area, which has
300 permanent residents. The population has probably more than
doubled in the last two years. Their closest competition is Jake's
Corner, thirteen miles away. It also has a restaurant and bar, but
Jake's closes at 8:00 p.m. The resort is a focal point for the community, with the community club using the conference facilities for
their meetings. Melody says, "We're forty miles from town, and
we've got a store, a laundromat, and we've got showers for the
people who don't have running water. I think we're a big part of
the community and I think people depend on us and rely on us.
Nobody has phones, but we've got the phone here. That's changing
in December 1989, when telephones will be installed. Further, we
hire local people."

Challenges

Gary characterizes their typical customers: "They're usually middle-
aged people, fairly well-established. They like to go out and eat
dinner and have a few drinks. You never have problems with those.
You're always paid, they're regular customers. You know they're
always going to be there."

Unfortunately one small segment of the local population regularly
makes complaints. The partners feel it's an attitude problem; these
few people do not realize the work and effort that goes into running
the business but take the business for granted. Melody says: "For
myself, it's been difficult to accept. But these people are going to
complain no matter what. We're doing our best and if we're not
making people happy, then you can't please everybody all the time."

Environmental Responsibility

The partners try to run their business in an environmentally responsible manner. Each partner attempts to limit or prevent any kind of destruction to the natural environment. Gary points out: "We're always careful when we're doing any type of development to keep as many trees as we possibly can. Garbage is hauled to a territorial dump at the end of the lake. We don't dump waste oil into the lake." They are ready for a fuel spill in the marina and carry foam pads supplied by the government that are designed to absorb oil or gas and not water.

As individuals, each partner puts importance on protecting the environment. Bill points out, "I believe everybody has to do their part. It doesn't matter how small or insignificant you think it is, it all adds up." This attitude is even more important because they live in the North and enjoy its natural beauty. Bill no longer buys aerosols and has tried to cut back on the amount of cellophane used. At home Melody uses cloth diapers. In their business, Laurie and Melody often discuss ways of modifying their practices in the kitchen, but acknowledge how difficult that is to accomplish with so many people. They try to set a good example for the staff and reuse plastic and tin foil. The resort recently helped a local individual distribute a questionnaire that focused on the need for a garbage and recycling pickup service in their community.

Future Development

Although they do not have a five or ten-year plan on paper, they share some common ideas for their future. In the short term, expanding the kitchen facilities is on the agenda. Melody would like to see another couple hired. "I don't want another couple to become part of the partnership, but somebody we could hire that could help us and give us some more time off. Gary and Laurie have two kids and we've got a baby now and family is important. This business is not more important than my family."

Expanding the conference facilities and booking more conferences were also suggested. As Melody points out: "It's good business. You know you're going to have fifteen people for dinner. Whereas if it's just a restaurant, it could be dead or you could have a hundred people, you never know." Another possibility is expanding the store to provide more fresh meats and produce.

Another option might be to hire musical bands more often and increase the number of dances held in the lounge. Although liquor sales are profitable, problems with drunk customers can be very difficult and unpleasant. Melody notes: "I think that we cater to one sort of group of people. There's a large population up here that would like to see us have more dances, more fun things. Now, we're trying to get by mainly as a restaurant. That is a big, big part of our business." Gary adds: "We've become selective about the type of people we'd like to have around, so we tend to cater to them."

Bill and Melody expect to put in ten or twelve more years; then they would like to sell out and move into another kind of business. Bill says: "It is the type of business that is labour-intensive and means dealing with people all the time. You get tired of them, especially by the end of the summer. Over time, it's just a lot of work. There's not much of a challenge left."

All the partners feel the business is a success. It pays the bills and allows them to support their families. Their business is growing and is probably four times busier than when they first purchased it. They enjoy working for themselves and like the flexibility it allows them with regards to their kids. They can bring their kids in if they want or they can run home and have lunch with them. Gary says: "My kids will always have a job waiting for them. It's a tremendous asset and the potential is almost unending."

Melody adds: "Even though I find that in this job I sometimes think I'm not really doing anything that is worth anything, it's not that way. People come here to spend their hard-earned money. If they enjoy themselves then that's worth something. Leisure time is important for everybody and I like working with my husband."

Summary and Conclusions

In summary, Marsh Lake Resort and Marina is an example of a successful partnership in a business that supports two families and provides employment for local residents. The purchase of the business was financed through private sources, which worked out better than a bank loan. A government grant and a bank loan were used in the building of the resort; that experience would indicate that an entrepreneur should canvas government sources early in the planning stages of his project for possible funding.

The partners had held jobs in which they worked for others. But the experience of owning and operating their own business has generally been much more challenging and fulfilling. It is hard work, but they work with their spouses, they can take a month off for holidays, and they have some flexibility in seeing their children while they are working.

Both couples have families and can always offer their children a summer job or eventually bring them into the business. It is interesting to point out that Fred Doehle had his own business before building the resort. His son Bill also had his own business before purchasing the resort. It is possible that he and his sister may pass this entrepreneurial legacy on to their children.

Although working with relatives can be a disaster, these four have been decidedly successful at working together. Part of their success can be attributed to the complementary blend of skills and knowledge that each partner brings to the group. Further, they hold common goals and objectives for their business and agree on the means of accomplishing them.

Their common attitude towards the business is to put in the effort that is required to make it succeed, in a manner that they can be proud of and that meets the needs of their customers. This approach has earned the resort an excellent reputation for high-quality food and service. They have established themselves in the community and serve as its focal point. Things are changing as the community grows and more people settle by the lake, but the resort continues to offer a place where community members can meet and socialize in a friendly atmosphere.

Finally, the partners see the beauty and fragility of their surroundings and follow environmentally sensitive procedures in whatever ways they can. They are cognizant of the impact the resort and the marina have, and they try to minimize that impact through recycling, following proper disposal techniques, and preparing for emergency fuel spills. They also practise these procedures at home.

Postscript – 1990

Business went well and each couple was able to take a four-week holiday in the fall. Conference bookings remained steady over the fall and spring. In 1990, the partnership arrangement was phased out, since all tax benefits were extinguished, and all business is now carried out under the incorporated name of Lakeview Resort and Marina, Ltd.

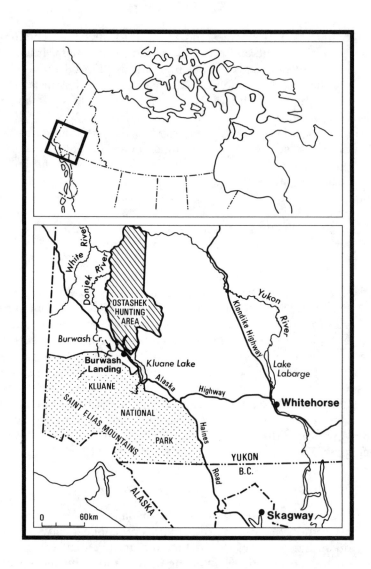

ENTREPRENEUR'S ENDORSEMENT

I, the undersigned, acknowledge that I have read my business profile. I approve of the contents of the profile and recognize its accuracy in describing my business.

Dated _May 3_, 1991

John Ostashek
John Ostashek

11

OSTASHEK OUTFITTING LTD
Burwash Landing, Yukon

John Ostashek has been an outfitter for thirty-two years in Alberta and the Yukon. His business is located 150 air miles west from Whitehorse in the Kluane Lake area and has operated for eighteen years. John handles fifty to fifty-five hunters per season in a hunting area of about 5,000 square miles.

This operation is very successful and attracts hunters from across North America and Europe. Many are repeat clients, who appreciate the professionalism and integrity with which John provides his services. John's wife, Carol Pettigrew, does the business's bookkeeping and manages the flow of hunters between Whitehorse and their ranch headquarters near Burwash Landing. This personal service is another element in their success.

In 1981 John started another business called Glacier Air Tours. It is a division of Ostashek Outfitting Ltd and provides tourists with a selection of six tours over Kluane National Park. Visitors can view Mount Logan, Canada's highest peak, and the icefields and glaciers of the St. Elias mountain range.

History

John began outfitting near Jasper in northern Alberta. He recalls the decision to move to the Yukon, "We were in the hunting business and we also offered trail rides in the park. The hunting business was getting real tough to operate because they were starting to set quotas on mountain sheep so I decided to look for an area in the north where there was more freedom."

There was also a tradition of outfitting in the Yukon. John comments, "It was the first tourism industry in the territories. It was the first reason for tourists to come to the territories, at the turn of the century."

Rocking Star Ranch – Headquarters for Ostashek Outfitting

When John arrived in the Yukon, he recalls, "We were taking mostly sheep hunters in Alberta, and that's what we started with here. We did that for a few years. Then we expanded into some moose camps in the northern part of our area. Then we started doing some spring bear hunts as well. That's when we worked up to fifty to fifty-five hunters a year."

Although the outfitting business was successful, John seized the opportunity in 1981 to start Glacier Air Tours. John recalls:

We had the [Cessna] 185 aircraft for servicing the outfitting camps and we found out we just weren't doing enough outfitting to justify the 185 so we had to get rid of it or find more work for it. The opportunity arose to find more work for it. It started by demand from the public. We had a Class 4 restricted licence, which allowed us to service our camps. Then we started getting people at the lodge in Burwash Landing enquiring about seeing the glaciers because someone had told them about our plane.

From the 1970s to the 1980s, the Arctic Institute at Kluane Lake were taking people out on glacier flights in a haphazard way to utilize their aircraft. They now offer flights at $300 an hour. But 1980 was the window of opportunity for us.

They flew twenty visitors in their first year of operation and they expected to fly 1,200 people eight years later.

Operations

Ostashek Outfitting Ltd
Beginning in May each year, John takes four hunters on a spring bear hunt. Then from August to the end of October, Ostashek Outfitting handles twenty-five hunters for dall sheep and mixed game and twenty to twenty-five moose and caribou hunters.

The sheep and mixed bag hunts are the most popular with the Americans. For the Europeans, the moose hunts are more popular. Our hunts are in the middle price range. I try to balance price against what my clients are going to get and I try to keep it within the ballpark.

The biggest thing we've found is the importance of truthfulness. If your client comes here and says "you promised me this" and it's not there, then you've got a problem. If you provide everything you promised, then really you don't have any problem. There may be a misunderstanding with some clients and you can't satisfy them, but at least you can go back and refer to the pamphlet or letter and say "Look, this isn't what I said or this isn't what I promised you."

Anytime we have a fourteen-day mixed-bag hunt, if a hunter takes three trophies, then that is what we call a good hunt. For example, he might take a sheep, a moose, and a caribou or a grizzly. Then, when you get the guy who gets the four and five trophies, which happens several times a year, that's the exceptional hunt. But as far as I'm concerned, a good hunt is when the hunter's gotten some trophies, regardless of the size, that he is quite happy with. He's happy even when he puts them along side the other guys' in the party, and goes home with a good feeling and we go home with a good feeling. We've met some great people in this business, but we've met a lot of turkeys too.

As owner/operator of Ostashek Outfitting, John works seven days a week during the season.

My schedule from the first of August to the end of October goes by the days that I have hunts changing, at the beginning and end of a ten-, twelve-, or fourteen-day hunt. I don't know whether it's Monday, Tuesday, Wednesday, or Sunday or what day it is. My main duty is to keep the camps running and make sure that everything is okay. For example, in the last two days, we've been changing moose camps. I got the camps all serviced and came out yesterday about 6:00. I was into one of the sheep camps this morning. Then this afternoon, I'll be back into one of the moose camps because it's possible that they got some moose already and I'll have to start flying moose meat out. So basically I live in an airplane. A short day would be two to three hours in the air, and then a long day would be seven and eight hours in the air, plus servicing the camps. I average twelve hours a day during the whole season.

But I do put in a lot of seventeen-, eighteen-, nineteen-hour days, day after day. I never do get caught up. There is always a pile of stuff to do, but I try to stay on top of it as best I can. We do our own aircraft maintenance. My son's my engineer. He's got his engineer's ticket. This year we're doing all our own maintenance and that's saved me a pile of time. Our airplanes are in far better shape then they've ever been in. We do the maintenance here because we've got everything we need. I have to be self-sufficient out here, in everything.

Of the 5,000 square miles in his hunting territory, John notes, "We're hunting a good three-quarters of it. There are pockets that we only go back to every once in awhile and some areas that we hunt every year. It depends on wherever the game populations are. We do a lot of reconnaissance by aircraft every year. There are large parts that I'll never be in because there is nothing there to go for."

Hunting areas may shift. "For example, we just started hunting the Nisling River three years ago because prior to a big fire there in 1974, there was no game. Then the moose moved in and there is a tremendous moose population in there now. There has always been a tremendous grizzly population but it just wasn't worth going in there just to get grizzly. There are other parts of our area that I just don't think are productive right now, so we won't spend the time or the money to go into them."

Hunters are flown into base camps, which are fully equipped and linked to the ranch headquarters by radio communications. Most of the hunting is done from spike camps – portable camps that the hunter and his guide set up in areas that are closer to the game. Clients and guides move throughout the area by saddle and pack horses. John says, "Right now we've got around sixty or seventy head [of horse]. We grow almost enough feed at the ranch but we do supplement it from outside."

John describes the classic stalk that a hunter might experience. "I was out with one of my guides for the first hunt this year. It was 10:00 a.m. when we spotted some sheep and it was 7:00 p.m. at night when we killed one. It was 11:30 at night when we got back to the horses and 2:30 the next morning when we got back to camp. The thing about that hunt was that we waited for one of the sheep for seven or eight hours until he moved into position where we could get him. Then the hunter shot the wrong ram at twenty yards. But that's just another day in the mountains as far as I'm concerned."

Glacier Air Tours
The tours cover the largest non-polar icefields in the world, in Kluane National Park and the St. Elias mountain range. The Donjek Special lasts thirty-five to forty minutes; passengers fly over the gold placer fields on Burwash Creek to the Donjek River and the Donjek Glacier for $50 per person. There are three one-hour tours available for $65 per person, with trips over the Donjek and Kluane glaciers, or the Kluane and Kaskawulsh glaciers, or Kaskawulsh glacier and Silver City. A one-and-a-half hour tour takes passengers over the Donjek, Walsh, and Logan glaciers and the icefields of Kluane National Park for $97.50 per person. Finally, there is a two-hour tour via Mount Logan and the St. Elias range for $130 per person.

John says, "The hour trips are probably the most popular because of the price. We've got the hour-and-a-half and the two-hour tours – once we get people up, there have been no complaints on the price on any of the tours. We get so many articles on it all over the world that business is going to snowball one of these days. We're getting writers taking the tours all the time. We've been written up in some of the leading magazines in Europe over the last five or six years. The glacier flights are also a major attraction in the Yukon, as far as tourism is concerned generally." Carol adds, "In fact, the Europeans know more about the glaciers than Yukoners or Americans."

John is considering expanding his marketing efforts. He says, "If we do market in Europe, it will be through tour companies, because it's very expensive to market in Europe. We only have one product to sell, we don't have a package. One company, who's been flying with us for four or five years, is expanding its marketing and it's going to have 150 people for us next summer."

Glacier Air Tours uses two airplanes, an M-6 Maule on wheels and a Cessna 185 on floats. John expects to handle between 1,000 and 1,200 tourists in 1989. He notes, "We fly whenever customers come in. The pilot's there on call. He flies them whenever they want, just as long as there's daylight. He's been out there at 11:00 at night in June and July and 6:00 or 7:00 in the morning. There's lots of times in between when we don't do anything. We've got a good pilot there now. He's an aggressive salesperson and great with people. If it gets busy, then I go up and fly the other airplane."

John Ostashek

Government Regulations
John feels that the outfitter industry's relationship with the territorial government is positive. He says, "Basically the government is pro-outfitter. I believe that the outfitting industry in the Yukon has a tremendous influence over government and has had over the last eighteen years. When they start making regulations pertaining to hunting, we've been vocal enough and adamant enough in our dealings with government that I'm sure they stop and think how outfitters are going to react to it before they bring anything in."

There are some restrictions regarding grizzly bear hunting and regulations regarding mountain sheep. In addition, regulations are in place that have had an impact on outfitters raising their own horses. The land claim by the Yukon Indians is another issue that affects an outfitter's business.

John notes, "There aren't really quotas, but there are some restrictions – like grizzly bear on a point system and different management techniques. We have enough country with enough wildlife, that quotas aren't required." John describes the point system.

We're allocated a certain number of points over a five-year period. Ostashek

Outfitting was allocated forty-four points over a five-year period. Then every time we kill a male bear, we lose a point and every time we kill a female we lose three points. So the emphasis of the harvest is to kill male bears. Hypothetically, we could kill forty-four male bears in five years. Then we renegotiate for the next five years.

We keep track of the harvest and the Wildlife Branch keep track and then in the fourth year of the agreement we're supposed to start renegotiating. All the bears are measured. We expect that we'll increase our points because we had a predominantly male harvest. The outfitters that haven't had a predominantly male harvest may lose some points. It just depends on what further biological information the Wildlife branch has.

We've come up with a fairly decent system that we can live with. The first one that the Wildlife branch wanted to institute was impossible to live with and then they liberalized it a little bit but it still wasn't good. But for the last five or six years, this point system is one that we can live with. I think the government likes the system and is quite content with it. The majority of outfitters are happy with it. There are one or two outfitters that aren't but they are in a very bad position because they have small areas to start with and the bear quota is based on bears per square mile. So the ones that have a lot of resident hunting pressure are not as happy as they could be.

The industry as a whole can live with the bear quota the way it is now. It's not really hampering us. It has made us change our methods of harvesting but it has also provided some rewards for us if we do. It all works out well. The government has changed some things. During the late 1970s, at our insistence, the government brought in a one-bear-in-a-lifetime regulation. They monitored the change and decided that it wasn't a necessary step, so they've changed it back to one bear every three years. It's working.

Female mountain sheep and their young are protected. Rams must have a full curl where the tip of the horn curves up past the eye. Since the institution of the regulations affecting grizzly bears and mountain sheep, John notes, "The quality of the wildlife is probably better. The quality of the harvest is better than when we first got here because there were no restrictions. When it was legal to hunt a three-quarter-curl ram, a lot of hunters and guides weren't as selective and would take an easy one a lot of times. After full curl came in, which the Outfitters Association had pushed for, it brought the quality of the sheep up. The quality of the grizzly bear went up because of the point system."

Guides in the Yukon must be licensed. John explains, "In the Yukon, we have a chief guide and assistant guide. With the outfitter and the hunting concession [hunting area controlled by government permit] controlling the harvest, we don't need restrictions on the guides."

Another aspect of regulation that John handles is insurance coverage for his aircraft. John explains, "We have liability coverage but we self-insure the hull of the aircraft. Hull coverage is a problem because it's very, very expensive.. It costs about 12% of the total value of the aircraft. It's so expensive because of the remoteness of where the aircraft flies and the cost of getting it out if in fact there is an accident."

Marketing

The recession in the early 1980s affected John's way of doing business. He recalls, "When we had the recession in 1981, bookings started getting harder to get. Before that we were able to just answer the telephone and stay booked but after the recession we had to get out and start marketing our hunts." He started presenting his company at trade shows in the United States.

We attend one trade show on the east coast at Harrisburg, Pennsylvania and one in Anaheim, California. If you find a good one, you have to stick with it. There are no results in the first year. However, it was our fourth year last year in Harrisburg and we did more than $100,000 in business. Next year is almost fully booked after that show. We've also got quite a few hunts booked for 1991. We have turned a lot of people down. Generally, people have talked to us before, so they visit our booth because they know we're going to be at the trade show. They don't bother booking by mail.

We have a newsletter for each season that is typeset and printed professionally with high-quality photos. I write it and Carol edits it. We include that newsletter as part of the information we send to prospective hunters and those who have hunted with us before. The new clients like it because they really want details of our operation and the newsletter provides names and places that really get them excited about hunting with us. Former clients love to see their names and faces starring in the headlines, too.

We do a mailing list at the trade show. We put anyone that looks interested on our mailing list. Information like that is fairly expensive. It costs us $5 or $6 to answer an inquiry, so we're pretty selective on what we answer. That's one of our best marketing tools. It's personal and there's continuity. That's what's good about the trade show, too.

Ostashek Outfitting offered a mixed-bag hunt to the winner of the 1989 sweepstakes, sponsored by a popular magazine called *Petersen's Hunting*. The winner took part in the hunt at the end of August 1989. The hunt was reviewed in an article that appeared in the March 1990 edition, and both the article's author and the winner called it the hunt of a lifetime. This was excellent publicity for the company.

Competition

The Yukon has eighteen or nineteen active outfitters, employing on average four to six people and handling twelve to fifteen hunters per season. According to John, "British Columbia has hunting areas; they are very small in comparison to the Yukon, but they have a far more productive country. They produce a lot more animals per square mile than we do. The Northwest Territories has big hunting areas, but it's basically in the Mackenzie Mountains where the mountain sheep are. I think there are eleven outfitters." Big game trophy hunting is popular around the world, so Ostashek Outfitting must compete at an international level in order to be successful.

Pricing

Comparing their prices to other outfitters, John notes, "I can tell you we're in the ballpark. We are not on the low end of the scale. On some of our hunts, hunters tell us we're extremely expensive and on other ones they tell us we're average. We take one-third deposit on booking and we take another one-third on June 1 of the year they hunt and then the balance on arrival. It's a nonrefundable deposit."

Setting the prices is not easy.

It's trial and error. With the way we book hunts, I have to plan prices a year or a year and a half in advance, sometimes two years in advance. So I'm out on a limb to a certain extent. Basically our rates have been going up about 8% to 10% a year. In 1986 or 1987, we took an enormous jump because we went to a new system.

We used to have a set price where hunters could come here and shoot anything they wanted. Now we charge them for every animal. So if they're successful, their hunting is very, very expensive. Our base price for a fourteen-day hunt for 1989 is $7,100 (u.s. funds) but if they're successful in taking a grizzly bear, then it's another $1,800, so that brings it up to $8,900. They take a moose and a caribou that's another $1,700 so that brings it up around $10,000. We've had guys pay us $11,500 for a hunt.

Only the hunters that are successful pay when they take a trophy; they don't mind paying for it. This system is getting more and more common. We were one of the first to pioneer it, then two or three outfitters went that route. And now there's a wide variation of basically that same formula.

It is important that pricing for an individual type of hunt reflect its success rate. John explains, "Our grizzly bear hunts have been very, very successful in the spring. So we've just made a price increase with them because we're producing, so we think we're worth it. Now our bear hunts are $4,500 plus $1,800 for the kill, which is $6,300. Next year they will cost $5,000 plus $2,500 for the kill. We're very limited, because we only take four bear hunters in spring. So it gives us a substantial increase and we hope to maintain the 100% success rate that we've been enjoying."

Staffing
The biggest problem for Ostashek Outfitting is finding suitable staff.

It's a personal business. You're sending a guide out there with a fellow for five days and you're asking a lot of that guide. If he can't produce it, then it's your neck that's on the line. He can go to work for somebody else next year.

There is a certain percentage of guides who are doing it because they like it and those are the ones you want to get. There is a tendency among guides to move around from outfit to outfit and from area to area – go to British Columbia for a year or two, go to the Northwest Territories for a year or two and see some different country. A guide's a young man in his twenties. Once he gets married and has a family, then it's over for him.

In a typical year we'll have nine guides, a couple of cooks, my son, who is the mechanic, plus ourselves. Our biggest problem is hiring good, qualified people. I try to keep a couple of the best guides. I run the spring bear hunts and a couple of late moose hunts so that I can work them about six months of the year and encourage them to come back. But I can't do that with everybody.

The people that I'm looking for are people that want to be here, and I can't always get that. They're interested in getting paid good wages but the money isn't the main reason they are here. They're here because they love to guide and they love to hunt.

At the beginning of the season, the guides are given a schedule of bonuses that can be earned through the season and an information sheet on what Ostashek Outfitting expects from their guides in the way of professional behavior.

Depending on the quality of the kill, good guides can make an extra $1,000 to $1,500 a season in bonuses. For example, a guide can earn an extra $150 for a moose kill and on a ten-day hunt if you're paying a guy at $80 a day and you give a $150 bonus that brings him up to $95 a day. If they get a grizzly bear, it's an extra $200.

I fine them $200 if they come in with a female grizzly and they get a $200 bonus if they come in with a male. So it's a $400 shot every time. We have a video to help them identify male bears. They say it helps. The Game Branch brought in an expert from Alaska on identification. He talked to them for a day and showed films and pictures.

A guide will lose all his bonuses for an entire season if an illegal ram is killed. Finally, according to the information sheet, bonuses will be paid at the end of the season and only to guides who complete the season.

John says that he will employ Natives if he can get them and all his employees are treated equally. John notes:

Native employees don't take time off to do their own hunting when they're guiding. They have to be reliable. Most of them that we hire are reliable, but on occasion, we get the odd one that we have to let go. But that has nothing to do with race or creed or colour; it's just that we do that. We go through some white guys every year too – we weed them out. After thirty-two years in the business, I don't have very much patience with them anymore. This has been a good year because I've only let two go, so far. But they were only here a matter of days not weeks.

If they don't work out, we have to let them go immediately because we're putting them out there with a guy that's giving us thousands of dollars and we can't be there, holding his hand. If we put them out there and they don't go a good job, then we have to give the hunter a refund or a discount or we have to do something to make amends. I feel we do as a matter of principle of doing business and it's part of the obligation to the clients. I basically try to keep one guide that I know in each camp and then I can put another guide with him. I know it is going to work out no matter what happens, because there is somebody there with experience to prod the new guide along.

Financial Information

Ostashek Outfitting Ltd has earned a very high return on equity over the last four years, ranging from 45% to 66%, as indicated in Table 10. This high rate of return is somewhat misleading because the absolute numbers used to calculate these ratios are less than $20,000 and in most cases, less than $10,000.

The sales-to-assets ratio followed a general upward trend through-out the four-year period. For a $1.00 investment in assets, Oshtashek Outfitting generated almost an equal amount in sales revenue in 1985, rising to 1.25 times in 1987, a 29% increase. There was only a

Table 10
Financial Information for Ostashek Outfitting

	1985	1986	1987	1988
Return on Equity (%)	54	66	50	45
Sales/Assets (times)	.97	.86	1.25	1.21
Wages ($)	50,734	47,415	159,009	156,356

slight decrease in 1988. This ratio is an indication of the company's utilization of its capacity to generate revenue.

Since total revenues ranged from $200,000 to almost $400,000 and net income (defined as revenues less expenses) fell below $10,000 over this same period, it is clear that John chose to follow a financial strategy that leaves little income in the business. Given the total wages paid in 1987 and 1988, it is clear that the majority of the income was paid out as wages.

Reasons for Success

Ostashek Outfitting has earned an excellent international reputation in a highly competitive market. John says, "For Ostashek Outfitting, the reason for our success is the fact that I'm running the outfit myself. I'm into the camps everyday. We get comments all the time from the hunters, 'Gee, it's nice to be hunting with an outfitter that just doesn't take your cheque and we don't see him again.' It's that personal touch. Carol and I, we're the thing that makes the ball roll."

He stays in constant touch "Even as large as we're operating, I still get around to all the camps or I talk to them on the radio or I send a plane. I am in communication with that camp if I can't get there personally at least. It's that personal touch that keeps you on top of problems and lets you solve small problems before they get to be big blowups."

This philosophy of personalizing the business carries on through John's use of newsletters and a photo "brag book." Every customer receives an annual newsletter about the hunts that year and is asked to contribute a picture of his or her trophies for a brag book that Carol compiles. Each hunter gets to know John and Carol. John notes, "We have a lot of friends we got to know first as clients. We go and stay with them when we attend the trade shows in the States."

Establishing a good reputation is very important. "It really doesn't matter what you provide, as long as you provide what you said you

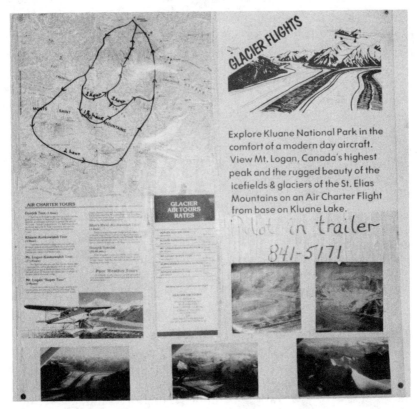

Map of Glacier Air Tour Routes

are going to provide. There are some hunters who are happy with just a packsack, while others want the first-class camp. What I've found interesting over the years is the truthfulness demanded by clients."

Nothing is perfect: "I've never had a major problem with our reputation. You're not going to satisfy everyone 100% of the time. There are going to be a number of years where you don't have a good harvest because of a number of reasons – you don't have quality guides or the wildlife populations are down in the areas that you're hunting. But I consider those problems over the long range and therefore they are very minor."

For John, his business is a success. "Self-satisfaction means my business is a success. I feel good about it. The fact that we have a lot of clients that are repeat hunters. We have a lot of clients that send their friends out with us. Those are the things that point to a successful business, I believe."

"Of course profit is important, but if you are in outfitting strictly for profit, then you'd best get into another business. There are businesses that will produce far more profit per dollar invested than the outfitting business will. Outfitting is basically a way of life. If you can make a good living at it and save a few bucks, then it is so much better."

Would his business weather a downturn? "I think that it is probably a recession-proof industry. We've survived over thirty years through good times and bad times. Maybe not as good as we would have liked it sometimes, but still there was enough there to survive. There are enough people around even in recessions that have money. If you look back to the 1930s, the outfitters did quite well. There was a pool of people that still had money to make those trips. If you are into wilderness guiding, they are the first ones that are going to lose in a recession because they are catering to the guy on the street. That's the guy that can't afford to go anywhere if a recession hits. They are going to feel the crunch a lot harder than a big game outfitter will. Our Glacier Air Tours will feel the crunch a lot sooner than our hunting business will.

Glacier Air Tours
According to John, "Glacier Air Tours is doing well. It's a business where you have a quality product. You make any reasonable effort and the business has got to grow. How big it grows depends on how aggressive you want to be in marketing. It's on demand after the first of May. We operate [regularly] from the first of June until the end of September. Then it's on demand until the end of October."

To this point, John notes, "Everything's operated under one company. Glacier Air Tours is just a trade name, but we're at the stage now where we're going to separate them. For several reasons, but basically, because we're thinking of selling the outfitting business."

John refuses to deal with one tour operator.

Relying on one tour operator is like putting all your eggs in one basket. I would never do that. I would never tie my hands that way, because then I'd be saying that's the guy I'm going to deal with and I'd have to be there for his people. I've got other people wanting tours. I think the business has got to be very diversified to meet a diversified market.

Right now, we're working with big tour companies that run the small groups of ten or twelve people. We've got a lot of them we're working for, and we picked up a few more this summer. We can service them quite handily because they want two or three trips of two or three hours and we can do two of them in the day. These people are coming on a regular basis all summer long. That's been the basis of our business over the last couple of years and what's given us a big surge. We've gotten into these tour operators' handbooks. They are using our product to sell their trips. It's one of their attractions on their northern trip – the glacier air tours out of Burwash Landing.

"We don't take chances with weather. We've had a fantastic summer this year. If the weather's bad then we just don't go into that area. We're located in a good place in the park because one side or the other side of the glacier is always open. You can see glaciers almost any day."

Areas for Improvement

There is a price for his success. "If I ran a smaller outfit, I could do a much better job of it. But I have to balance profit and what I want out of the business. I've always wanted to make a good living out of it. I always figured that I should be getting some return on my investment. For me it is more than just a way of life."

There is a great strain on family life. John says, "I'm at the ranch from April to November. Carol and I have no time to ourselves. We have people around us all the time. We just breathe a sigh of relief at the end of October when everybody's gone. Then we have six weeks or two months in Whitehorse that aren't too hectic. Then we're away for the next three months at the trade shows and that is basically the time we have out of a year to ourselves."

Finally, it is not a business that could be run successfully by a manager. John says, "If you can hire someone that could run it, then they will be running their own outfit. It comes down to the fact that you have to be able to do everything."

Environmental Friendliness

John is very aware of the fragile nature of the environment and the ease with which irreparable harm can occur. He says,

I've got great problems with the wilderness aspect of outfitting. I figure that it takes at least twenty wilderness clients to give you the revenue of one hunting client. You are doing twenty times the damage to the environment that one hunter is doing. I can argue that with anybody. If you've got twenty people in an area, then they are going to do twenty times more damage than one person is.

The person that is going in to hunt and is paying big bucks, is taking on the average of 2.2 animals a year from the Yukon. Now the Yukon is a great big place and nobody's missing those 2.2 animals that the hunter is taking and that's the average overall in the outfitting industry. There is very little impact on the environment. With the fragile environment you've got here, if you start using it twelve months of the year, then pretty soon you're going to have nothing. There is not enough snow cover to protect the environment in this country.

In the handout that John gives to each of his guides, he describes the procedures required for handling garbage. "We don't leave any garbage around. All the garbage is burned immediately. I think the fact that we've only had one or two bear raids in our camps over seventeen years, is an indication of the quality of the camps that we keep. We don't leave any meat in the camps, garbage is burned up immediately and the camps are kept neat and tidy."

John continues, "We don't pack food cans out from the camps. We burn all the cans because once you take that glaze off them, they just disintegrate and they're gone. So we have a garbage pit in every camp and we keep things burned up." Meat from the trophy animals is given to the local Native community at Burwash Landing. The meat is divided up and given to the elders.

Is trophy hunting an environmentally responsible activity? "As far as the harvesting of animals goes, outfitters are conservation minded. That's the idea of the bonuses for guides. They don't get a bonus just to get a moose; the spread between the horns has got to be fifty-five inches and it has to have at least three eye guards on one side. Sheep have to be at least nine years old or thirty-eight inches. Sheep only live to be ten or eleven years old, twelve years old maximum. A caribou has to have a minimum of five points on top and one side must have a shovel. Male grizzly bears must be over six feet. If they kill a female they lose $200. In four years, we've only taken three female grizzlies out of about thirty grizzlies since I instituted that system. We're not dumb. The wolves kill more game out here every year than I do."

Sustainability of the Business

John feels strongly that outfitting is an important component in any strategy for sustainable economic development in the Yukon.

I think we're very fortunate to be outfitting in the Yukon. Outfitting is accepted as a legitimate business in the Yukon by the majority of the people. If it was ever put on a ballot, "Do you want outfitting in the Yukon?" I'm sure that there would be a very, very high percentage that would answer "yes." At one time, it generated about 8% to 10% of the tourist dollar spent in the Yukon. That's quite a big impact for twenty businesses. There is always a little conflict with the resident hunters, some resident hunters. But we're very fortunate in the Yukon that we have such a large area and so few people.

... As people increase, there will be more and more pressure on the wildlife, and the outfitter will be the first one to cut back. Things are changing now from the way it was twenty-five years ago. The outfitter was just shut off in Alberta, and places like that. Now they are talking about dividing the allotment of wildlife in certain areas in the Yukon, but I still think that there is a great future for outfitting in the Yukon.

It is certainly a sustainable economic resource or development if it's left alone. It's not outfitting that is going to hurt the territories. It's the other pressures, from mines, putting more roads in, and more people getting into areas. Twenty outfitters couldn't begin to hurt the territories. There might be little pockets of it, but logistically, in two or three months, what can you do? How many hunters can you handle, when you have to have a guide for each hunter?

We fill out a form for every hunt for the government, before a guy can get out of the territory with a trophy. The government knows exactly what we are doing. They know exactly how many animals we take and the quality of the animals. No, it's not outfitting that will ruin the wildlife.

Future Development

John wants to sell Ostashek Outfitting and devote his full time and attention to Glacier Air Tours. He says, "I've been in outfitting for thirty-two years. I'm not getting out of it because it's not a good business, but I can turn it over and sell it to somebody else and they could have a good business of it for the next thirty-two years. Anyway, you lose interest in the business after a while. Outfitting is a young man's business. It's high pressure when you have your clients and you're trying to hire help. It's a short season in which to make your living and then you have the other nine months of the year when you have expenditures going out. It's high pressure to establish a reputation and keep that reputation. It's higher pressure now than it was twenty years ago. The competition is also far stiffer."

John has met the objectives of his five-year plan. He planned to increase his business to the point where he could show a potential purchaser what was possible with the business. After 1990, his fifth year, he plans to cut back to 75% of his current level of activity so that his life is not so hectic.

For someone to get into the business of outfitting, John says, "The only way is to buy out an existing outfitting business. However an outfitter can't sell his hunting area permit. The areas are not a saleable item, even though they do change hands. Basically, you sell your outfitting business and then apply to the government to transfer your area to the people who are buying your outfitting business, and the government has the final veto on it. It's costly to get into an outfitting business now. It's not something you can get into for $10,000 or $20,000. The last one that sold here was in the neighbourhood of $400,000."

Is it worth such a large outlay? "There are all kinds of opportunities. Nothing has changed in the eighteen years I've been operating here to hinder the outfitting business. Outfitting is going to be the same twenty-five years from now as it is today, unless some major development happens, for example, they discovered oil all over the Yukon. The demand will always be there. The demand is getting greater and greater because there are less and less places to go for quality hunting in the world. A new outfitter will survive as long as he provides quality service."

One factor that could affect the sale of his business is the question of land claims. A land claims settlement "would have an impact depending on who is going to buy it and what they intend to do with it. Certainly land claims are going to be a factor. I know it was a factor when I came here eighteen years ago. It's still a factor and it will probably still be a factor twenty years from now."

He has his doubts about a settlement.

First of all, the federal government doesn't have the money to settle land claims. It appears that the federal government is about to give them more land, but I don't know how far the Yukon government will go in fighting that. It may be a hardship on the outfitters. I expect to see a whole new round of negotiations and a whole new round of land selection before land claims are ever settled.

"We know where the land claims are, and if you listen to the land claims negotiators, no, we're not going to get hurt because we're going to be able to deal with the Indians or the Federal Government is going to pay us off. I would just as soon be left alone. I don't think land claims are going to put any outfitter out of business. But they may change the style of the business somewhat, but I don't even think that will be dramatic.

Glacier Air Tours
In terms of changes to operations, John says, "We are going to start narrating the tours next year with a PA system through the aircraft. We used to do it years ago. We found we were getting more people who spoke German than English, so it was not much good. We're going to give all people headsets next year then we'll narrate by just

punching a tape. The pilot can shut the tape on and off given where he is in the tour. We will do different languages eventually, such as French and German. Some of the people want it narrated, but most of the people are taken in by just seeing the view and just want the different peaks pointed out."

John may consider purchasing or leasing more airplanes. "If we require them, we will buy more planes. Right now, we've been able to handle the people this summer. I don't think we've lost a flight this summer. But if the market is there, then we'll look at expanding, either more aircraft or bigger aircraft. Right now a bigger aircraft would lose money because the volumes aren't there."

He favours buying, not leasing: "One thing about aircraft, they don't depreciate in value so you always have it to sell, if you decide you don't need it anymore. You're not going to lose money on an airplane as you do with vehicles or other things. I think the economics dictate you should buy it rather than lease it unless you buy an expensive aircraft."

At this point, John is not planning on actually landing on the glaciers.

We are trying to stay away from it because it's a hassle. Right now, we have a marketable product at a very reasonable price. If we were to begin stopping on the glaciers, then you've got the weather to contend with. You might not always be able to land on the glaciers, so then you'll have people complaining that we're supposed to land and we didn't land. There are all these variables, and given the size of the market, it's not worth it.

We are looking at expanding our services into the National Park under their new five-year management plan where they open up other areas for landing sites. Then we'll probably take hikers in and drop them off and pick hikers up with wheel planes from gravel bars on certain rivers. Right now, Andy Williams at the Arctic Institute's Kluane Research Station has a restricted licence for servicing skiers and mountain climbers. He's looking after that. We're not interested in that because there's not enough business as far as we're concerned to equip our aircraft to land at those high altitudes.

Summary and Conclusions

John Ostashek has followed a five-year plan that will make his business marketable and allow him to slow his frenetic lifestyle. Once the outfitting business is sold, he will be able to market the number of tours he desires on Glacier Air Tours. With a pilot in place already, John has the option to continue as the second pilot and fly only when it gets busy.

John's business philosophy has been to provide high quality with integrity and in a professional manner. This philosophy has served him well and has made his outfitting business very successful on an international level. He and his wife, Carol, provide friendly, personal service which is well-received by new and returning clients. A newsletter containing highlights of the past season, and a photo brag book, personalize the business for their clients.

John manages his hunting concession so that no area is over-hunted. Thus, he is able to maintain a high success rate and to price his product accordingly. He is knowledgeable about the financial aspects of the business and is able to set prices for one to two years in the future. Marketing the business by attending popular trade shows has worked, with a major amount of his business booked through the shows.

Although hiring good staff is a problem, John tries to attract good people and keep them. He offers the best guides the opportunity to work for six months each season. He trains them to offer professional service and to treat his customers properly, since the guides represent his business to the public. He lets staff go immediately if it is clear that they are unsatisfactory, in order to minimize any negative impact they may have on the business and to maximize customer satisfaction.

The business earns a good rate of return and maintains the standard of living that John wants. The business requires a lot of hours and effort over the season, with three or four months to recover and some time off for trade shows. It is a competitive business, necessitating a high standard of service and customer satisfaction in order to be successful.

John is sensitive to the environment and the impact his business has on it. His staff follow strict procedures for keeping the camps clean and burning garbage. He believes strongly that the environment is too fragile for wilderness outfitting. The amount of traffic that would make such a business feasible would wreak havoc on the environment. He notes that the culling of animals by his hunters raises the general quality of the wildlife. His bonus system encourages guides to take mature animals rather than any animal at all.

Big game outfitting is currently economically sustainable. As John points out, it appears to be recession proof, which is a big advantage. There is minimal damage to the environment and little impact on wildlife. The industry generates a good proportion of revenue for the local tourist industry, and all activities are monitored by the Wildlife Branch of the Yukon government.

Postscript – 1990

After the best season for sheep they have ever had, Ostashek Out-fitting was sold to John's son-in-law and a partner. John's son-in-law will be the on-site manager. John will continue to assist as pilot for the summer of 1991 but then they will be on their own.

The tourist season was slow in starting, and then the weather in the glaciers was very poor. This had an impact on Glacier Air. John states, "We were probably down 25 to 30% from 1989 due to the slow beginning and the weather."

With the sale of the outfitting business, John plans to concentrate on Glacier Air, develop it over the next four or five years, and then sell it.

We're doing massive advertising in 1991. We're going to put out 30,000 pieces of literature in the brochure racks at various stops along the Yukon highways. Our tours are very dependent on the weather, so you cannot pre-book. We give out information about another activity for tourists. The advertising will also go to the convention trade in Whitehorse. Several people might rent a vehicle and take a glacier trip if the weather's good."

We will continue to work with the ten tour companies that we established our business with over the last few years. We are looking at adding a larger aircraft such as a six-passenger Turbo 207. Glacier Air Tours is something to do eight months of the year. I want it to grow, but I don't intend to build it up into a big charter operation.

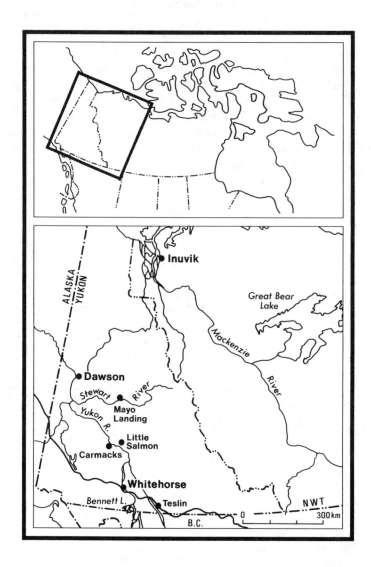

ENTREPRENEURS' ENDORSEMENT

I, the undersigned, acknowledge that I have read my business profile. I approve of the contents of the profile and recognize its accuracy in describing my business.

Dated _March 9,_ 1991

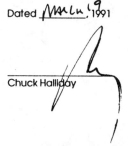

Chuck Halliday

12

TAYLOR CHEVROLET OLDSMOBILE DEALERSHIP WHITEHORSE, YUKON

Chuck Halliday, President and General Manager of Taylor Chev Olds, operates a successful car dealership serving a market of approximately 40,000 people in northern British Columbia, the Yukon, and north to the Mackenzie Delta in the Northwest Territories. Mr. Halliday was hired as secretary-treasurer on January 1, 1966 to run the business. Originally a banker from Vancouver, Mr Halliday became general manager in 1968. From Chuck's perspective, the key to the dealership's success is its reputation with its customers, with its staff, in the community, and with its major franchisors, General Motors and Tilden Rent-A-Car. Taylor Chev Olds is known for its friendly service, top quality products and willingness to accommodate the needs of its customers. Today, this dealership is the sole remnant of the Taylor and Drury trading post empire, which developed into a major Yukon business success story over the years 1899 to 1974.

History

*Taylor and Drury, Ltd**
The Klondike gold rush of 1898 appealed to Isaac Taylor, who had left Yorkshire to recover his health in dry Australia. William Drury, another Englishman from Lincolnshire, was also attracted to the Yukon. They met by chance and decided to pool their resources and open the first Taylor and Drury store in Atlin, British Columbia, on July 1, 1899. Taylor had $200 and Drury had a twelve-by-fourteen foot tent.

---

* All information and quotations in this section are taken from Warner, "Taylor & Drury," 75–80, and from personal interviews with Charlie Taylor.

Taylor & Drury Store, Whitehorse, 1901 (Source: Vancouver Public Library Collection, Yukon Archives.)

The two men went into the outfitting business and began buying gear from men who were disillusioned with the search for gold and were heading home. Their customers were the newcomers to the Klondike. After a few months of operation, Taylor left for Vancouver and Victoria, British Columbia, to stock up on goods. He returned via Lake Bennett, where a sizeable camp of gold seekers had become established. He was inundated with purchase requests from men preparing for the long trip by boat to Dawson City and urged Drury to move their tent and open shop in Bennett.

By the summer of 1900, the railway was completed to Whitehorse. Taylor and Drury were aboard the first train. They opened their store on Front Street, looking out across the Yukon River, to serve the town's 300 residents. Very quickly Whitehorse became a railway and river transport centre, with hotels and other businesses springing up as more than 1,500 men arrived that spring.

The partners decided to capitalize on the opportunity to trade furs with the Indians who were hunting and trapping throughout the Yukon. Taylor and Drury opened a trading post at the mouth of the Hootalinqua River, followed by one each at Little Salmon and Teslin. "Goods were paid for in kind, mostly in furs," recalls Charlie Taylor, one of Isaac's three sons. "The thing is barter is not a fair way of trade because you make the rules as you go along. The founders agreed upon that one thing that they would never allow barter. The

Hudson's Bay had a very bad name for that, for stacking furs against the rifle. They just made the barrel longer. These were the kind of stories the founders heard and they didn't want any part of it."

According to Isaac's wife,

In 1901, Mr. Taylor in taking a short trip of 70 miles down the river in a small boat, from one post to another, had occasion to stop to deliver a package at an Indian camp. The package contained a woman's skirt and was to be delivered to an Indian named Charlie. On inquiring at the camp, Mr. Taylor was informed that there was Big Salmon Charlie, LaBarge Charlie, Hootchi Charlie, and Shortie Charlie. As he didn't know which Charlie the package was intended for, Mr. Taylor remarked that there was "Too much Charlie." The Indian addressed replied at once, "Taylor, him roadhouse; Taylor, him wood camp; Taylor, telegraph man," and pointing to Mr. Taylor, "You Taylor. Too much Taylor."

In total, eighteen posts were opened in a circle that included Stewart River and Coffee Creek, although no more than twelve operated at any one time. Each post reflected the different attitudes of the men who operated them. However, they were similar: "Each post consisted of several buildings and they were set far enough apart so that if one burned, all would not be lost. This was a successful form of fire insurance – in 75 years only the Teslin store and the residence at Carmacks were lost to fire."

Taylor and Drury decided to issue its own money in the form of tokens, because paper money deteriorated very quickly. "Brass tokens were struck in denominations of $5, $10, and $20, and aluminum pieces worth 25 cents, 50 cents, and $1." Charlie Taylor recalls, "If the fur came to $500 or $600, that was a lot of money in those Depression days. Then the postkeeper would write a cheque. It was a thing about those cheques, Indians accepted them because then they came in and they would change them into trade money and carry on. Well, one fellow lost his cheque and he came into the trading house, and said, 'Oh, boy. I lost it. No paper, no good. Broke. I want $200.' I said, 'No problem' and I wrote another one out. 'Gee, that's easy money, you make money quick.'"

A post was opened at Mayo Landing on the Stewart River in 1919, after the discoveries of silver, lead, and zinc at nearby Keno Hill. In addition, several satellite stores were opened in the area. To supply these stores, Taylor and Drury purchased the "Thistle," a ninety-foot stern-wheeler, from British Yukon Navigation Co. Their interest in transportation continued when they learned in 1927 that they had been appointed by General Motors to handle four lines of automobiles, Chevrolet, Pontiac, Oldsmobile, and Buick.

One day in 1928, Charlie's father said to Charlie, "George Johnson is here from Teslin. If you can teach him how to drive, he'll buy a car." George had arrived in Whitehorse to sell his winter catch and had been very successful. "Well," Charlie says, "I figured the airport was the safest place; nothing up there to run into. George was a good trapper, one of the best around, but not much of a driver and when we finished the deal I offered him a good buy on an extra bumper – $26. I figured he would need it!" This was the first car the dealership sold.

The car had to be delivered to Teslin, but there were no roads. So the car was shipped on the "Thistle." "We did a lot of measuring and then we cut a hole in the side of the Thistle's deckhouse," Charlie recalls. "Even then the car was a little bit too high to get under the steam pipes and we had to let some air out of the tires to get it stowed aboard."

When the car arrived in Teslin, George Johnson built a short loop road by following a footpath and widening it to accommodate the car's width. He also made a parallel path for the other wheel. That summer, George did well by selling rides to the locals for $2 each. He was also very successful that winter in hunting timber wolves over the ice on Teslin Lake, which is eighty miles long. George painted the car white to camouflage it during the hunt.*

After the Alaska Highway was built, George drove the car back to Whitehorse for new tires. "He still had the original set, but the inner tubes had been replaced with strips of moose hide and the tattered rubber was stitched together with sinew." Thirty-four years after its original purchase, the car, still in operating condition, was repurchased by the dealership from George Johnson for the same amount George had paid for it.

By the 1930s, four sons were working for the Taylor and Drury empire, one Drury and three Taylors. Bill Taylor and Bill Drury worked at the car dealership. Car sales were slow until 1945, when the Alaska Highway and other roads throughout the Yukon Territory were constructed. At that point a separate company called Taylor and Drury Motors, Ltd. was formed and incorporated in 1947.

In 1953, sales volumes were such that General Motors decided to split the dealership into two groups, Chevrolet-Oldsmobile and Pontiac-Buick. Bill Drury sold his interest in Taylor and Drury Motors, Ltd. and purchased the Pontiac-Buick dealership, which he operated as Yukon Motors Ltd. Bill Taylor became General Manager

---

* "General Motors Yukon Dealership," 34.

Chuck Halliday and original 1928 auto

of Taylor and Drury Motors until Chuck Halliday assumed that position in 1968.

The other side of Taylor and Drury's operations continued to flourish. Construction of the Alaska Highway brought thousands of men to the Yukon. Charlie Taylor recalls, "Taylor and Drury became the first food suppliers on the Alaska Highway. We made deliveries to the civilian camps which replaced the United States Army as fast as the original construction came to an end." Travel by paddlewheeler and dogsled was replaced with aircraft and a trucking system that extended throughout the territory. Most of the posts closed as the demand for fur declined and Indians left traplines to settle in towns. By 1972, only the Whitehorse store remained.

Charlie Taylor says, "It was a department store. We sold a full line of ladies' wear. We expanded the store about two times. The non-food departments were on two floors. Men's wear, hardware, and the shoe department were on the main floor. Upstairs we had ladies' wear, notions, and fashion accessories." Charlie was general manager for some twenty years.

T & D's, as it was called, was a family business. This created some problems with customers who were also friends. Charlie explains,

"Family businesses are not the easiest thing to run. The customers were all friends and expected a better deal. It was a hard thing to handle. On the other hand we had a great deal of loyalty among our employees and we had some very, very fine employees. It was a family business with good service and friendship. We had credit business and we helped a lot of people out in rough times which we didn't always get paid for."

On July 31, 1974 Charlie Taylor retired. No heirs were interested in the store so Taylor & Drury, Ltd was sold after serving the North for seventy-five years. Only the car dealership remains in the family.

Taylor Chevrolet Oldsmobile Ltd

As previously mentioned, Chuck Halliday became General Manager of the dealership in 1968. The sales end of the business was conducted on Second Avenue in Whitehorse and service was provided on First Avenue. Chuck recalls, "It was quite a hodgepodge of buildings. The buildings had been built in 1942 and 1944, and part of them were dragged up from Taylor and Drury Ltd at about the same time. It did the job but not very efficiently. It was kind of hard on a cold day to find out what was going on."

At 5:00 a.m. on July 26, 1969, a fire was discovered in the Service Department in the First Avenue building. Chuck reminisces, "I got a phone call from the RCMP saying, 'You'd better get down here, there's lots of smoke and fire.' So I came down and I could see the smoke just going straight up. It was a damp, dull, rainy morning and I guess the furnaces had backfired and something caught and away it went." The parts department, service department, and body shop were completely destroyed, along with the entire parts inventory and shop equipment. The total loss was $280,000.

A new building was built and was ready for business by May 1970. The increased efficiency and larger display area warranted a new name. Taylor Chevrolet Oldsmobile Ltd was incorporated and became the operating company for Taylor & Drury Motors, Ltd which retained the fixed assets of the company. The dealership carries Chevrolet cars and trucks, Oldsmobiles, and Cadillacs.

Operations

Chuck Halliday has been the General Motors dealer since 1974. General Motors signs an agreement with an individual who is active in the business. Dealers have a long list of obligations and responsibilities to General Motors and to the community that they operate in. Chuck says, "We have to maintain a presence in the community,

Charles Taylor

we have to treat our customers properly, we have to maintain certain inventories, we have to have certain premises, and staffing for those premises. They're all just good business practices."

Sales targets and premise requirements for a dealership are set every five years. According to Chuck, they change according to the market and according to the size of the cars. "They are guides really. If you're starting with a vacant lot and a blank piece of paper, then that's what you're supposed to do. You can't just go by what they say, however. They're talking about Podunk, Saskatchewan, and Whitehorse, and downtown Toronto." says Chuck. If a dealer is making a legitimate effort to meet these guidelines in terms of service and customer retention but is unable to meet target sales figures, then he can expect as much assistance from General Motors as is necessary.

The dealership has twenty-six employees staffing several departments including sales, parts, service, the body shop, car rentals, and the office. Over the last twenty years, the firm has sold twice as many trucks as cars. Fleet car sales used to provide a significant portion of the revenues. Many of the large mining companies such as Cypress Anvil, United Keno Hill, Cassiar, and Clinton Creek bought virtually nothing but Chevrolets.

Chuck recalls, "We had a pretty good chunk of fleet business. Now that fleet business was hard to maintain because we had to go out there regularly. We'd be on the road every six weeks going to one or two of the mines." It all changed "when the world stopped in 1981 and 1982." Cassiar purchases few trucks as a result of its austerity program. United Keno Hill and Clinton Creek are shut down.

Reviewing his twenty-three years in the business, Chuck has seen many changes in the type of product demanded, the cost of that product, and market demographics.

The demand changes about every two months, and it's a little hard to keep up with when it takes about three months to get a vehicle in here. People want various models but yet they don't seem to want them for two-year runs. The demand is only there for six to eight months, or even less. Then the demand just goes away.

The trucks we have now are not trucks. They are fancy cars. You're looking at $20,000 for a nicely equipped Blazer. You're looking at $20,000 for a Lumina. So you don't save money by buying a truck, and you can get some trucks that will just blow your socks off. We had one roll out of here yesterday with a sticker price of $29,000 – a four-wheel-drive extended cab with all the trinkets and toys on it. I can remember ordering trucks with Bill Taylor's guidance. We'd sit down and price trucks out before we brought them in. Twenty-four hundred dollars and he was saying "You've got too much stuff on that thing. Get the price down. People won't buy it." Now we don't think about it; a $20,000 pickup is just run-of-the-mill."

Women coming into the market have changed the demographics. Chuck recalls, "If you look around town you see fewer and fewer women driving pickups. It used to be the "in" thing to drive the husband's pickup. Now they are coming in and buying small cars. We went on a six-month rampage where we sold twenty or twenty-five Cavalier Z-24s all to young women. They would come in and they would know what they wanted. There was a mixture of air conditioning and non-air and automatic and five-speed. We seemed to hit the right mix and we just sold them all."

This trend was fine but it ended, and women went on to something else. "They bypassed us completely. Beretta sales just went down one day. We didn't sell one in six months and we had eight here. Nothing's wrong with the cars but it's just that people are turned off them." This unpredictability has implications for the dealership which cannot predict demand in a timely manner. Chuck jokes, "We try. We use the swag method of forecasting. It's Scientific Wild Ass Guess."

Despite the long-standing relationship Taylor Chev Olds has had with GM, there can still be mixups when it comes to doing business in the North.

We have product campaigns where the manufacturer recalls the vehicles for whatever it may be. It's usually something that's going to wear out too soon but they're not life-threatening things. When a car or truck is delivered to a dealer, the unit becomes that dealer's responsibility for campaign purposes. If we sell it to another dealer, we can get it transferred to that dealer, but while it is our unit, any campaign in the next ten years will come to us if GM doesn't have a customer name. So things like product campaigns come to us.

A lot of vehicles go across the North on the barges in the summertime. We had some units farther North and we fixed the problem by having someone in Inuvik do the work. General Motors had approved it as a special claim. A lady in the Oshawa office caught it. We had thousands of vehicles on the next listing of uncompleted campaigns. She had taken everything north of 60° and assigned it to our number. This lady had learned that the dealer in Whitehorse could handle the North. But she didn't know how big the North was. So she just found all entries with NT or YT on the postal code and she programmed the computer to shoot it all at us. But she had to go back the following month and take it all out manually."

We thought it might help if she had a better idea of the distances involved. So we had some fun with her. We went to a geological survey company and got one of their big maps and had someone present it to her with a big ribbon on it so she could see where everybody is. There was a great big round sticker on Whitehorse and the other one on Frobisher Bay that is directly to the far north of St John, New Brunswick. Of course it was impressive on this map because it was about five feet long.

Financial Information

Unit sales have increased since 1966 from 100 cars annually to 400 or 500 cars per year. Return on owner's equity has decreased steadily over the last five years but remains healthy at 29.3% in 1988, as can be seen in Table 11.

The sales generated by the company's investment in assets fluctuated from a high of four times to less than one over the five-year period. This ratio shows how well the firm's assets are being put to use. A high ratio could indicate that the firm is working close to capacity. It may prove difficult to generate further business without an increase in invested capital. For every $1.00 invested in assets, the company generated sales at a rate of 0.9 times in 1986 to 4 times in 1984.

Table 11
Financial Information for Taylor Chevrolet Oldsmobile

	1984	1985	1986	1987	1988
Return on Equity (%)	40.3	25.4	31.0	31.5	29.3
Sales/Assets (times)	4.0	3.6	0.9	3.1	3.2
Total Salaries (000$)	648	699	746	826	914

Total salaries have increased almost $266,000 or 1.4 times over the five-year period from 1984 to 1989. The increase may in part be due to the high historical rate of return on owner's equity. The company may have chosen to pass on its excess earnings to its employees.

Reasons for Success

The reputation Taylor Chev Olds has earned over its fifty-two years of operation in Whitehorse is the major reason for its success. Chuck says, "Just be straight with people. If there's a problem tell the customer or tell General Motors. Here's the problem; we screwed up or you screwed up, or here's what broke. Just do it right the first time." Their reputation with their staff, their customers, the community, and their franchisors, General Motors and Tilden Rent-A-Car has been critical. Another reason for the firm's success is its pricing strategy.

Reputation with Staff
Company policies in dealing with staff seem to foster loyalty and responsibility in their employees. Chuck states, "I have great staff. I have brought them along to the point where they can do anything they want, and they know they can. Now they won't, because they know they can usually get hold of me within a day wherever I am. But if they want to do something then go ahead and do it, they've got to make the decisions themselves. Hopefully, the decisions are right."

When mistakes are made, Chuck tries to be as tactful as possible. "When they're not right, I will very, very nicely tell them about it. I'll say, 'Hey, guys, this is what you did; this is what you should have done.' Then next time, hopefully, they'll do it the right way. It's cost a few dollars, but I don't have to worry about what they are doing."

Loyalty is reflected in the long employment histories of many of the employees working at the dealership. Chuck proudly states, "At

Taylor Chev Old's Car Lot

one point in time we had over 400 years' experience amongst thirty people and the majority of that experience was with me. They've enjoyed working for me. I shouldn't say *for* me, I should say *with* me. I think it's a pretty nice place to work because we can all joke."

Chuck describes the atmosphere at Taylor Chev Olds as friendly and happy. "They know that if they come to me with something intelligent, that if they've thought it out and I can't argue with them, we'll probably do it unless it's going to cost a whole bunch of money. It's a culture; no, I guess it's a way of life. It's the way you'd want to be treated. I don't ask anybody to do anything around here unless I would be able to do it."

Reputation with Customers and Community

Excellent service and friendly staff help to keep customers satisfied and loyal to the dealership. Service is especially important because bad publicity from dissatisfied customers would spread rapidly. The service department staff are highly trained individuals with many years of experience in the business. They all go to courses held by GM to keep up-to-date on all the latest techniques. GM also provides a private number to call at the Technical Assistance Center. Service staff can talk to the engineering staff who have access to a computer bank of problems and solutions.

Regular customers who want to rent a car will often come in and fill a thermos with coffee for the ride. The coffeepot is always available to staff and customers. As Chuck says, "Friendliness. It's a small town and the guys seem to get out and around a lot so we know a lot of people. We try and have a friendly atmosphere for staff and for the customers. If the customers are happy then the staff are happy." Chuck is heavily involved in community groups and associations and has been for many years.

Chuck's staffing policies are the same for all his employees whether they are Native or white, male or female. His only concern is that his employees can handle the job. The level of expertise required for most jobs at the dealership has increased substantially, especially through computerization.

Reputation with General Motors and Tilden Rent-A-Car

A relationship of trust appears to have developed between Taylor Chev Olds and its franchisors. Regular contact with GM is the norm. Chuck says that most dealers get a telephone call every week to check their progress. At Taylor Chev Olds the situation is different. Chuck comments, "With our reputation we don't see them very often. We haven't had a GM rep in the building, and that's fine with me. I phone them if I need something, and if I don't phone them then they know everything's okay. We were one of the first dealers in the Vancouver zone to get warranty self-authorization. We could authorize any warranty job we wanted; we don't have to go to anybody. Some of the guys in the Vancouver zone are just getting to that point right now."

A good reputation with GM has other benefits. Chuck notes that, although they may make some mistakes through misdiagnosing a problem, these occurrences are rare. Chuck states, "If we want to replace an engine in your car and the car's a year old, we'll just go ahead and do it and we'll tell GM after the fact. We may not even tell them; they'll just get the bill. They'll pay with no questions. There are other dealers, that if they try to spend a hundred bucks on General Motors, the General wants to know why and wants to see the job."

Taylor Chev Olds holds the franchise for Tilden Rent-A-Car, covering the Yukon Territory with the exception of Watson Lake. They have had the franchise since July 1958. Chuck states, "It's had its ups and downs over the years, as all businesses have. It's still a big part of our business."

Pricing Strategy
Chuck has the choice to offer special financing deals to entice customers into the dealership or to offer a fair price. He has chosen to offer a fair price, based on the experience of two dealers in Vancouver. He says, "I could offer 1.9% interest right now. Two years ago two Pontiac dealers with Acadians went head to head. One was offering a good price. The other was offering 1.9% or 2.9% financing. Well, Santa Claus is dead, I'm afraid, and the cost of the difference between the current rate and the 1.9% was added on to the cost of the car. It's a fact of life. The one that was offering straight price sold 50% more than the other one. The only people that went in [for the special deal] were ones that didn't know what they were buying and they didn't know what kind of a deal they were getting. They only looked at one part of it."

Challenges

One particular weakness that affects the amount of business the dealership can do is the size of the market for GM products. Chuck does not feel that the market is growing enough to have a substantial effect on sales: "There is no way that I could double my sales. There are always people who buy Toyotas, Fords, and Chryslers."

Environmental Friendliness

Chuck feels that basically the dealership and its products are environmentally responsible. The dealership takes care that waste oil is picked up by a disposal service. Some of the waste oil is used for heating and some of it is dumped. The paint booths have special filters, and used batteries are picked up by a local recycler. There is no asbestos on site. Emission controls are standard equipment in all vehicles. The only option that currently is not environmentally responsible is air conditioning. Chuck notes, "However, we now have equipment that allows us to capture the freon during air conditioning repairs and to reload it into the vehicle."

Furthermore, "The vehicles we sell are virtually all recyclable. You can take a car and melt down the plastic and reuse it. Only the fuel is not reusable. Also, cars are much more fuel efficient than they used to be."

Summary and Conclusions

Taylor Chev Olds is a family-owned business with a rich history of operation in the Yukon. The current general manager, Chuck Halliday, runs the business in a manner that encourages staff loyalty and responsibility. His policies have resulted in an excellent reputation with General Motors and Tilden Rent-A-Car as well as with customers. The firm's standing in the community is exemplary.

The long employment records of the dealership's employees is an indication of the success of Chuck Halliday's open, direct, and respectful way of dealing with his employees. He does not seem to face the same staffing problems that many small businesses must deal with. The fact that he is dealing with skilled people may also contribute to this result.

Chuck's customers receive good service on their products. His service department staff are highly trained in all recent service practices. He has been able to deal with the problems of isolation and distance in serving his customers by using creative solutions. He will make deals with other garage owners in distant towns in order to meet the obligations of warranties and product campaigns.

The firm's excellent reputation with General Motors and Tilden Rent-A-Car has resulted in relatively little interference and monitoring of operations by these major franchisors. Because of its overall reliability, Taylor Chev Olds is not penalized for the few mistakes it makes.

Chuck Halliday and many of his staff are very active in the community. Chuck has been president of the Chamber of Commerce, is treasurer of the Yukon Anniversaries Commission, and has been a director of the Tourism Industry Association of the Yukon and a member of the Kiwanis and the Rotary clubs. The list continues. This presence in the community is part of an overall spirit of co-operation and concern for the community in which the company operates.

This concern extends to the environment. The impact on the environment is minimized to the best extent possible with current technology. Policies are in place which minimize the impact of repair work and vehicle operation.

Finally, in Chuck's words, "We've come a long way. These employees and I have grown up together in the business. There are some real experts in their various fields in this building. But I didn't put this group together; it came together and has thrived."

Postscript – 1990

Chuck continued on in his position as president and general manager. Sales remained steady throughout the year. He was named the Business Person of the Year in October 1990 by the Yukon Chamber of Commerce. The award recognizes outstanding members of the local business community for their business performance, community involvement, contribution to workplace improvements, business expansion, and job creation.

Charles Taylor was inducted into the Order of Canada. Charles was described in a federal government press release as a former businessman and politician who "made a significant contribution to the development of the Yukon through a wide range of activities, including the provision of trading services to accommodate a growing Northern population."

In early January 1991, Chuck Halliday purchased all outstanding shares of all the Taylor & Drury companies from various family members. He amalgamated these companies into one holding company, thus ending the Taylor & Drury era. In late January 1991, the land and buildings from which Taylor Chev Olds operates were sold to the government of the Yukon Territory and leased back for two years. It is Chuck's intention to sell the dealership in the next year.

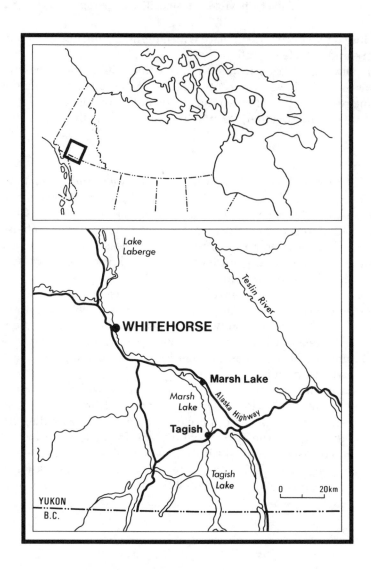

ENTREPRENEURS' ENDORSEMENT

I, the undersigned, acknowledge that I have read my business profile. I approve of the contents of the profile and recognize its accuracy in describing my business.

Dated July 9, 1991

Lorne Metropolit

13
YUKON BOTANICAL GARDENS
Whitehorse, Yukon

A surprise awaits visitors to the city of Whitehorse. A long-time resident has realized his dream of building the northernmost botanical show gardens in the western hemisphere. Lorne Metropolit conceived the idea, developed it over a year and a half, and then built phase one and opened his doors in the summer of 1985.

The Yukon Botanical Gardens are located on twenty-two acres of land on the southern outskirts of the city. Visitors are treated to beautifully landscaped gardens throughout the summer months. Approximately 750,000 annuals and perennials are planted each year and there are almost 1,000 plant species in the garden. These include indigenous flowering and non-flowering plants, as well as fruits and vegetables. Other attractions include the garden centre, where plants and vegetables are sold, farm animals that live in Old MacDonald's farm, an exotic bird display, and a duck pond, which was completed in 1989 as part of phase two.

Lorne has met the challenge of making his dream of a northern gardens a reality. It has been a struggle financially but in his mind it is a success. It allows him to work with plants, which he enjoys, and it has begun to give him a financial return on his investment. The future looks bright for the gardens as the number of visitors has grown each year.

History

Lorne grew up in Cudworth, a small town south of Prince Albert, Saskatchewan. He started his own landscaping company in high school, drawing on gardening skills that he had learned from his parents. His first jobs included working in provincial parks, where he had his first experiences in tourism. He went on to earn a diploma in recreation technology and his bachelor's degree in education. He taught survival courses at a local college, where he became familiar with edible and nonedible plants and other plant lore.

Lorne moved to the Yukon, where he taught school for a couple of years in Dawson City and Faro and worked for the government. He then worked as a miner, earning the initial funding for his business venture. When he decided to start his own business, he considered his favourite pastime of gardening and thought, "Maybe people would like to look at the wildflowers and the trees, with everything labelled, along a nice pathway." This was the beginning of Yukon Botanical Gardens.

Lorne spent some time drafting a business plan, which he used when he approached the Department of Regional Economics and Expansion (DREE) for initial funding. He recalls, "I went to them with a flimsy business plan. I think the thing was three or four pages. They said, 'Lorne, you've got to get more meat into it and do some talking to different tourist people.' I worked with one of their counsellors. He reviewed my progress and helped me develop my plan. From there, it was homework for me. I had to check the market, so I talked to WesTours, Princess Tours, and Royal Highway Buses in Seattle, and Atlas Tours and many other companies involved in tourism."

Since the market seemed to exist for this type of project, Lorne began planning the layout of the gardens. "Since an indigenous wildflower bed looks fantastic for only about three or four weeks, I began to research vegetables and fruit. I built a cardboard replica of my plans in order to make presentations." The next step was to find and acquire the site for the gardens.

"The area I was interested in had basically turned into a garbage dump. People were just backing in and dumping their garbage, digging up soil, or digging up trees for transplanting. The year before I moved in, the fire crews were called in five times for abandoned campfires that were just left burning. The area was destined to be a charred mess. I was determined I wanted to get into that area: the location was good and the rock formation gave the area a unique character."

The city of Whitehorse got involved: "They walked right in and took over. They came up with a clause which stated that if I got the land, then the city would lease the property from the government and then lease it to me. So now the city is my landlord."

The construction phase took two years. Lorne had originally planned to complete the whole gardens in two years, but it quickly became apparent that his funding was insufficient, and he revised

Lorne Metropolit

his strategy. He decided to build the gardens in phases. At the peak of construction, he had twenty-two employees working for him. They moved approximately 3,000 cubic yards of soil onto the site for the gardens.

DREE approved only a certain percentage of the construction budget and released these funds thirty days after the gardens opened. This meant that there was a shortfall and Lorne also had to find interim financing during construction. He worked during the winter and his wife Jean worked full time in order to generate cash flow. They used these savings, but additional bank financing was required.

Lorne recalls:

Even with a written statement from the government guaranteeing a portion of the funding, every bank in town turned us down because it was botanical gardens in the North. They said, "Lorne, it sounds great, it looks fantastic with the amount of work you've already done. I think you've got something here. But there's no precedent. We can't help you. If you want to open a restaurant or a hotel, how much money do you want? But for a show gardens in the North, sorry."

Even if I had owned the property, they would not have jumped in because of the nature of the project. Too different. I finally found a bank that was interested, the Royal Bank. I talked to them and it looked like we might be able to negotiate something. It was Christmastime and we decided to take a break for a month because it was hard getting government people and bankers to the same meeting. We reconvened in January but the fellow from the bank was transferred. He never even told me. So it was a new guy and we had to start all over again. My proposal was rejected again. But the first guy had given me his word that he could probably get me at least $40,000. So we finally got the $40,000 from the bank. With my savings and the $40,000, we got through.

When that funding was gone, Lorne and his wife decided that they would sell their house and move onto the site in order to cut down on costs. They were going to save the money, but Lorne recalls, "We sold the house and my wife didn't know it but I spent all the money. It was a bit of an accident because I overspent on construction. It was the result of poor financial planning and not sticking to the plans. I worked hard all day, every day, twelve hours a day plus evenings. Then I'd come home at 10:00 or 11:00 o'clock every night. With the short growing season here, I had to work hard. I didn't have time to add up how much money I spent that day or that week and compare it to my budget. I kept it all in my head."

He found himself in the same position in the second year. He needed some interim financing until DREE's money was released. Lorne recalls, "I went to the Federal Business Development Bank, who I consider to be legalized loan sharks. They were charging phenomenal rates. Everyone else was getting charged 7% to 10% and they wanted 15-1/2%. I paid it. I took a loan out with them for twenty-four days. I was furious but what can you do? There were no private loan sharks in town. So I got the money and it was enough to carry us through until DREE paid and that got us through that year. We opened the second year of construction, in midsummer."

Operations

The tomato greenhouse starts up in February, and bedding plants are started in early or mid-March in the three other greenhouses. Most of the annuals are grown from seed. They usually are ready for planting by late May or early June. Planting takes five weeks but is still risky even at that time. Forty thousand plants were lost on June 24, 1989, due to a late frost. Imported flowers include shasta daisies, delphiniums, Iceland poppies, and asters. Lorne notes, "The

Yukon Botanical Gardens

wildflower garden includes saxifrage, fleabane, and cinquefoil. The vegetable show garden displays twenty-two varieties of potatoes. The orchard is bountiful, with crabapples, plums, gooseberries, pin cherries, cranberries, and strawberries."*

Initially, the gardens were just Lorne's dream. He recalls, "In the beginning, there were some shaky moments with my wife, Jean. She didn't have much choice. It's hard for one person to impose a dream on another, looking at it from her point of view. There I was totally upsetting the entire household and gambling everything, including our livelihood and our way of life. Now the shaky moments are gone. She's gotten much more involved in it, too. She dreams about this and that so it's part of her dreams, too, and is no longer a nightmare. Jean does the books and manages the gift shop. She does all the ordering and the staff scheduling. I do everything outside. The dream is now our dream."

During the peak of summer operations, there are close to twenty staff. Lorne tries to attract workers who are interested in the gardens but says, "My wages are the pits. However, the older they are, the less money-hungry they are; then they get involved in the gardens.

---

* Serup-Jansen, "Garden of Earthly Delights," 24.

It's a personal thing. It's their gardens and I'm the manager. It's up to me to create that commitment. I've always felt I've been able to create enthusiasm and people take it with them. But then again, there are days when I just say, 'Why do I have to be nice to that person to have them work hard?' I'm tired of it. But I find I get more work out of people when I'm nice to them. I say, 'Would you? or when you're finished, do you think you could?' instead of ordering them around."

Native and non-Native employees are treated equally. Lorne says, "If any of my employees were late then I'd have to have the whole scenario laid out. In most cases, I'd give them another chance. But I run a pretty tight ship. I'm fair but I'm tough. So everybody gets two chances and that's it." The staff work hard and may be offered overtime in the busy summertime. "If we have some extra work to do, I ask those who want to work, and those who want to, do."

When Lorne did his market research, he discovered that if he wanted to have a really successful show garden, he needed to have 200,000 people within a fifty-mile radius. There are only 23,000 people in Whitehorse and the number of tourists passing through Whitehorse from June through September was 115,000 in 1987 and 141,000 in 1988. So Lorne wants to attract tourists and residents of Whitehorse to his Gardens. To that end, he holds a number of events throughout the summer to involve the local residents and attract them to the gardens.

The Yukon Gardens received national attention when they were featured on the Canadian Gardener television program in September 1989. Lorne says, "They do a garden show out of Vancouver and they came up and did the gardens as part of a Northern garden program. Super. They are going to do a segment on the tomato house sometime this winter."

The rates for viewing the gardens are as follows: adults, $4.75; students aged 12–18, $2.75; children 11 years and under, $1.00; children under 1 year, free. A family season pass costs $25 and an adult season pass is $10. Lorne explains, "I am contemplating an increase in the gate admission in 1990. It will be the first increase since we've opened. Consider the local tourist-oriented stage shows, which are an hour, and compare the amount of money they've invested in that business. I spend that amount in a week and they're charging $12 to $14 per person. Investment in river tours is small compared to the gardens and they're charging $8 or $9. For some reason, people don't think twice about getting on a boat and paying $9. Yet to walk through a big botanical gardens and pay $9, are you crazy? It takes a lot of educating. It's going to be tough for us."

Both Lorne and his wife work during the winter to augment their income from the gardens. Lorne is a substitute teacher until Easter break in March, when he returns full-time to the gardens. For Christmas 1989, he planned something new.

We're going to start a crop in here of poinsettias that we'll market at Christmas. My product will be ten times better than what other stores sell now, if not this year, then next year. The imported plants get beat up, they are in boxes, and they are in the dark for a long time.

The tomato house isn't making that much money now. My prices might be a little high and my production isn't up to where I want it. My tomatoes are selling for just above production costs. But it's to the point where it's still worthwhile keeping. So the poinsettias are going to be a total bonus crop. The boilers have to be going anyway, but the greenhouse isn't going to cost much more to heat. So it should be a good performing cash crop.

I think of all the wood I have to cut or buy or both, and having to get up every morning and evening with the boiler. If it doesn't work next year, I'll shut the whole works down at the end of September and have a [good] fall. I used to do a lot of hunting and fishing but I haven't for a long time.

Financial Information

Yukon Gardens has a typical financial history for many start-up operations. There has been no net profit earned since the gardens opened. Sales revenues have increased from 1986 to 1989, but at a decreasing rate. For example, 1987 sales revenues were up by 310% over 1986 but 1989's sales were only up 49% over 1988. This is not a surprising trend, as this is a new attraction, some of the early visitors were probably from Whitehorse and very little revenue was generated in the first year. The 1989 sales revenues probably reflects a truer picture of how often tourists to the Yukon are frequenting the gardens.

Wages paid to employees have grown from $14,000 in 1986, when the gardens operated for only eight weeks, to $59,000 in 1989. Lorne has expanded his gardens each year and has added the new attractions and the greenhouses. This expansion has increased the required manpower, which is reflected in the higher wages.

Reason for Success

Lorne is generally pleased with the positive feedback he has received about the gardens from tourists. The growing interest in the gardens is reflected in the increasing number of visitors each year. He at-

Yukon Botanical Gardens

tributes this success to the uniqueness of being the most northern botanical show gardens in North America.

It's a different type of garden. It's not your average botanical show garden. What we have in common with the botanical show gardens is that we do have a large display of flowers, shrubs, trees and different types of plant life that don't flower, that are all labelled. What we have on top of that are sections that display indigenous species. Then we get into a vegetable show garden showing all the different types of vegetables that can be grown up here. Also, I've got all the different types of fruit that can be grown in our area.

We want to show our visitors everything we can regarding nature. For visitors to walk in and see all the flowers that grow naturally in the Yukon, they would have to spend ten summers walking the territory. One interesting flower we have is the fireweed. It's the Yukon colour, it's in ditches, and it's the Yukon Botanical Gardens emblem. It's very pretty but it can be a pain. Each plant produces hundreds of seeds and they go everywhere they are not supposed to. So we hoe and continuously fight the fireweed, but they look pretty. There is also moss campion. It looks like a basketball that has been sunk into the dirt, with only a third of it showing. Its flowers are small and brilliant pink. They look like pink beachballs. Its natural habitat is high in the mountains.

As far as berries go, the crowberry or moss berry is good to eat. It's a humorous berry because you can be walking along and you'll sit down to take a break and you get up and you'll have little purple spots on your bum from sitting on them. There's also a buffalo berry that I learned about from Native friends. It's also a humorous berry. What they do is to pick it, crush it, and whip it until it turns into a pink foam. Then they sit around the campfire and eat the foam. Pretty soon everybody starts burping because it causes gas. It turns out to be quite a party. It's a way to pass the evening.

Areas for Improvement

Lorne identifies lack of capital, the need to educate the public, and the gardens' susceptibility to the weather as his biggest obstacles in making the gardens a success. He now thinks he should have opened a portion of the gardens much sooner in order to have generated some cash flow. For example, he could have opened the Garden Center for commercial sales or he could have built parking stalls for recreational vehicles. That course of action might have minimized the need for financing from outside sources during the construction phase.

Secondly, Lorne feels that the public needs to be educated about botanical gardens and what is possible to grow in the North.

We're well off property-wise but cash flow is still a problem. What I've found is that even though the gardens are growing, I still have to do a phenomenal amount of marketing. People from Vancouver have no problem coming to the gardens. People from Alberta and Saskatchewan have never had [botanical] gardens in the prairies. They don't know what to expect. They go to a gardens and it's like visiting their neighbours. They can't conceive of paying to go see these gardens."

People come up here and they say, "What kind of gardens are you going to have in a northern climate? It can't be worth much, so why go?" They look at the comments in the signature book and they peek around the corner saying, "Give us a glimpse," and then they come in.

Most of the comments by the visitors are positive.

"I have the daybook where there are thousands and thousands of signatures by tourists with comments like–"fantastic"; "terrific"; "unbelievable"; "unexpected"; "wow"; "a delight to see." However, once last year and once this year, a person has come through and said "This is a total waste of time and a farce." It was locals more than tourists. I guess, I'm sensitive and it hurts me. I remember the first one I got. I had hundreds of people saying how nice the gardens were, and one person wrote in the day book, "Not bad, I could have done better with all the government money you got." That went through my head a million times, over and over and over again even though I got one negative comment and hundreds of compliments.

I look at those negative comments and I realize that they have no background to judge because this is probably the first show garden that they have ever seen. The negative comment turned out to be a case of jealousy due to the government grants. However, there is hardly a business in the Yukon that hasn't received some form of grant, from student-assisted programs to power subsidies.

Intensifying his marketing efforts may attract those people who have not been to the gardens yet. There will always be people who will not appreciate his achievements, but the thousands of people who do will more than compensate for those few who do not.

The gardens are highly susceptible to poor weather. Lorne says, "It annoys me quite often. We work so hard to create something worthwhile here. The weather doesn't have much bearing on any other attraction, but with mine, it's impact is total. That's the bad thing about my business. I can have the best thing in the world, but if it's drizzling outside, I can take a shot in the parking lot and I won't hit a thing." In order to deal with this shortcoming, Lorne is looking at expanding the gardens to offset the effects of poor weather on attendance. The options he is considering are discussed below.

Environmental Friendliness

Environmental responsibility is an important issue in the way Lorne has developed the gardens. He built the Yukon Gardens in a way that integrates the natural flora with transplanted flowers, fruits, and vegetables. In fact, he reclaimed what was essentially a garbage dump. He now identifies himself as an environmentalist. This was not always the case.

Lorne recalls, "In past years, I would probably say I was the opposite to an environmentalist. I suppose in my younger days, like many people, I mistreated the land by not being environmentally sensitive." The policies he has in place in the Gardens reflect his concern for the environment. Lorne says, "To show wildflowers, you have to go dig them up or take the seed. Digging them up is forbidden in North America. We only go with seed."

Theft is a potential problem. "I have to be careful. For instance, there's an indigenous boreal forest orchid I have in the Garden that orchid fanciers would pay a great deal of money to own. For that reason it hasn't been labelled yet. I don't know if I will label it. I've been approached by many outsiders to buy certain plants."

Future Development

Lorne is contemplating several options. He may decide to continue expanding or he may sell the gardens.

I'm pretty proud of the gardens now because it's my own business that I scraped out of the bush. I've created something beautiful that is unique and different. I have to slap myself every now and then. But right now – since there's no money – I'm living on a little ego, I guess. That's what's paying my salary right now. I cash a cheque of ego every two weeks. In 1989, we had to break even. We did. So that was a big, big milestone. So the next thing would be able to start paying me a wage.

The gardens are not creating a profit yet, so I want to change and diversify it. In the short term, phase two will develop the gardens back to the rocks and that's on-stream for next year, 1990. It's a small area that I think we can pull off without too much trouble. In addition, I am going to turn the Garden Center into a large show greenhouse. I'm going to have long English cucumbers, tomatoes, pumpkins, zucchini, and cannonball watermelons. They are miniature watermelons that are twice as sweet as the regular ones. Then we'll introduce indoor plants. We're continuously asked for them. There's really no one that markets them here. Hopefully, these changes will mean that we can meet our goal, financial independence for the gardens.

As for the long term, "The original concept was that there would be five different attractions off the parking lot in five main directions. It would be the type of thing where the family can come and spend a day at a restaurant, some rides, and the gardens. We were thinking of water slides at one time. This year would have been great, but last year we would have lost it all because of the weather. So basically the designs, the ideas and the desire are there, but when you start these things you need phenomenal cash flow and we just don't have it. We've been very fortunate to get this far."

It is frustrating continually having to build additions to the gardens.

I've got to stop building. I hope that the gardens can begin to live on its reputation and start supporting itself, which I'm fairly confident it can. However, at the moment because things are changing rapidly, I'm finding since I have created a business that raises the question: do I want to be a businessman or a creator? Will I be satisfied with being a businessman? It might not be a nine-to-five job, but if it's still a challenge, then I know I will.

I have to start examining my dreams. How many are economical? If I build phases six, seven, eight, and nine and they're all gardens, then it's not going to make a heck of a lot of difference to the visitors. It's still a garden and they're just little additions now. The other thing is I have all my eggs in one basket. So now I'm changing philosophies and dreams. It's nice to get a little money in the pocket. It's the first year that we didn't go in the red. I had my banker come out with his assistant to congratulate me midsummer that we hadn't used our floating loan in seven weeks.

Mind you, the money's not coming in fast enough. I've worked too hard and I've created something that, I guess, was never designed to be a big money-making dream. I've worked so hard, now I'd like to build something where I could make some money. It's hard when I've spent every ounce of energy, every minute of thought on construction and design of some monstrous thing, and everybody's saying, "It won't work out, you can't do it, you're stupid." The effort is continuous and there is no way I can stop. Whether it was determination or stubbornness, I built the gardens, but the responsibility to do that has always been mine. I get tired of that. I've gone so far, but I have to watch it because all of a sudden, my energy and my enthusiasm disappears. I don't want that to happen so I might change my goals. I find that starting companies is fun and challenging.

Lorne has found that his priorities have changed since he started the gardens.

Now I'm picking out things I work on, where before I would do anything for a nickel and I would work like an idiot. But my family relationships suffered. My daughters don't know me because of the hours I put in. Now I'm starting to reevaluate my priorities. I'm in a position to do that because I've paid my dues. That's another milestone.

In 1988, I taught all winter just to pay off debts that had been incurred that fall. I was almost in tears every second day for about a month because we had incurred so many debts and had such a crappy season that it was tough. It was a severe setback and mentally depressing. I just wanted to close it all down and get into anything else. Now I'm finally getting the time and a few dollars to take a break rather than work here day in and day out. That takes the love out of it. So if I don't do something soon, I'll hate it and we'll be bankrupt and I'll be out of the gardens in a year. I'm always burned out in the fall anyway, because from March, it is go, go, go.

Summary and Conclusions

Lorne's experience with creating and building the Yukon Gardens out of wilderness has been a rich learning experience which provides a number of lessons for inexperienced entrepreneurs. It has been an all-consuming exercise to build the gardens, in terms of time and money. In realizing his dream, he faced lack of support from public officials and the financial community, but he accepted the challenge and persevered. The initial marketing he completed before the gardens were built indicated that tour companies would support the gardens. That indication of interest was not binding and their support is slow in materializing, but that may change in 1990 with the new city tour package offered by WesTours.

Lorne's family relationships were strained financially and emotionally. He worked long hours, which meant he had little time to spend with his wife and daughters. Expenses got away from him during the construction phase, resulting in the need to use his personal savings. Although, initially the gardens was solely his dream, his wife has always supported his efforts and is now more involved herself in the daily operations. This special support has enabled him to accomplish his goals for the gardens.

Lorne's experience with financial institutions and government funding agencies was difficult. Few people had faith in his ability to build the gardens or in their financial viability, so that it was difficult to get funding. He persisted, revised his strategy, and was able to secure the necessary funding. In addition, he learned some hard lessons, which show the need for overall planning, constant checking of actual dollars spent with budgeted dollars, and the wisdom of getting early cash flow from a major project.

Lorne is proud of his creation, but is at a crossroads. His pride in making the gardens a reality must be balanced with his financial and personal goals. If he continues with the gardens, he will have to consider the economic feasibility of each phase and when he will build it. He has to be careful not to lose his enthusiasm and love for the project. Intensified marketing of the gardens could be an immediate priority rather than building another addition. Will the gardens remain primarily a show garden, or will he build other family attractions? By diversifying the attractions to include indoor ones, Lorne might lessen the effects of weather on attendance.

Lorne enjoyed creating the gardens, but he wonders whether or not he will get that same satisfaction from merely running them. He may want to continue operating the gardens but consider creating other business enterprises on the side. This option could supplement the cash flow from the gardens and provide a source of enjoyment and income in the winter months. This option could incorporate Lorne's love of horticulture and be both environmentally responsible and profitable. One option might be starting a garden catalogue service, specializing in Northern plants for the local market. There is probably a market for providing indoor and outdoor plants that grow in the North at a better price and higher quality than are currently available.

The frustrations and concerns that Lorne is now facing are common among entrepreneurs moving from the start-up phase of their project to the operating stage. The support of his family and the level of commitment and energy that Lorne has demonstrated in bringing this project on-stream will certainly contribute to making the next decisions personally satisfying and ultimately right for him.

Postscript – 1990

This was a pivotal year for the Yukon Botanical Gardens because the future of the business was at stake. If the year had been a slow one then Lorne would have some hard thinking to do about the future. But 1990 turned out to be a good year. "We increased our advertising by 60% with a new brochure for tourists and a catalogue-type listing for the Garden Center. We were in a local trade show for the first time and we did regular advertising throughout the summer on the radio and newspapers. We really tried to get more locals involved and it worked. Revenues were up 15% to 25% but so was our budget in advertising. I also joined the Yukon Tourism Association for the first time."

The Garden Center was expanded, with more products and staff. A landscaping service was introduced but targeted at a narrow market for fancy gardens. Lorne does the design and actual construction of the gardens, which cuts into his time. There is a market, but in order to manage the demands on his time, Lorne tells potential customers that they will pay 20% more for the gardens than for other landscapers. This screens out all but the serious customers.

Two more phases are in the planning stages. One side of the lake is going to feature natural forest, as seen throughout the Yukon, and will be called the Yukon Black Forest. The other side of the lake will also be developed and will highlight the natural rock bluffs with birch trees growing out at 90° angles. They are considering adding a garden restaurant with a view of the scenery. Lorne would also like to train several key people in the Garden Center so that he can spend more time handling marketing and general business issues.

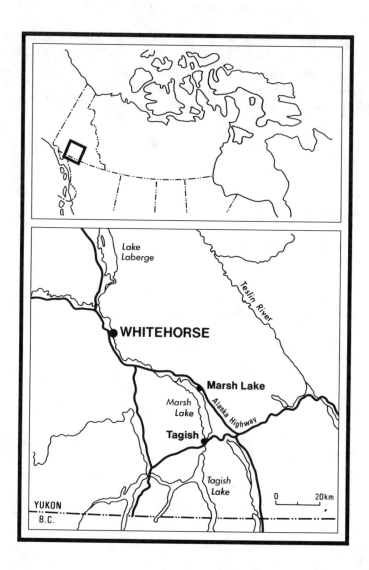

ENTREPRENEURS' ENDORSEMENT

We, the undersigned, acknowledge that we have read our business profile. We approve of the contents of the profile and recognize its accuracy in describing our business.

Dated ___July 4___, 1991

Danny Nowlan

Uli Nowlan

14

YUKON GAME FARM LTD
Whitehorse, Yukon Territory

Danny Nowlan operates a successful game farm, located just outside of Whitehorse. Over the past twenty years, he has established an international reputation with world zoos as a first-class breeder of northern animals. In 1989, he began work on upgrading the farm as a result of an agreement with a tour company to bring tourists to view the animals on his game farm.

Danny operates the farm with the assistance of his wife Ulrike (Uli). He has recently hired staff to assist in the family-run operation. His children, who are grown now, have worked on the farm in past summers. Among many other duties, Uli handles the accounts and business records as well as organizing the paperwork and laboratory tests required for the upkeep and sale of animals. Danny is usually busy with the heavy manual labour required to operate a farm. There are always fences, roads, or equipment to build or repair.

In Danny's mind, "I think it's a success when you do something that pleases yourself, benefits a species of wildlife that we need on this earth, and you make some people happy along the way." This sentiment is shared by friends and neighbours of the game farm and his clients, especially at the Calgary Zoo. He and Uli are in tune with their animals and it shows in the amount of success that they have achieved.

History

Twenty years ago, Danny decided to build a game ranch for tourists because he predicted tourism would become an important industry in the Yukon. Danny recalls those days. "When I started out I had a picture in my mind of a full-blown game farm, but I didn't have the dollar bills in my hand. For several years, I looked for a suitable habitat. The problem was I was looking too far from Whitehorse. It never dawned on me that I would find a thousand acres of the kind of habitat I wanted, right on my doorstep. At that time, I was with the forestry department on fire patrols. One day I was coming back in a helicopter from a fire that I had been fighting north of Whitehorse, and I flew over this place. As soon as I landed I came out and looked at it and said 'That's exactly what I'm looking for.' That started it all."

Danny made a deal with the Yukon government to buy increments of 150 acres at a time, up to 2,000 acres. However, the government changed and the deal fell through. Danny now owns 200 acres and operates the farm on an additional 500 acres, which he used to lease.

Clearing the land for the farm was done in Danny's spare time. "I was working full time at the Forestry Service; then on evenings and weekends, I was out here clearing land. It wasn't very easy. There was bush and swamp. I cleared the first ten acres with an axe and a saw and then I started to drain the swamp, which had heavy willows and big roots. It took me a couple of summers to drain it. I couldn't get equipment in without getting it stuck, and of course I didn't have the proper equipment anyway. But it worked out all right."

Danny hoped to attract tourists to his farm. He caught some animals and then opened it to the general public. "I had practically all the predators – wolves, bears, and otters in pens and in pastures. Then I bought a train and train tracks to take tourists around the farm. After several years, I decided that the tourist flow and the local population were not enough to support the thing."

He therefore changed his focus. "I went to phase two, in which I would use it as a breeding farm until tourism picked up. I always had faith in tourism. Even though the governments of the day and the federal government said I was dreaming, I knew that tourism was coming. If there was ever an animal that was going to be a real payer, it was the tourist. I'm quite happy to say that I was absolutely correct."

He gradually built up the operation. "Except for the first two years, we've been a breeding farm, supplying game farms and zoos all over the world. The major countries of the world all display our animals and are reproducing them. When I started selling animals, I had to sell things that were hard to get, like Dall sheep. The only Dall sheep that had ever been caught before I caught some were by the Brooklyn Zoo. I helped Al Oeming from Alberta catch some sheep and I could see the mistakes that he was making in trying to raise the babies. Then I caught my own sheep and supplied Oehming and the Calgary Zoo with offspring."

Wanda Wuttunee with Danny Nowlan

Danny has sold a number of different animals over the years. He recalls, "I suppose even to this date I've shipped more wolverines to game farms and zoos then any other trapper in the Yukon put together. I've sold a lot of lynx, Dall sheep, and stone sheep. Mountain goats have been the biggest seller for the last ten years. Now I've got everybody else raising mountain goats and the price is dropping which is perfectly normal."

One of the major hurdles in the operation of the farm occurred in 1984, when he and Uli and five others were charged in Operation Falcon. The RCMP charged Uli and Danny with taking gyrfalcons from the wild and selling them through the game farm. They did not believe his story that they raised gyrfalcons successfully under the country's first private experiment in controlled captive breeding, initiated in 1981 and monitored by a Yukon government biologist.

It cost them $147,000 in legal fees over the two years that it took to be acquitted on all charges and to clear their names. Danny and Uli survived the ordeal with the help of friends and the Bank of Montreal. During this period they were prevented from exporting captive-bred falcons which added to their financial hardship.

Danny tried to sell his land during this period. When that failed, he thought he would divide it into fifteen-acre lots and sell those.

Then he changed his mind: he decided that he was too stubborn to let the game farm fail. In the past, Danny had never tried to make the farm pay for itself but in 1987 he decided to look for customers. Danny entered into negotiations with Holland America WesTours, a large company that owns cruise ships and several large hotels. He ended up signing a five-year contract with them under which he received an amount to cover the initial expenses of upgrading a road through the farm and expanding his selection of animals. If WesTours cancels the contract in the next five years, they will pay him a lump sum. As a result of this contract, Danny was able to double the size of the farm's operating line of credit.

Danny recalls, "The farm always made money through the sale of animals. But it got to the point, with the project I had with peregrine and gyrfalcon breeding, where it not only paid the bills and allowed for expansion, but there was a little money left over. My breeding stock of gyrfalcons was coming of age. I was ready to break out and sell twenty gyrfalcons a year which would have been a viable business. Operation Falcon cooked the whole thing's goose. But, on the other hand, we survived it."

The next section describes the daily operations of the game farm, especially staffing, competition and regulatory regimes which impact on the game farm.

Operations

The Yukon Game Farm operates on 615 acres and is located twenty miles west of Whitehorse. A ranch-style house sits on a hill overlooking pastures, cliffs, and pine forests. In the summer of 1989, the farm had elk, mountain goats, mountain sheep, musk oxen, mule deer, and a bull moose. Several buildings are located at the bottom of the hill and house birds, including peregrines and gyrfalcons, snowy owls, Himalyan snowcocks, and numerous quail, pheasants, and geese. The falcon business is almost nonexistent. Danny plans to keep only a few breeding pairs of gyrfalcons. Several pairs have been sold to breeders in the United States, British Columbia, Ontario, England, and Germany since Operation Falcon.

Under the agreement with WesTours, Danny plans to upgrade all the roads through his farm and add fencing. He also plans to add moose, woodland caribou, wood bison, and bighorn sheep. These additions were completed by the spring of 1990 for the first bus tour in May. In the summer of 1989, Danny commented on his progress. "It's going well. Yesterday, we put up 2,000 feet of wire in the rough back country. When we're done, there will be sixteen miles of wire. I've also got my stock under control."

Muskox

After the modifications to the farm are completed, Danny plans to take time to pursue his hobby. "After I'm done, I'm going to placer mine [mine an alluvial or glacier deposit for gold]. The gold mine is going to be my diversion. I'll probably spend $20,000 a year on that property and if that $20,000 is gone in one or two months after I've started, then I'll shut it down, go home and carry on with the farm. But for that time, it's going to be my recreation. If I find some gold, that will be good. If I don't find gold I'm not going to lose my equipment and my farm."

Danny's down-to-earth attitude about his hobby permeates other areas of his life. He says, "I think life's quite a bit of fun. If you had a pile of gold there and a pile of pretty rocks, I'd probably be looking at the the patterns in the pretty rocks."

He feels his age – but not too much, "There's nothing romantic about getting old. God, when I look across and see a beautiful young lady, I think about making her a cup of cocoa now. That's the sad part. Don't you ever believe the golden age is after sixty-five; the golden age is between eighteen and thirty. I've got the same ideas in my head and I like the same things as I did when I was twelve years old. The carcass is getting old, but the grey cells are still young."

Danny describes the work of a game farmer.

The average week for me means fencing and farming – like any other farmer. It includes looking after my stock and keeping equipment and the buildings in working order. In the spring, Uli's job is monitoring the hatching of the falcons' eggs and seeing that their feed is proper. She's constantly testing for parasites in everything.

You might think that tomorrow is going to be an easy day. But something always happens. An animal gets sick or hurt or a bird gets loose. So every day is full, including Saturday and Sunday. Generally, my day is from dawn to dusk like any ordinary farmer. We're mixed farmers and we have to treat it like a mixed farm. Of course, we've also got the book work. It gets bigger and bigger every year because the government gets bigger and bigger every year. They always have new forms to fill out and they will never stop.

Work on the farm continues throughout the year. "Granted there's more work to do in the summer, but it's a lot easier than working with frozen ground. But then if you have a sewer problem in the winter and everything's frozen six feet down – give me the summer any day. Every year so far we've had to fix something in the frozen ground, so I don't think of the winter as being a lax time."

The farm has become more financially viable over the years. "In the past, I've taken other jobs and contracts because I needed the cash flow. I don't have to take other jobs now. I was always convinced that the game farm could pay if that was the avenue that I wanted to take. It took a good court case to make me really understand that money is a very important item. It buys everything that is precious to us. Once I realized that, then it took me a matter of a couple of months to identify which route to take and that was to look for business."

Danny reached this decision after he almost sold the farm during Operation Falcon. He recalls, "The first tour company I hit was WesTours and they said, 'That's what we're looking for.'" The bus tours were seeing less and less game each year in the Yukon and tourists were complaining about it. Now WesTours' advertising brochures incorporate the addition of Danny's game farm into their tour. They describe themselves as the only tour company that guarantees wildlife sightings.

Competition

The Yukon Game Farm is the only game farm operating in the Yukon or the Northwest Territories. It is one of the few game farms which meets the high standards of record-keeping and quality of animals required by world zoos. Danny notes, "I don't have competition in this business. There are game farms I'm trying to get started with other people in the Yukon. But I think anybody would be foolish to try and duplicate my farm as a tourist attraction. They're going to have a hard time trying to find 615 acres that are set up like this for a game farm. The big thing we have is the terrain. We've got bush, fields, cliffs, forest, and water in a little package here."

Staff

The Game Farm has always been a family-operated business with seasonal help hired only as required. In 1987, Danny hired one permanent person. Danny says, "Once we started to expand we needed a full-time person since we have a lot more animals and construction. Since then, we've hired a second person, so I have two permanent employees plus Uli and myself."

Danny looks for two main characteristics in his employees. "They have to have a genuine interest and concern for animals. If they don't have that, then they can't fit in here. I've found out over a long course of hiring people, not only for the game farm but for other jobs, that there is a work force in Alberta of farmers who don't have farms but who work for other farmers. They are the best employees that I can find. If I needed another man, I would go straight to Alberta. I've got two excellent men from Alberta and every day I think how lucky I am."

When Danny hired his employees, "I told them, 'The law says that you cannot work overtime or weekends, unless I pay you double time. I'm not going to pay you double time because we cannot afford it. If I decide that I want to give you a month's holidays with pay, then that's what I'll do. So you come to work at 9:00 and you quit at 5:00. Take an hour off for lunch and then you don't have to sign time slips.' So my crew said 'Okay, but what we do after 5:00 and on weekends is our business, right?' So I thought they were going to fix up cars and make a buck on the weekend. Christ, it's all my stuff that they fix on their hours off. Where are you going to find guys like that? Forget 5:00, they'll work until midnight down there. They must like it here or they wouldn't be here."

Danny feels that he built up their loyalty by treating his employees properly and paying them a decent wage. "If it doesn't start as a decent wage, you bring it up as they progress so that it is a decent wage. It's also important to share the same interests. They are as concerned about those animals and birds as I am. That's very important. They keep their eyes open and they notice things that they pass on."

Elk

Regulations

A number of federal and territorial government regulations and policies govern the importing and exporting of the game farm's stock,
as well as trapping and the title to the land where the game farm
operates. When the game farm imports animals from other countries, it is a complicated process. The farm or zoo that is shipping
the animal must handle the testing and the paperwork. "For example, the musk ox I bought in Minnesota will be held in confine-
ment for two months. They test for tuberculosis, blue tongue, and
other diseases and if the tests are negative, then two months later
they'll repeat the tests. If the results are negative again, then they
ship them to us. Then I'll hire a person at the border called a broker,
and he will handle the paperwork for us."

When an animal is shipped from the farm to a customer within
Canada, a general health certificate is required. Uli says, "The local
veterinarian examines the animal and signs the certificate that in his
opinion, the animal doesn't have any infectious diseases." There are
no further problems so long as there are no stops where the animal
is off-loaded before it reaches its destination. Danny points out, "The
reason they won't let you off-load is because of diseases. If you have

to off-load in a stock yard, a disease could be transmitted between the animals."

There is a lot more paperwork required when the game farm exports an animal from outside Canada. Problems arise because a federal veterinarian is required and none lives in the Yukon. Danny notes, "Sometimes we have to fly a federal vet in, or if a local vet is satisfactory to Agriculture Canada then he may do the inspection. Our vet records the particulars and if the animal goes through Vancouver, the federal vet stops the shipment and examines the records before the animal leaves Canada."

Some misunderstandings about game farming have influenced government policy and regulations. For example, some people believe that game farmers will capture animals from the wild and put them in pastures.

If a wild elk comes into my pastures, I'll have the Game department get that elk out of here or I'll shoot it. It's as simple as that. Our whole living is based on how healthy our animals are. We know what our elk have, but we don't know what diseases a wild elk might have.

I can see there's going to be a problem for a while with the restrictions imposed by B.C. and Alberta. But it's one of the glitches you have to go through. They're worried about a lot of things including escapement, that is, when an elk escapes from the farm and mixes with wild animals. It's a rather screwy thing to worry about because elk will not leave the area if they do get out. There are some people who don't want animals in captivity, period, and there are some hunters who seem to think we're a threat to their hunting, but they won't win in fighting against game farming because it's a good thing.

The territorial government has played a major role in the way title to the game farm land is held. Danny says, "Two-thirds of this land is not mine. I don't even have a lease on it. I refused to sign it because I maintain that I want to be treated like every other farmer is in the Yukon. I don't feel like spending $500,000 on 500 acres with a lease which says you can take it back and give me thirty days to move my assets off it. How do you move fences built in rock? How do you move roads and dams?"

Originally, the territorial government told Danny that if he worked the land he could eventually purchase it. This verbal arrangement fell apart with the election of a new government. Danny recalls,

The new deputy minister said, "If we give you thousands and thousands of acres of land, then every other Tom, Dick, and Harry will want thousands and thousands of acres of land." I got mad and said, "You'd better do your homework. I'm not every Tom, Dick, and Harry. I'm Danny Nolan and there's only one of them in the Yukon. It's the only game farm in the Yukon. I've been here for forty years and I'm not asking for thousands of acres, I'm asking for 500 acres that I've done $100,000 worth of work on. The hangup is simple; it's your policy. But whenever it suits you people, you change your policy. You're not changing it this time. But if it was the other way around and I had you over a barrel, you would change the policy.

The Game Farm's recent association with WesTours has improved the relationship with the territorial government regarding the issue of title. "This issue is going to be resolved one way or the other. I've never ever kissed anybody's backside in my whole life and I've made a living. Not the best living, but I've got by on it. It's too late now to start that sort of thing."

Financial Information

The Game Farm earns revenue from the sale of its animals and it utilizes an operating line of credit from the bank to balance out any irregularity in its cash flow. The new WesTours contract is an additional source of revenue but is not included in the following analysis. Finally, government funding received over its years of operation included a grant of $60,000 to purchase elk, muskox, and deer breeding stock in 1985 and a no-interest loan which covered 40% of the expenditures for one year related to upgrading the farm for tourism.

The game farm raises and sells animals to zoos and other game farms around the world. Table 12 sets out total wages and return on equity and sales to asset ratios for 1984 to 1988.

The return-on-equity ratio (ROE) of net income to owner's equity fluctuates dramatically over the five-year period, from 0% to 173%. This reflects the high legal expenses and restricted activity during Operation Falcon. Once that court case was settled, regular operations were possible again, as reflected in the 42% ROE earned in 1988. In other words, for every $1.00 invested by the owners of the Game Farm, they earned a very respectable 42¢ in net profit.

The sales-to-assets ratio is an indication of the capacity to generate revenue due to investment in the company's assets. It should show that the capacity of the company to generate revenues is reasonable for that business. For example, when the restriction on gyrfalcon sales was placed on the game farm in 1985 and 1986, the sales-to-assets ratio was very low (0.3). The value of the birds was listed as

Table 12
Financial Information for Yukon Game Farm Ltd

	1984	1985	1986	1987	1988
Return on Equity (%)	14.4	0.0	8.5	173.0	42.0
Sales/Assets (times)	.8	.3	.3	1.4	1.2
Total Salaries ($)	13,632	16,048	6,774	38,600	24,205

an asset of the company, but since they could not be sold, they did not generate income and brought the ratio down. The sales-to-assets ratio returned to a more normal level in 1987 (1.4) in 1988 (1.2) after regular operations were resumed.

Total salaries indicate the amount earned by the hired help on the farm. It does not include the salaries taken by the owners. It grew in the last two years when full-time help was hired.

Reasons for Success

The success of the Yukon Game Farm is a result of Danny's tenacity in accomplishing his goals. In addition, Danny and Uli have established a reputation among the world's zoos for supplying animals of the highest quality. Their dedication as a team, their care for their animals, and the hard work they put in have helped to make their farm a success. Finally, their operation is set in an ideal location to enable them to meet these standards and live the lifestyle that they want.

Danny explains the philosophy which helped make the difference in the farm's survival. "One way to be successful at something is to be tenacious and never quit. Set your mind on a goal and get there no matter what, as long as it's honest and you're not hurting anyone. You don't walk over anyone to reach your goal, at least I don't. Perseverance has gotten the game farm where it is today."

For Danny, profit is not the overriding indication of the game farm's success.

Our success is due to the basic desire of good zoos and game farms to perfect the breeding of animals. Every last one of us believes that if we don't learn how to do it, there won't be any animals in certain species left. We perfected the way to mass-produce gyrfalcons and mountain goats. Nobody did it before we did, and our techniques are being used by every zoo and game farm that raises mountain goats.

Before we developed a technique that worked for raising mountain goats, a zoo might get one kid one year out of half a dozen females, and then the next year they'd get two, and both would die two weeks after they were born. So I think the whole game farm is a success because of the fact that I learned how to raise these animals when no one else could. I've got a grade three education but it's not schooling you need when somebody says, "Here's a pair of mountain goats, reproduce them."

When I started my research, I phoned good zoos and asked, "Have you got any information on raising mountain goats?" They said, "If you find out, tell us." It took five years to figure out the way to raise goats was by using an antibiotic to kill parasites and offering a particular feeding regimen. Being able to share that information is another reason this farm is a success. If you gain the knowledge of how to do something in this business, you are bound to pass it on to other zoos and game farms. It's also been a financial success because I raised a family on it and I paid my bills and that's what a farm is supposed to do.

Peter Karsten, the director of the Calgary Zoo, has known Danny for many years. Peter recalls:

Our dealings started in about 1967 or 1968, when the previous director of the zoo, who knew Danny, suggested we contact him about getting some mountain sheep. We had started to look into opportunities to get more native animals in our exhibits, such as the Alaskan Dall sheep. We got a permit from the Yukon government to collect six or eight lambs, and we hired Danny to help us. He knew exactly where they were, how to find them, how to collect the lambs, and how to hand-raise them with no losses. This is very important to us because we can't afford animal stress or losses.

Danny took several people from the zoo out in the back country. He would observe a ewe through a spotting scope and he could tell by her behaviour that she was going to deliver a lamb within the next six hours. So the group would watch it and when she delivered a lamb, they went up and collected it. It meant a fair amount of climbing, but there was no such thing as just waiting around, then rushing and (by chance) stumbling across a young one. Danny felt if it was older than a few hours, then the young would run and (a) you may not catch it; (b) you may separate the mother from the lamb, or (c) you may lose the lamb by causing it to fall. Dannywould never waste wildlife. I think that's a religion with him. For us, that was a very reliable way to collect animals. Danny did a marvelous job.

Establishing an excellent reputation with world zoos was important in the success of his farm. Danny notes, "We built our reputation up by never sending out a bad animal. If it wasn't a perfect animal, then it never left here. So we became known in the zoological world for raising low numbers of quality northern animal stock. It's spread to the point where I get orders from Japan and Eastern Bloc countries and I've sold to all of them."

Peter Karsten elaborates on the unique position that the Yukon Game Farm holds in the zoological world.

Game farms are not a part of the primary network for zoological gardens. We do work with game farms in the acquisition of certain animals we need, but we are somewhat reluctant often to work with game farms unless we know their operations in detail. That is due partly because of policies that we've established, and guidelines under which we are accountable under the ethics code from the American Zoological Association.

For example, we do not deacquisition animals to recipients when we are not absolutely sure that they have the competence, the long-term capability, to maintain the animal and can guarantee animal welfare standards to the level that we have. We are even concerned where people would take valuable wildlife genetic material and hybridize these just to bring up some interesting animals. We need to be custodians of wildlife in order that the subspecies and species are kept separate.

We follow a species survival program where certain animals are centrally managed by a data bank as to their genetic makeup. We must be absolutely sure that the players in this are always reliable and that they do not tell a better story than reality. We have had problems in that area with animal dealers and some commercial operations. So with game farms we need to know that the operation, the record-keeping, and their stewardship of the animals meet our standards. Few do, so that's why we normally don't deal with them.

However, we have a unique situation with Danny. Initially the Yukon Game Farm was a place where we knew somebody who was intimately knowledgeable about wildlife, knew how to capture wildlife with a reasonable amount of effort, and was effective at it. When we started our relationship with them, we weren't interested in them as suppliers of animals. But our relationship has evolved that way.

Danny's so much in tune with nature that it's almost eerie. Danny is like a part of the wildlife, I think he can catch anything you want and do it on the wavelength of the animal. He understands their behaviour and he's a keen observer. It's a sixth sense. He has an incredible gift of reading nature.

In considering the small number of game farms which meet the zoo's strict criteria, it is clear that the Yukon Game Farm is rare. Peter points out, "Danny is the only one in Canada that has the kind of skill that meets our standards. In fact, he's the only game farm operator that I know who is so incredibly dedicated. It's not just Danny, it's also his wife Uli. They are amazing people. When they decide to rear some animals, then that becomes a priority. I would trust them with anything I could think of, including my own babies if I had any any more. To them, life is a reverence and I think that's what makes the difference. So you can't really compare them with anybody."

For example, Peter recalls their gyrfalcon operation.

It was unfortunate that they had a fair amount of frustration to suffer because nobody believed their success rate at raising falcons. I didn't have even a moment of hesitation in believing that Danny and Uli could raise as many falcons as they did. I know how they operate. They read nature like nobody else. There's never been a reference guide or any documentation about raising falcons that you could study and then follow.

Danny and Uli have a relationship with their birds where they know exactly how to reduce levels of fear, frustration, anxiety, and trauma. It's on a psychological wavelength that has nothing to do with physical contact. The animals are so relaxed and trusting that they will rear a number of young. Danny and Uli do whatever the birds don't do. They do it with a twenty-four-hour, around-the-clock dedication that can't be duplicated in a commercial organization. You couldn't hire somebody with the same dream that Danny has and do as well as he can. You couldn't pay them enough. It's a wonderful arrangement. So we always marvel at their success rate for reproduction and survival of their animals.

Danny's a gutsy guy. He will take on the government, he gives up only what he has to, and it's very little. He is wilderness and freedom itself and he's someone you can't corral. If you ask him to help you, he'll help you more than you could yourself. But you can't just badger him and demand it. He disdains people who are driven by rules and regulations rather than common sense. The remarkable thing about Danny is that he doesn't have a lot of formal training but has a very lucid and brilliant mind. He's a good researcher, and formal training doesn't necessarily reflect the level of someone's intelligence.

I think the other part to Danny's success, is his organization and determination. He can envision something and he can get it done in a very short period of time. For example, I went and stayed with him and one day he said, "I'm going to turn that area into a mountain goat enclosure. The cliffs are great because the sun will warm their hide in the morning. They probably will stay there because that's the best place there is, so I don't think we'll need much of a fence." I said to him. "That's going to be a bit of a job." He said, "Oh yeah, I know but I'll get my cat [bulldozer] out." He worked like a bear and did everything. It didn't take long and the whole thing was done.

The physical attributes of the property that makes up the game farm and its location in the Yukon have also contributed to the viability of the farm. Peter explains. "Danny was so clever when he selected that piece of property. He saw the cliffs, a wonderful meadow, a little marsh and some water. Also it backs on real wild country, so he has several different habitats in a small area."

The results have been excellent. "The mountain goats that come from Danny have always been the best. They are the healthiest animals and are excellent breeding stock. There's enough of nature's testing that's built into the equation that you're not going to get animals that are so artificially raised that they die with the first infection. He's made of rugged stock and so are his animals."

Danny also recognizes some of the advantages of operating the game farm in the Yukon. "There are no significant animal diseases here yet. I've noticed that when I take an animal, for instance, to the Calgary Zoo, they've got a tray of needles they give it for vaccinations. When we bring an animal here, we don't vaccinate it for anything, which is a big savings of money, time, and trouble. The only thing that seems to happen to an animal that you bring in from outside, is that the next year he looks ten times better than he did when you got him. So something is right in this country for raising game animals."

Danny identifies other personal benefits from living in the Yukon.

I've got the lifestyle I want. Streams of people come here because I like people, but I like them one on one. I don't like to be in crowded places. If I had my way, I wouldn't go anywhere but to my trapline, because that's where I'm the happiest. I can go to a back pasture and it's like travelling back 5,000 years. I'll see a grizzly bear or moose sometimes, but I don't run into anybody else. So I'm ten minutes from 5,000 years ago. Uli likes this lifestyle to a certain extent, but she also enjoys travelling."

I've got to say it's a lifestyle that I like; that's why I'm here. I like to get up in the morning and see the animals and I enjoy the farm. We've got good friends and we're always making new ones. I remember some people wrote a letter that they had wanted to see muskox for thirty-five years. They had sent a card and written a nice long letter before their visit to the farm. When they came Uli was very sick with the chicken pox. She got the muskox for them anyway. That was pretty nice of her because the lady may never have seen a muskox in her entire life, if she hadn't come here."

Areas for Improvement

Danny's relationship with the territorial government has been difficult. It has had an effect on the game farm but Danny has followed his principles in dealing with the various government departments. He says, "There is another way of going about running a business in the Yukon. I could have been a lot more diplomatic with bureaucrats and politicians. But I like to think I've got the brains to do it, without having to cultivate those people. I don't want to cultivate them. I like him and I like you and I'll go to hell for you if I like you. But no, I won't cultivate those people, but I'll be as diplomatic as I can. There are two ways I could have gotten here and probably the diplomatic way with the bureaucrats would have been the fast way. But I don't care, I'm quite happy the way I did it."

Danny feels some of the tension in dealing with the government is a result of lack of understanding on the part of the bureaucrats and other interest groups of a game farm's value in dealing with the Yukon's renewable resources. Lobbying could help to educate them.

The hunters are against game farms and environmentalists are not happy with it. I think the territorial Game Branch is not happy. They develop a strange attitude that wildlife is "our turf." "Thou shalt not have anything to do with it except kill it when we say you can kill it." But if you buy a permit and they tell you where to go to hunt, then they are controlling it. So they see the game farm as stepping on their turf. They have told me that.

The director of the Game Branch said I ought to be ashamed of myself because I'm making a living out of those animals. I'm only making a partial living because I do odd jobs with my tractor. I told him that he was making his entire living off of animals. It staggered him because he never thought of it that way. They're awfully hard to educate. If they weren't hard to educate, they wouldn't be working for the government. That's my honest opinion, because I can sit down with anybody else and talk reasonably and logically with them, and we can come to a conclusion at the end of the discussion. I cannot do that with either politicians or civil servants. They get hung up on some little glitch and there we sit.

Environmental Friendliness

Danny takes responsibility for minimizing the impact of his operation on the environment very seriously.

I don't do a lot of things that would make my life easier. I will not use any herbicides, which makes it tougher because I get foxtails and weeds. I will not allow spraying to be done for mosquito control. There are no mosquitoes because I have a lot of birds. The one year that I got eaten by mosquitoes, was when they sprayed and we almost had a court case over it. They sprayed the hot springs up the road and then they sprayed me. My swallows left, and I haven't got them all back to this day. If you look up in the sky, you will see birds that eat bugs, flies, and mosquitoes. The very fact that I can raise animals without using herbicides and control the mosquitoes with the normal environmental forces that are here already, proves that it can be done.

I also leave a lot of bush when I develop the land. I'm not a standard farmer who has to have square fields. I believe that I have to have wind-breaks. I can't leave 150-acre fields open because the land dries out and doesn't grow anything. I leave the willows for birds to nest in and try not to overgraze any of my property so the land keeps producing well and the weeds don't take over.

In the long term, Danny feels that his work with raising animals will be beneficial to our quality of life. "The whole idea behind the game farm is the fact that we'd better learn how to raise and reproduce these animals in captivity because in fifty years, they may be the only ones."

Sustainability of the Business

The economic sustainability of the game farm – in Danny's words, "earning a profit, hiring employees and going on forever" – was not a major reason for his starting the game farm. He recalls, "Two reasons that I started the game farm was, first, because I liked animals and I wanted to find out more about them. The second reason was I wanted to find out if I could practise livestock agriculture in the Yukon and make a success out of it. I tried raising cattle, horses, geese, and chickens but it didn't work. The cost of feed was too expensive and the winters too long. There isn't a long grazing period, so feed costs were double. So I tried local animals. I thought I could raise mountain goats for a dual purpose. They have excellent wool and some of the males weigh 450 or 500 pounds – that's a lot of meat. It takes twelve mountain goats or sheep to eat the same amount that one beef cow does and they have more meat per pound of feed."

In the past, Danny's game farm was less subject to the pressures of a poor economy because he was the only one successfully raising certain northern animals. With the shift to relying on tour groups as a source of revenue, there may be a greater impact on the farm if tourism slows down because of a poor economy. However, Danny can always rely on his special expertise and find a market in the world zoos and game farms. Further, his creativity in dealing with slow times in the past will see him through the inevitable slow periods in the future.

Profile in the Community

The game farm has a special place in the community. Part of the legacy from the farm will be an understanding of animals passed onto the local children. Danny notes, "There are a lot of kids who go through this farm during summer holidays or on weekends. Over the years, a lot of kids from the schools have come out here." One lady recently told Danny, "I can remember when we were nine years old following you around. You were in your old coveralls and you weren't shaved, but you dropped whatever you were doing and you went with us and you explained things for an hour."

At one point, Operation Falcon and its court expenses left Danny so financially strapped that he was finding it difficult to feed his animals. One morning, he found a piece of paper with two red bows, left next to a pile of quail feed that had not been there the night before. The note read, "Danny and Uli, over the years you have done so much for so many different people. With this gift we are showing only a small amount of our friendship, respect, and good-will. We are your friends and it is our intention to ease your minds, if only for a short time. The Feed Fairies."

Future Development

With the signing of the agreement to expand the game farm to accommodate WesTours' needs, Danny has considered making changes to his organization, expanding his elk herd, pursuing his hobby of developing his gold mine, and continuing his favourite research projects. "I agreed to make changes because it will still operate as a working game ranch. It will be bigger and have more species, but it won't be a zoo. In other words, you're not going to see all of the animals all of the time, but you're going to see a sufficient number to thrill the heck out of you."

Other changes will follow within the next couple of years.

Eventually we'll have to have a manager. There's no question that I would want the first fellow I hired to manage the farm. He's been here three years now. He's a good stockman and heavy equipment operator and he seems to be happy here. As far as making financial decisions, we'll keep pretty close tabs on that. If I'm going to go broke, I want to know it right away. I'm not sure how big I want to get in the future. I seem to plan the "last project," but before it's completed, my mind is already turning over other things.

Eventually I'll have less staff. Uli will always look after the books. But once this farm is operating, the beauty is it could almost run itself except for looking after the daily needs of the animals. This place should only have one farmhand because we will have all the machinery he might need, like the grader, the cat, and the backhoe. There is not going to be that much to do. He'll probably replace a number of fenceposts each year until they're all metal or treated wood. There's no need to feed the animals in the summer, since their food supply grows in their pens. The watering setup we've got now means you just turn taps on, which is not a big deal. So one person will look after the physical labor.

When WesTours comes in, we'll train their drivers, and if they hire a new driver, they have a videotape of it [the farm tour] and they don't need me. I see the farm becoming a full-blown tourist attraction. I see its financial success with the tours, but I think the game farming aspect will continue.

Danny sees several options for his elk herd. He would like to expand his own herd and begin selling elk to other game farms and as an alternative source of meat in the Yukon. He has encouraged several local people to start elk farms so that they can develop a local source of meat which is cheaper than what can currently be obtained from the south.

I keep preaching to these guys to try to sell their elk locally. I'd even cut the price on some of mine to sell them here. We need to worry about ourselves. I fed seven elk for the same amount I fed one beef cow. We also need a herd of elk so that in the future if anyone wants a quality bull elk, then they have to come to the Yukon to get the best.

You develop that herd by producing lots of elk and mercilessly cutting out the poor ones. You tag the elk to find out if you've got a good bull. For example, if you've got six cows and four of them are having good calves but two aren't, then you know those two cows have to go. Elk sell from $1,500 to $15,000 each. In addition, each bull elk has thirty-eight pounds of antler velvet that sells well. The velvet is used as a tonic by the Chinese and Koreans. An elk farmer will probably take four years to start making money. If he concentrates on bull elk, he could start making money in his second year. One local elk farmer started from scratch and in five years, he could sell his business for half a million dollars.

Danny has plans for his elk herd.

When the elk herd gets big enough, we'll certainly have to branch out from this piece of land. I would like to have a place in the east Kootenays for elk. Right now, it's against b.c. policy to raise elk in captivity, but you can raise fallow deer, bison, and reindeer. So the next step they tell me will be elk. Soon I'll be raising 100 calves a year, but it's really expensive to feed animals here. I'd take them to B.C., where I can buy feed at a third of the price I pay for it here and I'm closer to markets. I'll keep a basic herd here for tourism, which will be producing elk all the time.

There will be a market for elk as seed stock. Recently, I read that six planeloads of red deer were imported into Toronto from New Zealand. They sold like hotcakes because people can't get enough elk. Silver is the poor man's gold. Red deer are the poor man's elk. So then those people buying red deer are going to be buying elk. They'll try to upgrade their red deer since they're only a third the size of an elk.

One local elk farm owner put an ad in the paper in Alaska and he's getting quite a few calls. People have a lot of land that the government cleared for barley. I don't know why it failed, but now those people are looking for some type of animal to raise such as buffalo or elk. There's a future in game farming even if cattlemen don't like it. They see it as competition. New Zealand has a million deer under fence now as breeding stock, but there are no less cattle.

Once the farm is running, Danny would like to work his gold mine. He says, "I'm going to placer mine in the summer. I'll set how much I'll spend each year on it and when that's gone, I'll come home. I will not go broke chasing a dream, but that will be my retirement. I'd want to be on the farm when the young are being born, because that's the most fun time. I have a theory about people who have done manual labour all their lives – if they quit they just die. I ain't fixin' on dying for a heck of a long time."

In addition to placer mining, Danny enjoys researching techniques for raising wild animals in captivity with more success. For example, he has looked into the technology for turning an animal's food into pellets. Danny says, "They've always had trouble raising moose in captivity because 80% of their diet is browse. Now there is a sawdust pellet available and moose are doing well on it. Norway has got a machine that cost the government a million dollars. Aspen, rosehips, and blueberry bushes are picked up, fed into the machine, and out comes a pellet. I'd like to see what can be done here."

Advice to New Business

Danny would advise anyone thinking of starting a game farm operation in the North, first to apprentice at a game farm. Second, they should like animals and want to succeed. They should be prepared to find other sources of income to supplement their cash flow in the early years of operating a game farm. Managing their land effectively and efficiently is important. They should be careful not to overgraze the land and give serious consideration to following environmentally friendly practices. He feels that it is not possible to make a living in the North in conventional farming, but it is possible to farm game and make money.

New operators must be prepared to study. Danny and Uli subscribe to a variety of technical magazines with information about diseases and the conditions that can lead to medical problems. Uli notes, "Basically I concern myself with nutrition, diseases, and new medications. Our philosophy is to be prepared should things go wrong. We also try to keep our animals healthy through proper nutrition. We make sure the animals get a balanced diet. In the winter, we get our hay tested for mineral content. We keep in touch with the feed company nutritionists who suggest changes or supplements to the feed."

Summary and Conclusions

The Yukon Game Farm has survived and thrived because of Danny's vision and tenacity, despite enduring severe financial hardship. He realized that he wanted to make the game farm survive because that money could be used to protect all the things that are important to him. With Uli's unstinting support, they have prospered and face a bright future. Through their efforts, certain animal species can be raised in captivity for future generations, no matter what their future is in the wild. They have relied on their own revenue, except for one government grant in 1985.

A family business, the Yukon Game Farm is moving into a new phase with the expansion to accommodate bus tours and the new relationship with WesTours. It will continue to be a working farm but it will probably be run by a manager in the next couple of years rather than by Danny. The manager will be one of the dedicated employees who currently works on the farm. Their dedication to their work was promoted by Danny's upfront management style and their own interest in animals.

There is currently no other game farm in the North that has the reputation with the international zoological community that the Yukon Game Farm has developed. They are known for their high quality of record-keeping and their fine, healthy northern animal stocks. The farm faces some paperwork in exporting their animals, further complicated by their remote location and the lack of a federal veterinarian in the Yukon.

Danny and Uli have a remarkable rapport with their animals, so their stock does well. They constantly cull their herds and keep only the best animals. They have developed a special place in the community and are known to accept injured animals and care for them. Their work follows principles that minimize any disruption of natural ecosystems. They do not use herbicides or pesticides and they leave the land as natural as possible. Overgrazing of the land is avoided by rotating their animals through the farm.

Danny and Uli enjoy their lifestyle in the North, and Danny plans to develop his placer mine as his retirement project. He will expand the elk herd and encourage other elk farmers in the Yukon to develop both an alternative local meat source and breeding stock for the international market. In his spare time, he will continue his research into techniques for successfully raising wild animals in captivity and sharing it with the world.

Postscript – 1990

The tours through the game farm were a big success. Six or seven busloads of people went through the farm five days a week from May through to mid-September. Uli notes, "It kept us very busy but it was an interesting challenge. We now have 234 animals that all stayed basically healthy through the summer. People liked to see animals in large enclosures rather than in pens."

15

TRANSLATION AND INTERPRETATION SERVICES*
North of 60°

Ethel operates a successful translation and interpretation service in a community in the Northwest Territories. The majority of her work is translating English to Inuktitut, the language of eastern and central Arctic Inuit. Ethel offers her translation and interpretation service to local businesses on a part-time basis throughout the year. She does travel to other communities, but this service is reserved for her established customers. She manages to schedule many of her projects around the times when her children do not need her. She hires additional staff in the community on a contract basis to handle any overload.

Translation and Interpretation Services was originally conceived as a way for Ethel to supplement the family budget while raising her children. It allows her to utilize her training on her own time. Her business is thriving due to a loyal clientele who receive reliable, reasonably priced translation and interpretation services in a prompt and friendly manner. With the support of her husband, she is able to handle the demands of her work and raise her family.

History

Ethel recalls growing up in the Northwest Territories.

I was born in an outpost camp where I was brought up until I was six years old. Then I went away to a boarding school for seven years. I would spend

---

* At the request of the entrepreneur, her name, her company name, and the community are anonymous to protect her privacy.

summer in a camp on the land with my parents. I finished my grade 8 there, which was the highest grade offered at that time. My parents didn't want to send me away to high school, so when I was sixteen, I started Adult Education.

After I was married, I held various secretarial office jobs until I got into interpreting. I had a year of special training when I learned simultaneous oral translation and written translation with the Territorial Language Bureau of Culture and Communications. I worked for them for several years then I left and went to work for a local organization as an executive assistant.

During her time with the Language Bureau, Ethel bought a computer and took on contract work after hours. In this way, she was able to build up a business when she finally decided to go out on her own. "I kind of fell into my own business. I wanted to spend time with my children before they started school, and my own business seemed to be the answer. I resigned and started Translation and Interpretation Services. I relied on the customers I had been working for on my off hours to form the core of my business."

Operations

Ethel works several days a week translating written material from English to Inuktitut or providing oral translation services. She puts in her time on the computer early in the morning, at lunch, during the children's bath time, and on evenings and weekends in an office located in her home. She may take her daughter with her to work at the client's offices, or she hires a babysitter.

Ethel owns a Macintosh computer, a software package for Inuktitut syllabics, and a printer. She purchased her equipment with the money she earned doing extra contract work while she had a full-time job. The bulk of her work is translating written reports or dictation, but she also does simultaneous and consecutive oral translation.

Ethel explains, "Simultaneous translation is done instantly so there is no time lost between the English-speaking person and somebody who wants to answer him during a meeting. I also do consecutive translation, in which the translator waits until the person is finished speaking and then translates."

Ethel charges $25 per page for written translation. Simultaneous translation ranges from $250 to $350 per day, based on negotiations with the client, resulting in an oral or a written contract that lists estimated time for the job and the rate of pay. The fee is based on the complexity of the work and on whether she is working alone. Ethel has never had a problem collecting her accounts. She invoices her customer and may receive payment immediately upon delivery of the finished product or in the regular accounting cycle, which is usually two weeks.

Regular customers include local Native organizations, oil companies, government agencies, and auditors who want their accounting reports translated. Ethel also works for several territorial departments, including the Language Bureau and Education. The auditors provide the majority of their work in the summer months. Meetings for the rest of her clients begin in the fall, go on until Christmas, and then resume at the end of January and last to mid-June.

Ethel does not advertise her company. The major source of her business is word-of-mouth. She has enough business to keep her busy year-round. When she requires additional assistance, she has a number of women she can hire. "Translation and interpretation provides an easy way to earn money if you are willing to work on evenings and weekends. The ladies I hire are good translators. I've trained with some of them, and some I've worked with for the government. I give them the project and they find their own equipment to do the work."

Competition for freelance work is scattered across the territories. Many translaters are Ethel's former co-workers. Ethel holds a Translation Certificate and carries memberships in the national and regional interpreter and translator associations. She has a business licence which costs a few dollars, but she requires no insurance.

Ethel's husband works full-time and supports her decision to operate her own company. He looks after the children when she puts in hours on evenings and weekends. She makes a significant contribution to the household budget through company profits. When she needs a break, she takes her family clam-digging or berry-picking on the land.

Financial Information

The initial capital purchase of equipment was paid for from part-time contract work. No government funding has been used in the start-up or the continuing operations of the company. Expenses for telephone, paper, and office supplies are financed through company revenues. A private accounting firm handles all of her requirements for financial reporting.

Reasons for Success

Ethel has worked hard at establishing a reputation for high-quality, accurate, and reasonably priced work. She prides herself on being punctual and reliable and on meeting deadlines. She feels these are the key factors that account for her success. The support of her husband has also been invaluable.

Ethel sets her rates somewhat lower than the $400 per day charged by the Interpreters Association for simultaneous translation. She notes, "I could raise my rates if I wanted to, but I don't find the need to charge that much. Some of my customers have complained about the rates but we agree on rates before I start a contract. They are more understanding once I advise them of the rates charged by the Association."

The copy she produces is of excellent quality, in part because of her software. "The interpretive fonts [part of the computer equipment which makes the syllabic characters] have been revised and they are excellent. There are different types of print available and the program also has English characters."

Areas for Improvement

For the most part, Ethel is very happy with her business. She feels no discrimination due to the fact that she is an Inuit businesswoman. She notes that it is most commonly Native women who work in this field. However, sometimes the working conditions can be a strain on translators if clients are not sensitive to the need for regular breaks.

When a contract requires Ethel to provide oral translation, it takes a great deal of concentration. It can be very tiring when the client does not provide a break for the translator every two or three hours. Ethel explains, "Some people that hire you don't think about the interpreter needing a short break. When I'm interpreting for a few days steadily, it's very hard on my family. When I go home, I can't say anything for an hour at least. I get a bit distant because of what's going around in my head. I deal with it by taking a few days off between contracts."

Another area of concern is the limited service available should the computer or the printer break down. The Macintosh computer representative rarely comes to the community. If Ethel's equipment breaks down, she must send it south for repair. In shipping her equipment, she runs the risk that it will be returned in worse condition then when she sent it for repair.

Environmental Friendliness

In providing her service, Ethel generates very little waste and has minimal impact on the environment. In her computer work, she generates little wastepaper because she generally prints out only the final report. She does not use recycled paper yet, but would consider it if the quality was up to her high standards. By the very nature of the service she provides and the way she is raising her children, Ethel is also involved in preserving and protecting her tradition and culture from extinction through the Inuit language.

Sustainability of the Business

Ethel believes that her business is recession-proof. Her clients have budgets that include translation services, so her business would only suffer if there were severe budget cutbacks. However, she identifies the major threat to her business: "The time that my business would start to slow down is when the Inuktitut language is not taught or used. I see a lot of our young people just speaking English among themselves. The older Inuit are dying and I don't see there will be a need for interpreters and translators in the distant future. I am raising my children in both languages, but even so I see the end."

Future Development

Ethel enjoys her work and plans to expand her business once her youngest child is in school. She would consider taking a partner and purchasing additional equipment with a government grant. "I want to have full-time work once my kids are in school. I believe there is a lot of work and by then I'll be free to travel more easily. I would hire staff, but I would encourage them to work out of their homes. I think that you are more productive when not distracted by people coming and going."

Advice to New Business

Ethel's advice to new translators is to get the training and equipment, then consider building a client base up slowly before going into the business full-time. She recommends the computer and software that she uses, although servicing requirements should be considered.

Ethel comments, "The training is free through Arctic College or Culture and Communications with the Territorial government. I estimate that the initial cost of buying a computer and software ranges from $4,000 to $5,500. In order to cut costs, get together with a group of people who want computers and get a better price with a bulk order."

Ethel feels that it can be a very demanding profession at times, and she must remain impartial to avoid any perceived conflict of interest. She says that does get difficult sometimes because many of the issues discussed in the meetings conducted by her clients are very important to her as a Native person. Translators must also be disciplined, well-groomed, and responsible in order to build demand for their services.

There is a need for the service she provides and she was quite surprised at how busy she has become. "I didn't think there was going to be this volume of business. In the beginning, I had three-month periods where it wasn't busy at all. However, if I want to, I can work more hours in the week."

Summary and Conclusions

Translation and Interpretation Services is an excellent means for Ethel to use her skills as an interpreter-translator while raising her family and making significant contributions to the family budget. Ethel built up her client base while working full-time for several employers. This was a low-risk way to ease into the business and establish herself before making the decision to start her own business. She was also able to finance the purchase of equipment through these extra revenues rather than by government grant or bank loan.

Ethel has built a loyal client base by working hard at establishing a reputation from the very beginning for good-quality work at a reasonable price and for reliability, punctuality, and meeting deadlines. She does not advertise but relies on word-of-mouth to generate business. She has more than enough work to handle without advertising. She sometimes passes her overload to other women in the community who are trained as translators.

Overhead expenses are kept to a minimum. Ethel does most of her work out of an office located in the house or at the client's place of business. She requires her overload staff to provide their own equipment, which they use in their own homes. Her plans for eventual expansion do not include providing office space for additional staff. Instead, her business would provide employees with the opportunity to work on their own time and on their own equipment.

Ethel finds that translation and interpretation work are satisfying but can be stressful due to the concentration required to do a good job. This sometimes impinges on her relationship with her family, but she minimizes this by taking time off between projects. The other problem that she has to contend with are the limited alternatives available for service if her equipment breaks down.

Ethel does not foresee a slowdown in the demand for her services in the near future. However, the biggest threat to her business is the decline in the use of Inuktitut, which she considers to be inevitable over time. Until then, she feels the demand for translation and interpretation services is fairly recession-proof. As a service, translation and interpretation have very little impact on the environment. Waste paper is kept to a minimum with the use of computers.

This business has provided Ethel with the flexibility to follow her profession while allowing her time for her family. She is providing a valuable service to her community while meeting her personal needs for earning a good income on her own time.

16
CONCLUSIONS

This study reports on a sample of successful businesses operating in small Northern communities at various stages in the business development process. Each entrepreneur or business team offers a personal perspective on issues surrounding the growth and maintenance of their businesses. Common themes appear throughout the chapters, but there are also unique approaches which allow the reader to review some options in developing his or her own business plans.

Personal skills and business philosophies for the sample are summarized in the following paragraphs. A potential entrepreneur may use it as a starting point for planning a business, and a practicing entrepreneur may use it to review key decisions. A practical checklist of the fundamental issues that arise during the start-up and operating phases of a business is set out in Appendix Two.

Starting a new business is never easy. Northerners also face obstacles unique to isolated communities, but these businesses are doing just that with success and style. Small business is alive and well in the North. Some of these entrepreneurs are local and others have come from "away," but all share a common desire for a good life for themselves and their families. Being in business for themselves has allowed this group of people to capitalize on business opportunities on their own terms, with dedication, commitment and hard work. Their insights and strategies follow:

1 *Putting thoughts into action is difficult.* Generally, ideas for a business are not hard to come by, but actually taking the necessary steps to get a new business off the ground is much more challenging. As Elmer Ghostkeeper notes, he knows of many people in his small

community with good ideas, but they do not know how to get an idea going, how to conduct a demand survey, or how to get the necessary financing. With all his experience in the tourism business, Bill Tait states that the first mile of a thousand-mile journey is the toughest.

2 *Set goals; plan; be tenacious.*   By setting goals and taking the time to write them down, the entrepreneur clarifies the means for accomplishing plans. For example, John Ostashek decided he would build up his business over five years, to show potential purchasers what his business could do. Once the business was put up for sale, he planned to start cutting back operations in order to slow down his busy lifestyle.

Written plans can be reviewed and revised as circumstances change and are a useful tool for understanding why basic assumptions or expectations either are not met or are exceeded. Elmer Ghostkeeper drafted a business plan and forecast demand for his store. He understands why his original forecasts were off: changing customers' buying habits, developed over a number of years, is a slow process. Bill Lyall recognizes the role five-year plans have in planning for a co-op's future and is encouraging all co-ops to draft plans based on suggestions from their community shareholders.

In Danny Nowlan's opinion, success comes from being tenacious and never quitting. "Set your mind on a goal and get there no matter what, as long as it's honest and you're not hurting anyone. You don't walk over anyone to reach your goal, at least I don't. Perseverance has gotten the game farm where it is today." Perseverance describes the reaction to various serious setbacks experienced by some of these entrepreneurs, in particular, Danny Nowlan and the lawsuit that almost put his business under; Mo Grant's experience with a partnership breakdown, a landlord's bankruptcy, and a fire; and the disastrous Lakeview Resort fire. All of these entrepreneurs built their businesses back up and are doing well.

3 *Be flexible.*   Unforeseen opportunities can be capitalized on when an entrepreneur is not locked into the details of a plan. For example, Fred Coman has no master plan but over the years he has built up a successful group of businesses by seizing unexpected opportunities. He does, however, have basic standards that guide him in assessing new opportunities and in operating his businesses.

4 *Break the rules.*   Relying on your own common sense rather than on what is the norm in your industry can have many benefits. For

example, the Jaques had never worked at a newspaper and did not know the conventions of establishing editorial policy. They set their own editorial policy in line with their personal convictions and derive a lot of satisfaction from it. They also followed their own instincts in making their business a success and brought a fresh perspective rather than being bound by traditional newspaper practices.

Fred Coman follows his own packing routine that he developed after many years of moving experience in the North. He does not follow United Van Lines standards and will not deal with certain agents whose standards do not measure up to his. His customers are his first concern.

5 Know your own strengths and weaknesses. Knowing your own strengths and weaknesses can allow you to rise to opportunities. Mo Grant recognizes that she is not as competitive as she would have to be in order to be successful in the south. She says, "When I get an idea I think about it for long enough and if I think it's going to work then I'll give it a try. It's a lot simpler to do that in the North. Money is secondary for me. It's mainly getting an idea, working on it and seeing it work that gives me satisfaction."

Partnerships work well when skills are complementary. For example, it took Kim and Elmer Ghostkeeper some time to identify and respect each other's personal strengths but this understanding has benefited their partnership. Personal challenges differ for each of them, and personal fulfillment comes from a variety of sources rather than just from the business.

Other partnerships have also benefited from these personal insights. For example, the Jaques brought different skills and complementary interests to their ventures. The Putlands and Doehles also have developed a strong partnership because of complementary skills, shared standards for products and service, and mutual understanding of each other's philosophies.

6 Make a sensible commitment to the business. Commitment to making the business a success is critical. Danny Nowlan and his wife commonly give round-the-clock attention to their animals whenever necessary. Lorne Metropolit has overcome many obstacles in making his dream of a northern show garden a reality. He and his family, as well as the other families profiled in this book, juggle business and family responsibilities, looking for an elusive, constantly shifting, satisfactory balance among the many demands on their attention.

7 Have fun.   With all the challenges and obstacles to overcome, these entrepreneurs still enjoy their businesses. They can laugh at silly things that happen in the course of the day. Many admit to a keen pleasure and excitement when they get up in the morning and go to work. Don Jaque notes, "We're always expanding in different areas of business and that is fun and exciting. We're doing a good job at it and making money which is our recipe for success."

There are as many ways to achieve success as there are definitions of success. The profiles of these entrepreneurs offer some insight into their paths to success. It is not a question of following in their footsteps, but creating a new path that is uniquely individual. Use their experiences to shed some light on your personal path to business success and capture that spirit of adventure.

APPENDICES

APPENDIX ONE

Key Definitions

These definitions are organized into three sections: business structures, financial statistics, and miscellaneous.

1 Types of Business or Economic Development Structures

Sole proprietorship: A legal term referring to a business that is owned by one person and is unincorporated.

Partnership: A business that is registered as a partnership owned by two or more people and that is unincorporated. Provincial and territorial legislation define the rights and obligations of each partner. These terms may be modified by partnership agreements executed between the partners.

Corporation: A separate legal entity owned by one or more shareholders. Shares represent this ownership and may be bought and sold privately or publicly. Businesses are usually incorporated on an accountant's advice when revenue and tax considerations make incorporation beneficial.

Community Development Corporation (CDC):   Typically an "umbrella" organization, a CDC usually serves a broad range of social, cultural, and economic functions. CDCs are incorporated and rely on volunteers and paid staff and work towards long-term local community development. Profit-making activities sometimes supplement funding from public sources.*

Co-operative: A collective economic activity, controlled by the workers or co-op members and meeting specific legal guidelines. The main principles distinguishing co-operatives from private enterprise include: open

---

* Brodhead, Lamontagne, and Pierce, "Local Development Organizations," 12.

membership, management appointment by members, member sharehold-
ing; distribution of surplus earnings through dividends based on members' level of support; education of members and the general public; and
co-operation with other similar organizations.*

2 *Financial Statistics*

Financial ratios: Data from a company's financial statements is commonly used by managers, shareholders, creditors, and potential investors
to evaluate that company's performance over time and relative to other
companies in the same industry. In this book, historical financial information is presented in the form of absolute numbers (*e.g.* total salaries)
and ratios (*e.g.* return on equity and sales to assets) for the majority of
case studies.

Ratios allow a certain level of evaluation and comparison for the
reader; more importantly, they protect the confidentiality of the actual
numbers representing the private company's financial performance. In-
depth analysis of ratios recognizes the limitations of this technique, but,
for the purposes of this study, the ratios give the reader an indication of
changes in the company's performance over time.

Return-on-equity (ROE) ratio: Net profits (sales less expenses) are divided by total owner's equity (amount invested in the company by the
owner). The ratio indicates the amount of money earned for every dollar
invested by the owner. For example, if the ROE is 8% then 8¢ was earned
for every $1.00 invested. The reader can compare this to the interest
earned on every dollar put into a bank account, which ranges from 6% to
10% at the time of writing.

Of course, investment in a business is generally for the long term, and
some years will show a low ROE, especially the early years, when the
potential for much greater returns is slowly being developed or when
major investment in the business has not yet had its impact on sales.

Sales-to-Assets ratio: Total sales are divided by total assets to give the
rate at which investment in assets is increasing sales. This ratio shows
how well the company's assets are being put to use. For every dollar invested in equipment and other company assets, a rate representing more
or less actual revenue can be determined and compared over time. A
high ratio could indicate that the firm is generating the maximum sales
possible with that level of investment. It may prove difficult to generate
further business without an increase in investment.

---

* Arctic Co-operatives Ltd., "The Co-operative Movement," 4.

3 *Miscellaneous:*

Sustainable Development: As pointed out by M. Pretes in "Sustainable Development and the Entrepreneur,"* "the term 'sustainable development' means different things to different people." Common themes include:

- Recognition of environmental problems as being global in nature,
- Acknowledgement of the relationship between economy and environment,
- Advocacy of local control of resources,
- Avoiding reliance on non-renewable resources,
- Recognition of the importance of social and cultural traditions,
- Need to eradicate poverty, hunger, and disease,
- Recognition that these factors must also be viewed with future generations in mind.

Popular definitions include the Brundtland Commission's description: "development ... that ensure[s] that it meets the needs of the present without compromising the ability of future generations to meet their own needs, and it "requires meeting the basic needs of all and extending to all the opportunity to fulfill their aspirations for a better life."*

According to the definition developed for the Northwest Territories' Special Committee on the Northern Economy,

Sustainable development challenges existing economic structures and practices and demands a fresh look at the definition of economic "success". Sustainable development redefines economic winners to include those whose activities maintain or improve environmental quality and to exclude those who ruin the potential for resource use by future generations.*

---

* Pretes, *Sustainable Development*, vi.
* World Commission on Environment and Development, *Our Common Future*, 8.
* Osberg and Hazell, *Towards a Sustainable Approach.*

APPENDIX TWO
Checklists

This checklist addresses common decisions that an owner must consider at different stages in his business. The list is not comprehensive: for example, the specifics of conducting a feasibility analysis or drafting a business plan are not addressed. The list is best used to supplement the information available from more technically oriented sources such as economic development officers, bankers, lawyers, accountants, and support agencies such as the Federal Business Development Bank and local chambers of commerce.

Start-up Phase

1 *Am I an entrepreneur?*

a. *Personal characteristics*: Although strengths vary from person to person, in general the subjects of this book:

- are dedicated to making their business a success;
- are willing to work hard and put in the required effort while foregoing immediate financial returns;
- possess technical or managerial expertise that is critical to their continuing success;
- hold business philosophies that reflect their personal values and that help to maintain interest and excitement in operating their venture;
- respect their partners' and employees' skills and work well together;
- enjoy strong family support;

- take into account more than bottom line profit;
- enjoy doing something that is personally satisfying and of benefit to the community;
- are involved in their community, which indirectly enhances their business reputation and promotes customer loyalty.

Judging from the variety of people, opportunities, and strategies that characterize the small sample of businesses presented here, literally anyone can give entrepreneurship a try. Deciding whether you have what it takes to make a business grow and prosper is a personal decision. It is reached by researching requirements of the new business or an existing one and by knowing your own personal skills, attitudes, and desires. These assessments should be confirmed by other business people and close friends.

b. *Previous Experience*: Previous experience is not a requirement but it helps to determine whether or not you would like to be in a particular business. (See Paddle Prairie Mall, Cascade Publishing, and Coman Arctic for examples of entrepreneurs with no previous experience. See Lou's Small Engines, Western Arctic, and Lakeview Marina for examples of entrepreneurs with previous experience).

c. *Training*: Most of the businesspeople in this study say that bookkeeping courses are an asset. Understanding simple financial statements is crucial in charting the financial health of your company. This knowledge is critical in putting partners on an equal footing for understanding financial matters and working with an accountant. By understanding financial terminology, a businessperson has increased confidence in dealing with his or her peers and other professionals.

2 *What type of business?*

a. *Buying an existing business*: Buying the business where you currently work will allow you to take advantage of your expertise. (See Lakeview Resort, Northern Emak, Lou's Small Engines, Translation Services.) Opening a similar business makes sense *if* the market can support it.

b. *Hobby or skill*: Turn a hobby or skill into business. (See Yukon Game Farm, Coman Arctic, Yukon Botanical Gardens.)

c. *Community Needs Assessment*: Use a community needs and marketing survey to identify business opportunities. (See Paddle Prairie Mall.)

3 *Planning for my business*

a. *Family*:   Will your spouse or children play an active role in the business? Consider speaking to other couples who are in the type of business you are considering starting. (See Paddle Prairie Mall.)

Involve your older children in discussions about the business. Whether or not they take an active part, their lives will be affected by the long hours and few family vacations during the early years. (See Paddle Prairie Mall.) Be prepared to put in long hours in order to make your business a success. (See Cascade Publishing and Lakeview Resort.) It can be lonely being the only business tycoon in town. Search out other successful business people in your community or surrounding area to share experiences and ideas.

Spouses or relatives may help with the accounting, planning, personnel, or scheduling. Plan for their roles and consider upgrading skills prior to the business start-up. (See Yukon Game Farm, Paddle Prairie Mall, Lou's Small Engines.) Family participation may not be an asset. The business person should *not* feel obligated to hire all relatives. Hiring decisions should be based strictly on the needs of the business.

b. *Product or service*:   Is the product or service essential to your customers? Will your business survive the boom-bust cycles associated with nonrenewable resource development through mega-projects? How could it be affected by a recession? Planning for these inevitabilities can help your business survive.

c. *Infrastructure*:   Are the services required by your business available in your community? (See Northern Emak.) Bookkeeping and accounting services are very important in the start-up phase. The entrepreneur should be sure that dealings with these professionals will be kept confidential.

d. *Staff*:   Are skilled staff available locally? (See Northern Emak.) If not, then what are the costs associated with hiring in the south? (See Coman Arctic, Raven Enterprises, Cascade Publishing.) Consider paying a local person a better wage rather than paying housing and moving costs for importing personnel from the south.

e. *Environment*:   Is your business environmentally friendly? If not, can you improve procedures so that the impact on the environment is minimized?

f. *Pilot project*:   Consider running a small, inexpensive pilot project before committing financial resources to the business. (See Northern Emak.) If you are considering buying an existing business, negotiate for the opportunity to operate the business for a month before making an offer. (See Raven Enterprises.) Consider retaining the previous owners as consultants for six months or one year. (See Lou's Small Engines.)

g. *Sell options*: Would you be able to sell your business in a few years? (See Paddle Prairie Mall, Lou's Small Engines, Western Arctic Air, Ostashek Outfitting.)

4 *To partner or not to partner?*

a. *Active partners*: Working with one or more partners who take an active role in the operations of the business can be a real benefit. Business risk is shared and each partner has a strong interest in seeing the business succeed. It is easier to take holidays and share the workload. But a partnership can strain personal relationships and all profits, no matter how small, must be shared. (See Raven Enterprises, Northern Emak, Paddle Prairie Mall, Lakeview Resort and Marina, Cascade Publishing.)

b. *Silent Partners*: A silent partner is not active in the business but provides needed financing. He or she is repaid and shares in business profits. (Northern Emak, Western Arctic Air, Taylor Chev Olds, Paddle Prairie Mall.)

c. *Partnership Agreement*: If the business will be owned by more than one person, then serious consideration should be given to formalizing the relationship in a partnership agreement. This sets out the duties and obligations of each partner and defines such items as the means of resolving disputes and actions to be taken in the event of death. These issues arise even if the partner is a spouse or other relative. (See Northern Emak.)

d. *Sole proprietorship and incorporation*: If you decide to run your own business, you are called a sole proprietor. You carry all the financial risk, make all decisions and keep all business profits.

e. *Incorporation*: At some point in your business, you may wish to incorporate your business on the advice of your accountant. This may make sense depending on sales, tax implications, and personal liability. (See Lakeview Resort, Cascade Publishing.)

f. *Community Economic Development Vehicle*: Form a community- or band-owned development corporation to achieve the social and economic goals

of the community. (See Champagne-Aishihik.) Consider starting a cooperative owned by local shareholders. (See Co-op.)

5 How can I finance my business?

a. *Personal Savings*:   Use personal savings and minimize the use of debt.
Perhaps operate the business on a part-time basis and use revenues to
finance purchase of equipment. This is an easy way to determine
whether or not you should go into the business full-time without incurring much debt. (See Translation Services.)

b. *Loans*: Take out a bank loan (Lakeview Resort, Lou's Small Engines,
Raven Enterprises) or borrow from family members, which may mean
more flexibility in making loan payments when business is slow. (Lakeview Resort). Or borrow from partners and pay the loan back from business profits (Northern Emak). Going into debt may be your only option,
but debt should be minimized so that the risk of default is kept low.

c. *Government Programs*:   Use government grants and loans to finance
start-up expenses or the purchase of a business. Local economic development officers can help with drafting business plans and filling out appli-
cations. (See Yukon Botanical Gardens, Lou's Small Engines.) Grants are
non-repayable and loans may be easier to get than from a bank.

d. *Issue shares*:   Incorporate the company as a public company and issue
shares. This is one means of raising capital without incurring debt. (See
Paddle Prairie Mall.) Ownership is shared among voting shareholders so
that control of your company may be at stake.

Operations – Phase One

1 What operational policies and procedures will I set for my business?

a. *Financing decisions*:   The bank will probably play some role in providing funds for an operating line of credit, for consolidating debts, or for
expansion. An excellent history of debt repayments, little past use of debt
financing, and good collateral will help make bank financing more easily
accessible. The risk of bankruptcy rises when bank financing is heavily
relied on and business is slow. (See Cascade Publishing, Coman Arctic,
Lou's Small Engines.)

   Government loan or grant programs may provide funding for updating
equipment, training, and business expansion. (See Cascade Publishing,
Lou's Small Engines.) Another option is to use business profits to finance
operations and expansion. (See Northern Emak.)

b. *Location*:   If possible, keep overhead low by operating out of your house or providing your service at your customer's place of business. Subcontract extra work out to other businesses. (See Translation Services.)

New businesses must remember to be visible to their customers through advertising and readily accessible by telephone during business hours. An answering machine is a useful purchase for new businesses that cannot afford a full-time receptionist.

c. *Business philosophy*:   Decide how your operating philosophy can differentiate you from your competition. Most of the businesses put the customer's satisfaction first and communicate this to their customers through words and actions. This is an excellent means of cultivating customer loyalty. (See Cascade Publishing, Lou's Small Engines, Coman Artic, Translation Services, Ostashek Outfitting.) Be straight with people. If you make a mistake, admit it and fix it immediately. (See Taylor Chev Olds.)

A good business reputation is an important factor in alleviating issues of bias or prejudice for women and minorities in business. (See Translation Services, Raven Enterprises, Champagne-Aishihik, Western Arctic Air.) It can still be difficult, however, to crack the old boys' network. (See Champagne-Aishihik, Western Arctic Air.)

Nurture your business carefully. Buying additional assets and hiring personnel before your business can afford them can mean the premature death of your business. Consider leasing assets rather than purchasing them outright.

d. *Customers*:   Know your customers. Be consistent in meeting their expectations for your products or services. For example, customers expect home-cooked meals using fresh ingredients from Lakeview Resort. Lou's Small Engines is noted for excellent service. Fred Coman's word is good and his business deals can be sealed with a handshake. Ghostkeeper's Store is always open according to its posted hours of operation.

e. *Suppliers*:   When possible use northern suppliers. (See Paddle Prairie Mall.) Regularly canvass suppliers for the best prices and services and pass these savings on to your customers. (See Cascade Publishing.)

If appropriate, consider using the best computerized equipment for inventory control, billing, and accounts. Service should be investigated. It is possible to order equipment in bulk with other business people in order to qualify for a discount. (See Paddle Prairie Mall, Cascade Publishing, Translation Services.)

f. *Pricing*:   What pricing policy will you establish? Most of the businesses in this book set their prices in the mid-range of prices charged by their competition. Setting high prices when you offer an essential service is a temptation, but it may be shortsighted. Competition may be able to come in easily and break your monopoly by undercutting your prices. (See Coman Arctic, Ostashek Outfitting, Translation Services.) There are a number of approaches to this question and no one right way. You must know your customers and your market to make an effective decision.

Offer regular clearout sales to move inventory that has not sold within a reasonable time. Regular customers may be notified of the sale before-hand in recognition of their loyalty.

g. *Credit policy*:   In the beginning, consider requiring all customers to pay cash. Business accounts may be opened, but with tight controls and close monitoring of accounts receivable. Advise these customers of upper limits. After the business is established, consider allowing only your best customers to charge to accounts or write cheques (Lou's Small Engines) or be more liberal in who can charge or write cheques. Have a clear set of guidelines to follow in credit collections to avoid problems. (See Co-op, Paddle Prairie Mall.)

By maintaining a healthy cash flow, a businessperson is able to take advantage of opportunities such as occasional sales by suppliers and bulk purchases that reduce unit costs, and can hold out through slow periods. Surplus cash is not necessarily profit. It is also handy as an emergency fund and should not be touched.

h. *Environmental policy*:   Are your products or services environmentally friendly? Choices in this area often make the art of doing business more personally meaningful and in the long term more sustainable. Strategies include:

• Offering environmentally safe products (Paddle Prairie Mall, Cascade Publishing.)
• Recycling materials from your business and the community (Coman Arctic.)
• Choosing means of production that are more environmentally friendly than more commonly used options (Yukon Game Farm, Cascade Publishing.)
• Building for energy efficiency and environmental qualities (Cascade Publishing.) – but beware of equipment that is costly to repair.

i. *Hiring staff*:   Competition for good staff is a common obstacle in the North. It is difficult to attract qualified employees because of the superior benefits offered by corporations and both levels of government to a very small skilled labour pool. This results in high staff turnover in the small businesses that are not able to compete effectively. How do you attract good staff to your operation? Some of the strategies used by the employers in this study include:

- Finding an underemployed segment in the local labour pool that you can tap. (See Cascade Publishing, Translation Services.)
- Offering the opportunity for staff to move into various positions in your organization if they show an interest in doing so. (See Cascade Publishing.)
- Advertising in the south and hiring qualified employees to meet your needs. Turnover is often high, but establishing a minimum stay requirement may minimize this problem. Other options include paying a bonus for each year that the employee stays and establishing some sort of penalty system for employees who do not stay for the minimum length of time. Hiring couples can broaden your labour market but you will likely have to provide housing and other benefits such as annual trips out of the North. (See Coman Arctic, Cascade Publishing, Yukon Game Farm, Western Arctic Air.)
- Hiring employees who have strong interests in their field. (See Yukon Game Farm, Cascade Publishing, Ostashek Outfitting.)

j. *Retaining staff*:   Consider the following:

- Offer staff a chance to purchase equity in the organization. (See Paddle Prairie Mall.)
- Offer health benefits to your employees. (See Paddle Prairie Mall.)
- Increase salaries as soon as possible and encourage a good working environment. For example, have an open-door policy for discussing problems. (See Yukon Game Farm, Cascade Publishing, Coman Arctic.) Consider offering guaranteed wages during slow periods to buoy staff morale and loyalty. (See Coman Arctic.)
- Advise staff of the high standards you expect from them and treat them as professionals. Document your policies and procedures in written form for easy reference by your staff. (This also makes training easier where there is high staff turnover.) (See Paddle Prairie Mall.)
- Encourage their input in purchasing decisions and, when feasible, give them more responsibility. (See Paddle Prairie Mall, Ostashek Outfitting, Co-op.) Rely on their judgement and back their decisions. Allow them to make mistakes and learn from them. (See Taylor Chev Olds.)
- Acknowledge good employees with monthly or annual awards or other benefits such as subsidized travel. (See Coman Arctic, Co-op.)
- Set clear targets for standards of performance which will be rewarded by promotions and pay raises.

- Keep business and personal debt low and develop the skills to step in yourself if staff leave or must be let go. This also gives your business the advantage of being easily streamlined if sales are low. (See Cascade Publishing, Lou's Small Engines.)
- Plan for your own regular holidays as soon as feasible, for mental and family health. (See Paddle Prairie Mall, Cascade Publishing.)

k. *Advertising*: Advertise your business in community newspapers. Consider projects, charitable contributions, and sales promotions that will attract community support and encourage customer loyalty. Some examples might include a grand opening picnic, a midnight sales blitz, or giving prizes for the best snow sculpture. (See Paddle Prairie Mall, Co-op, Coman Arctic.)

If appropriate, cultivate customer loyalty with a regular newsletter. It is also a useful means of reaching new customers. (See Ostashek Outfitting, Paddle Prairie Mall.)

l. *Competition*: Where you have competitors, consider establishing and maintaining a co-operative relationship with them while still giving good stiff competition as required. For example, you may make an agreement to split the market (see Lou's Small Engines) or you may make an agreement to share revenues while carrying the same product (see Raven Enterprises). This strategy may be appropriate when competing in a very small market (see Western Arctic Air).

m. *Competitive edge*: Maintain your competitive edge by constantly monitoring trends in consumer demand, technology, and other relevant areas. Stay informed about advances in your field by reading trade journals, belonging to trade associations, and developing a network among other people in the same industry, including competitors. (See Cascade Publishing, Yukon Game Farm.) Regularly consider ways of positioning your business to take advantage of trends and using your resources in an innovative fashion. (See Cascade Publishing, Yukon Game Farm, Yukon Botanical Gardens.)

n. *Accounting*: Hire a good accountant. If you are not skilled in this area, look for one who works well with you and is helpful in training you to handle the bookkeeping so that accounting expenses are minimized. Your accountant should help you to understand your financial statements and should also recommend the monthly financial information that you should monitor to ensure short-term financial health. Monitoring accounts receivable is critical. (See Lou's Small Engines.)

Operations – Phase Two

1 What's next? Expand, hire a manager, or sell the business?

a. *Business expansion*:   Should more than one business be operated in an effort to diversify sources of revenue? After operating a business for a while, the entrepreneur often becomes aware of other customer needs or options for improving the use of his equipment. He or she may expand the products and services offered in the present business. Alternatively it may make sense, after assessing available resources, to start another business. Complementary services are important when a firm is sensitive to economic cycles (Coman Arctic, Cascade Publishing, Western Arctic Air, Paddle Prairie Mall) but are not an absolute prerequisite (Ostashek Outfitting, Raven Enterprises, Co-op).

Sometimes, the demand for the new business can be tested inexpensively by running a pilot project. Once sufficient demand has been identified, then a more substantial investment may be made. Although there is a greater commitment of time and resources required, a new business may even out cash flow variation and may add a new level of interest to the daily routine of running a business. (See Paddle Prairie Mall, Co-op, Cascade Publishing, Raven Enterprises, Western Arctic Air, Coman Arctic, Champagne-Aishihik, Ostashek Outfitting.)

b. *Hire a manager*:   Do you want to retain your business but cut down on your responsibilities? Hiring a manager to handle operations is one alternative. (See Yukon Game Farm, Lou's Small Engines.) This frees your time but you risk lowering operating standards if the right person is not hired.

c. *Sell the business*:   Due to isolation and the relatively high value of capital assets, it can be difficult to find a purchaser for your business once you decide to sell, because the purchaser must want to live in your small community. Sometimes relatives are potential purchasers. (See Lakeview Resort, Lou's Small Engines, Ostashek Outfitting.)

Sometimes your competitors are interested in acquiring your business. (See Western Arctic Air.) If possible, give potential purchasers the opportunity to run the business for several months. This allows them to assess their interest in the business and can be a positive experience. (See Raven Enterprises.)

Community Enterprises

Public input into the types of businesses that people would like in their community can be used in developing an investment strategy. Choose a dynamic, committed individual to lead any community-based development vehicle, but plan for training other people to share responsibilities and to move in time into the leadership position.

a. *Objectives*:   If a band chooses to start a band-owned business as a major source of training, then band members must be educated about the problem of also trying to maximize profit. Expensive training costs eat into the profit margin.

b. *Staff*:   Although staffing from the local community is important, sometimes it must be balanced with hiring the best-qualified person for the position. Champagne-Aishihik finds that the pressures generated from a management decision taken by a band member can be minimized if the same decision is taken by a non-band member.

The Co-op gives anyone the opportunity for employment, including handicapped people.

c. *Training*:   The Co-op's experience has been that older people seem to appreciate the need for skills more than young people. Consequently, more mature community residents are upgrading their skills while many young people drop out of school. With a small local labour pool, business investments that are not labour-intensive are the main options for further expansion. The importance of education and training is actively promoted among their young people.

d. *Small business*:   Encourage band members to start up small businesses to carry out subcontract work from the band-owned business. This is one means of encouraging individual initiative and can alleviate some of the pressure on the band-owned business to provide all the training opportunities for band members.

ENTREPRENEURSHIP CHECKLIST
START-UP PHASE
1. Am I an entrepreneur?
a.   Personal characteristics
b.   Previous experience
c.   Training

2. What type of business?
a. Purchase an existing business
b. Hobby or skill
c. Community needs assessment
3. Planning for my business
a. Family
b. Product or service
c. Infrastructure
d. Staff
e. Environment
f. Pilot project
g. Sell option
4. To partner or not to partner?
a. Active partners
b. Silent partners
c. Partnership agreement
d. Sole proprietor
e. Incorporation
f. Community economic development vehicle
5. How can I finance my business?
a. Personal savings
b. Loan
c. Government programs
d. Issue shares

OPERATIONS – PHASE ONE
1. What operational policies and procedures will I set for my business?
a. Financing decisions
b. Location
c. Business philosophy
d. Customers
e. Suppliers
f. Pricing
g. Credit policy
h. Environmental policy
i. Hiring staff
j. Retaining staff
k. Advertising
l. Competition
m. Competitive edge
n. Accounting
OPERATIONS – PHASE TWO
1. What's next? Expand, hire a manager or sell the business?
a. Business expansion
b. Hire a manager
c. Sell the business

COMMUNITY ENTERPRISES
a. Objectives
b. Staff
c. Training
d. Small business

BIBLIOGRAPHY

Arctic Co-operatives Ltd. *The Co-operative Movement in the Northwest Territories: An Overview 1959–1989.* Winnipeg: Arctic Co-operatives Ltd, 1989.

Berger, T.R. *Northern Frontier: Northern Homeland. The Report of the Mackenzie Valley Pipeline Inquiry,* Vol. 1. Ottawa, Supply and Services Canada, 1977.

Brodhead, D., F. Lamontagne and J. Pierce. "The Local Development Organization: A Canadian Perspective." Local Development Series Paper No. 19. Ottawa: Economic Council of Canada, 1990.

Energy and Canadians into the 21st Century: A Report on the Energy Options Process. Ottawa: Department of Energy, Mines and Resources, 1988.

"General Motors Yukon Dealership Dates Back to 1927 with T&D's." *Whitehorse Star,* May 28, 1970: 34.

Industry, Science and Technology Canada. *Small Business In Canada: Competing Through Growth.* 1990.

Northwest Territories Data Book, 1990/91. Whitehorse: Outcrop, 1990.

Osberg, Z. and S. Hazell. *Towards A Sustainable Approach: Natural Resource Development and Environmental Protection in the Northwest Territories;* a Background study for the Special Committee on the Northern Economy of the Legislative Assembly of the Northwest Territories, 1989.

Pretes, M. *Sustainable Development and the Entrepreneur: An Annotated Bibliography of Small Business Development in Circumpolar and Developing Regions.* Calgary: Arctic Institute of North America, 1989.

Robinson, M.P. *Native and Local Economics: A Consideration of Nine Models of Business Development.* Calgary: Environmental and Social Affairs, Petro-Canada, 1981.

Robinson, M. and Ghostkeeper, E. "Implementing the Next Economy in a Unified Context: A Case Study of the Paddle Prairie Mall Corporation." *Arctic* 41, no. 3 (1988): 173–82.

Robinson, M., and Ghostkeeper, E. "Native and Local Economics: A Consideration of Economic Evolution and the Next Economy." *Arctic* 40, no. 2, (1987): 138–44.

Serup-Jansen, Sheila. "A Garden of Earthly Delights." *Up Here* (Jan.–Feb. 1991): 24.

Warner, Iris. "Taylor & Drury, Ltd, Yukon Merchants." *Alaska Journal* 5, no. 2 (Spring 1975): 74–80.

Watt, Erik. "Freddie Carmichael: Flying into the Future." *Northwest Explorer* (Spring 1989): 19–22.

World Commission on Environment and Development. *Our Common Future.* New York: Oxford University Press, 1987.

Yukon Data Book 1986–1987. Whitehorse: Outcrop, 1986.